PRAISE FOR

The New Honeymoon Planner

"*The New Honeymoon Planner* allows newlyweds to become a creative force in planning the best part of their wedding— the honeymoon! Lots of ideas and inspiration to create an unforgettable first journey as husband and wife."

—**Elizabeth Arrighi Borsting**, travel writer

"Full of cool advice for planning an idyllic honeymoon. You'll feel the pre-wedding stress melt away just thinking about your first romantic vacation as a couple."

—**Sarah Francis**, managing editor, *Rhode Island Monthly* and editor, *Rhode Island Monthly's Bride*

"I applaud Sharon Naylor for introducing honeymooners to the romantic world of spa vacations. It is this kind of fresh thinking that makes this book a must-read for anyone planning the best way to start a healthy marriage together."

—**Susie Ellis**, vice president of industry development, *Spa Finder* magazine

Other Books by Sharon Naylor

1001 Ways to Have a Dazzling Second Wedding

The Bridal Party Handbook

The Complete Outdoor Wedding Planner

How to Have a Fabulous Wedding for $10,000 or Less

How to Plan an Elegant Wedding in 6 Months or Less

The Mother of the Bride Book

The Ornament: A Novel

Please visit Sharon Naylor's Web site, www.sharonnaylor.net, for more information on these titles and to contribute your best wedding-planning stories, ideas, and questions for possible inclusion in her upcoming books.

The NEW Honeymoon Planner

Selecting the Ideal Location and Planning the Trip of a Lifetime

Sharon Naylor

PRIMA PUBLISHING

Published by Prima Publishing, Roseville, California. Member of the Crown Publishing Group, a division of Random House, Inc., New York.

PRIMA PUBLISHING and colophon are trademarks of Random House, Inc., registered with the United States Patent and Trademark Office.

Interior illustrations by Kate Vasseur.

Library of Congress Cataloging-in-Publication Data
Naylor, Sharon.
    The new honeymoon planner : selecting the ideal location and planning the trip of a lifetime / Sharon Naylor
        p.   cm.
    Includes index.
    ISBN 0-7615-3731-7
    1. Travel. 2. Honeymoons. 3. Couples—Travel. I. Title.
G151.N43   2002
910'.2'02—dc21   2002074971

02 03 04 05 06 BB 10 9 8 7 6 5 4 3 2 1
Printed in the United States of America

First Edition

Visit us online at www.primapublishing.com

To all those who make it safe and enjoyable
for us to travel the world.

Contents

Acknowledgments

For their wonderful guidance of this book, as well as my previous titles in their series, I thank my editors, Denise Sternad and Michelle McCormack, and my publicist, Jennifer Dougherty-Hart, of Prima Lifestyles. Special thanks to Laura Gabler for a great copy edit of my work.

No book is written without the help of many, many players. I am so grateful to know the following generous travel experts and magazine editors who provided just the right contact or survey when needed: Cathy Keefe of the American Travel Institute; Robert Isler of *Modern Bride;* Denise Schipani, Diane Forden, and Lisa Dickens of *Bridal Guide;* Mark Orwoll from *Travel and Leisure;* Kelly Holland and Elaine Luce from The Container Store; Laurie Borman from Rand McNally; Chris Whiteside from Sprint PCS; Susie Ellis and Cassandra Cavanah from *Spa Finder;* September McIntyre from Weber Shandwick; Kristina Stone from Princess Cruises; Stefanie Michaels from www.adventure girl.com; and East Hanover Public Library's Gayle Carlson (who bent a rule for me and saved me five days of work—Gayle, you're the best!).

Special thanks go to all the couples who shared their honeymoon stories with me, particularly Julie and Bobby Dubin, Jill and Mark

Wood, Susan and Darrin McDermott, and Karen and Greg Beyke. For their behind-the-scenes support, I'd like to thank my family and my closest of friends, plus the guys at FedEx and the East Hanover post office who deliver my work and make my job possible. And a big hug to the taxi driver in Bermuda who delivered great wisdom for any traveler: "Not to worry!"

Your Honeymoon-Planning Timetable

The following is a timetable to help keep you on track with scheduling, planning, and executing so everything goes perfectly for your big trip:

Nine Months to One Year Ahead

- ❏ Sit down together to discuss your desired honeymoon style, dream locations, and wished-for activities.
- ❏ Assess available funds for your honeymoon.
- ❏ Establish honeymoon registry (if applicable).
- ❏ Decide on a realistic honeymoon budget.
- ❏ Begin researching various destinations via the Internet, travel magazines, and other sources.
- ❏ Check with travel agent associations to find the travel agent that's right for you.
- ❏ Meet with the travel agent to receive information on desired honeymoon destinations.
- ❏ Make airline or other travel reservations.
- ❏ Make hotel reservations.

❑ Make reservations for transport to and from hotel, or inquire about free shuttle availability.

❑ Make note of confirmation numbers and other details and store in organized filing system for future reference.

Six Months Ahead

❑ Begin researching passport and visa requirements, if necessary.

❑ Send for copies of your birth certificates and other documents needed for passport and visa applications.

❑ Apply for passports, visas, or other documents.

❑ Reserve rental car or secure train/transportation passes.

❑ Contact a tourism agency in your chosen destination for updates on special events, discount perk packages, and additional information.

❑ Begin studying any foreign language or customs for your destination.

Two to Three Months Ahead

❑ Check with your doctor about immunizations required for your trip, and make appointments to get your shots and tests.

❑ Assess your luggage situation, and purchase new luggage and carry-ons to suit the new FAA regulations.

❑ Start shopping for honeymoon outfits and other items on your packing list.

❑ Make arrangements for house sitters, pet sitters, relatives, or friends to watch your children (if applicable).

One Month Ahead

❑ Reserve locational activities such as special performances, tours, sports, special dinners, etc.

❑ Confirm hotel reservations.

❏ Confirm travel reservations.

❏ Continue shopping for needed travel, wardrobe, and lifestyle items.

Two Weeks Ahead

❏ Pick up airline tickets and boarding passes.

❏ Pick up any additional travel package vouchers, coupons, or rebate forms.

❏ Buy travelers' checks.

❏ Exchange an amount of cash for foreign currency.

❏ Begin any beauty or pampering treatments for the trip.

The Final Week

❏ Ask a trusted neighbor to take in any package deliveries, watch your house, care for your lawn, etc.

❏ Submit post office "hold mail" form.

❏ Arrange to have any electronic mailing lists at home or at work postponed so e-mail doesn't clog up while you're gone.

❏ Set up "out of office" auto-reply on your work computer's e-mail system to alert any clients that you're not available to reply.

❏ Arrange for newspaper delivery to be put on hold.

❏ Confirm child care and pet boarding arrangements.

❏ Collect clothing and other items to pack.

❏ Begin packing process.

❏ Shop for toiletries and travel gear.

❏ Pack carry-on bags.

❏ Confirm flights and hotel reservations again.

❏ Check with travel warning sites to be sure your location is in good standing.

❑ Check weather reports for your location.

❑ Leave itinerary with family members.

❑ Leave house key with trusted neighbor.

❑ Leave contact information with boss or colleague, just in case.

❑ Discuss contingency plans at work (e.g., who will handle your caseload) while you're gone.

❑ Charge cell phones and other tech toys.

❑ Have prescriptions filled and pack in carry-on.

❑ Pack all of the children's gear if they will be staying with relatives or friends during your time away . . . or . . .

❑ Pack for the children who will accompany you on your trip.

❑ Set light timers in and around your house.

❑ Set house thermostat on auto program.

❑ Discard trash in house, and arrange for a neighbor to take out your trash barrels on the next collection date.

❑ Correctly label your luggage with your contact information, and include a card with your hotel location and phone number *inside* the luggage, in case your things get lost en route.

❑ Write down credit card numbers and credit company phone numbers on an index card, and place the card in a suitcase for easy access in case you need to cancel your credit cards should they be lost or stolen during your trip.

❑ Confirm ride home from the airport after your return, and give your driver your arrival information.

❑ Go for waxing and beauty appointments.

The Day Before

❑ Confirm domestic flight reservations.

❑ Double-check all packed items.

❑ Double-check packing list for all carry-on items.

❑ Lay out any snacks or bottled water you will pack in your carry-on.

❑ Go get some cash to have on hand for expenses, tips, etc.

❑ Be sure your wallet contains all needed IDs, checkbook, etc.

❑ Be sure airline tickets and confirmations, passports, visas, and other must-haves are packed and ready to go.

❑ Make arrangements to have your luggage brought to your wedding night hotel suite or other appropriate location.

❑ Confirm your ride to the airport or travel center for the wedding night or next morning.

Introduction

Swimming with stingrays in the Cayman Islands . . .

Gliding through tree canopies in a Costa Rican rainforest . . .

Climbing the ancient pyramids in Egypt . . .

Sounds like the programming lineup for "Adventure Vacation Week" on the Travel Channel, doesn't it? Actually, these are snapshots from the "new honeymoon," the exciting postwedding getaways for couples who want special, unique, breathtaking honeymoons, unlike any other vacation they've ever experienced. In fact, *Bridal Guide* magazine reports that of their readers, 89.6% chose a honeymoon location they've never been to. That said, you're in good company if you too want a unique adventure in a whole new world—to start your new life with a giant leap outside your familiar surroundings.

Of course, the tropical island resort honeymoon is still a top pick for many honeymooners—with Hawaii being a top destination for many—but today's couple is looking beyond the sun, sand, and surf for one-of-a-kind honeymoons.

We didn't want the average honeymoon, where we'd spend a week lounging around
on the beach, sipping piña coladas, and watching the same sunset every night seven

times. We've been on vacations like that before. For our honeymoon, we wanted to do something that neither of us had ever experienced before, something exciting but still romantic, something that we could share as a first-time experience for both of us.

—DIANE AND THOMAS

We've vacationed together many times over the years, and we've always done the beach resort thing. This time, we wanted to do something incredible, something we'd always remember, and probably something we might never have the chance to do again. So we're going on an African safari, which has been a dream trip for both of us for a long time.

—ELAINE AND WES

Whichever style of honeymoon suits you best—from relaxing on a pink sand beach to cruising in luxury through the Mediterranean to wreck diving off the coast of Australia—whatever location you desire, whatever your budget, this book will help you journey through your countless travel options and plan the honeymoon of your dreams. This is going to be the trip of a lifetime, and you have a world of possibilities at your feet. After all the fuss and scramblings of planning your wedding, after the stress of making sure everything runs perfectly on your big day, and in the aftermath of the sparkling joy of your wedding from start to finish, your well-deserved reward is your escape into a honeymoon that's pure release and pure enjoyment.

Before we start designing your honeymoon from step one, I want you to take a look at where other couples have spent their postwedding weeks.

The Top 30 Honeymoon Destinations

The editors of *Bridal Guide* recently surveyed readers for their picks of the top honeymoon destinations. Of the 98.4% of couples planning to take a honeymoon, here are the readers' choices, with some readers voting for more than one destination:

Rank	Destination	Popularity
1	Hawaii	25.5%
2	Bahamas	23.7%
3	Florida	19.5%
4	Jamaica	19.1%
5	U.S. Virgin Islands	15.2%
6	Cancún	14.6%
7	Cayman Islands	14.4%
8	Aruba	13.0%
9	Acapulco	11.3%
10	Europe	11.3%
11	Poconos	11.1%
12	British Virgin Islands	9.9%
13	Bermuda	9.1%
14	Las Vegas	8.8%
15	Tahiti	8.2%
16	Australia/New Zealand	8.2%
17	Lake Tahoe	7.4%
18	Puerto Rico	6.6%
19	Fiji	6.2%
20	Colorado	6.0%
21	St. Lucia	5.8%
22	Bali	4.3%
23	Los Cabos	4.1%
24	Vermont	3.7%
25	Costa Rica	3.3%
26	Belize	3.3%
27	Asia	2.3%
28	Thailand	1.6%
29	Africa	1.6%
30	Indian Ocean	0.4%

Information provided with permission from *Bridal Guide* magazine, www.bridalguide.com.

Sounds exciting, doesn't it? Already picturing yourself in a floral sarong in Bali? Already primed for scuba diving in Belize? Well, we're about to start planning your dream honeymoon, and you have the best available tool in your hands right now. I researched thousands of honeymoon spots all over the world, and within these pages I've spotlighted a few possibilities to give you a better sense of the types of trips out there. I'll guide you from start to finish through steps of planning to find the best online and travel association resources, taking care of all the logistics like getting your passports and immunizations for foreign travel, making smart investments in your trip, and keeping yourself safe and secure wherever you go.

Since money is often a powerful and determining factor for choosing a destination and planning a honeymoon, I've also included several chapters specifically on making the most of your travel budget and avoiding unnecessary expenses. These trips aren't cheap, you know. Most couples tell me they broke the bank to plan this, the biggest and most important vacation of their lives. In fact, *Modern Bride* magazine recently surveyed readers and found that the average amount couples spent on their honeymoons was $3,336. Your budget might be far more or far less, but you will certainly benefit from learning how to get more honeymoon for your money.

Speaking of smart trip budgeting, editors from the most influential bridal magazines and representatives of the top travel associations will share their insider advice with you in this book, and real couples from across the country will tell you their triumphs (and their warnings) from their own once-in-a-lifetime trips. The various checklists and worksheets will keep you organized, and the Resources will point you where you need to go for further information.

The fun begins in just a few pages. First, check out these four couples' honeymoons for some inspiration.

SHAELYNN AND CHRISTOPHER'S BERMUDA ADVENTURE

We chose Bermuda because it was just a two-hour flight to get there, and since we only had five days off from work for our trip, we didn't want to lose two days traveling there and back. We chose a great resort right on the azure-blue waters, and we spent the first day just laying out by the pool, decompressing from all the excitement and stress of our wedding weekend. We drank brightly colored frozen drinks, snacked on freshly caught seafood, slow danced on the beach in front of the glowing setting sun, fulfilled a Bermudian good-luck ritual by kissing beneath the circular arch of a stone moon gate, and recharged for the days ahead.

Our hotel featured an underground cavern and natural pool of ocean water, and the hotel had lit it from beneath the surface of the water with blue and green lights so the entire cavern glowed and glimmered. The ceiling of the cavern was spiked with natural rock formations, and you could see down to the rock formations and fish on the bottom of the pool. We were able to rent that cavern out for several hours, giving us complete privacy to swim there together, explore the underwater formations with our snorkeling gear, and share some very intimate time in a dreamlike setting. It was like a mermaid's castle there, and it was one of the most unforgettable afternoons of our lives.

We filled the rest of our short visit with moped rides across the island, riding horses on the beach at dusk, and snorkeling in the crystal-clear waters around old shipwrecks just off the coast. Another highlight was a botanical garden where they made perfume from the natural essence of the flowers plucked from right on their own grounds. The garden tour was lovely, and Christopher bought me a bottle of the rose-essence scent as a keepsake. I wore it throughout the rest of our stay, and I'll wear it for as long as possible in the future.

It was an unbelievably magical and romantic honeymoon, and we'll go back there again on our fifth anniversary.

JULIE AND BOBBY'S SPANISH SPONTANEITY

Bobby had never been abroad before, so it didn't take us long to decide on Spain as our honeymoon destination. Since our wedding was in November, we also knew that it was the off-season in Europe, when crowds would be fewer and expenses would be lower. It was a perfect fit.

We only booked the first night of our honeymoon at one particular hotel in Madrid so that we knew we'd have a place to stay when we reached Spain. From there, we planned everything day by day, which made the entire trip a completely spontaneous adventure. Each day, we'd call a hotel in a city we were headed to, and we made reservations then, moment by moment. We'd armed ourselves with travel books on Spain, so we knew the main cities we wanted to see, and our entire trek just unfolded before us as we took the train from city to gorgeous city.

While in Seville, we took a twilight horse-and-carriage ride through the city streets. During the day, we visited Plaza del Salvador, which was hopping with tons of locals sitting outdoors at the cafés and enjoying their tapas and drinks.

In Cordoba, we'd booked an amazing suite with a sitting room, king-size bed, marble bathroom and all-marble floors, plus a terrace overlooking the city. (Never could we have gotten a room this extravagant if we'd gone there in high tourist season, when such a room would be booked solid and at a far higher price!)

After that, we hopped a train to the south of Spain's Costa del Sol, which is part of the Spanish Riviera and is a beautiful and extravagant vacation spot for so many celebrities and royalty. This area of the Parador Nerja was absolutely beautiful, with whitewashed houses, enormous mountains all around, and the Mediterranean right there before us. After our days in the Riviera, we rented a car and drove along the coast to Marbella, where we stopped to walk along the Puerto Bonuse, which reminded us of the South Beach strip in Miami with its jet set crowds, designer shopping, and nonstop nightlife.

We made the most of every opportunity we came across, and our honeymoon—for all of its spontaneity—turned out far better being left to chance than it ever would had we attempted to plan the entire trip according to a strict schedule of our own . . . or (even worse) as part of some group charter tour. We visited street markets and museums, restaurants and hotels, and we took a romantic ride on an overnight train through some of the most incredible countryside scenery we'd ever experienced.

Our no-itinerary-allowed trip was the perfect getaway—and a welcome retreat from the fast-paced, ultraorganized world we'd left behind for the first nine days of our marriage. We truly were explorers in a different world, and we would do it all again in a heartbeat.

NATALIE AND MARK'S BREATHTAKING HONEYMOON

We knew our Alaskan cruise would deliver us to a beautiful part of the world where glaciers floated past at imperceptible speed, eagles soared overhead, and whales breached just yards away from our ship. We knew we were in for countless once-in-a-lifetime photo opportunities and sights we'd never dreamed of. But it was all far better than anything we could have imagined. For the first few days, it seemed like we were just pointing at one amazing new sight after another, in awe that the world still offered untouched places of natural perfection—which was so far from the city world we lived in with all of its man-made accents: pollution, graffiti, taxis, noise, and hurry-up pace. We saw caribou and bears on the shoreline looking at us like we were no threat at all. We saw amazing ice formations floating by us and a clear blue sky with air that was so clean we had to get used to it at first.

At night, the sky . . . it's impossible for words to do it any justice. With such a lack of air pollution, the night sky was filled with millions of stars, every constellation you could think of for that season, shooting stars, satellites, and planets visible to the eye. On the other edge of the horizon, the Northern Lights flashed in a shimmery dance, almost like a ghost in the sky—an unforgettable phenomenon that I still dream about to this day.

When we could be persuaded to step inside our cruise ship, we entered another exciting world full of amazing restaurants and some of the best food we'd ever had, never-ending buffets and delectable treats we ordered for a romantic dinner in our cabin one night. We took in Broadway-type reviews, tried our hand at roulette in the casino, and danced until dawn with other honeymooners we'd met during our two-week adventure. Even if I had to, I couldn't think of one thing that was missing from our honeymoon. We went to a whole new world, and the entire trip was glorious from beginning to end. Even more so because all of our parents and grandparents chipped in to pay for it, with one request—that we have the time of our lives. And we did.

SARAH AND JACK'S HONEYMOON . . .
WITH SIERRA, JACK JR., AND HANNAH

This was a second marriage for both of us, and with all the preparations for our wedding and our marriage, we were also preparing to blend our two families together as one. Sierra is my daughter from a previous marriage, and Jack Jr. and Hannah are Jack's children from a previous marriage. We made the kids a huge part of our wedding day, since we were taking vows not only as a couple but as a new family, and so it was only natural that we'd include the kids in a family honeymoon.

We thought about doing one of those family vacation packages on an island, with the kids whisked off for group activities like biking, surfing, and snorkeling while we had our days free for whatever we wanted to do as a couple. But that didn't sit well with us, since we wanted time together to share activities and bond as a group. So Jack planned an incredible itinerary that we started in Boston, taking in all the historical and cultural sights available, seeing a basketball game, and enjoying the wharfside, after which we took the train, stop by stop, down the East Coast to Washington,

DC. Along the way, we stopped in Rhode Island, at Providence and Newport, where we did the beach things and went boating together. Then we traveled farther, down to New York City, where we saw a Broadway play; attended a taping of *Emeril Live,* Sierra's favorite cooking show (she wants to be a chef someday); and looked for celebrities. Jack had even researched the time and location of a television drama that was scheduled to tape during the late-night hours out in front of Tavern on the Green, so the kids were thrilled to see a real TV-show taping. Actually, I think I was the most thrilled of all! From there, we hopped the train back down to Philadelphia, where we saw the Liberty Bell and caught another professional basketball game. Then we ended up in Washington, DC, where we did the whole historical tour thing. This was by far the highlight of the trip, since the kids have an incredible sense of patriotism and they looked so amazed at all the things they saw around them. We bonded during our tours and activities, especially while on the train, sharing DVDs and lunch, amusing ourselves during the hours of travel.

Sure, we could have left the kids at home and enjoyed two weeks alone in the Italian countryside, but this trip was a far better experience for all of us. Our group honeymoon brought us together as a family, and nothing could please us more or make our marriage richer than that.

Your Honeymoon Dream Sheet

Here's where you get to put your dreams down on paper for the first time. Whatever your fantasy of the perfect honeymoon entails—from the regions you want to see to the sporting activities you want to do to the special romantic moments you want to experience, like that passionate kiss at the ocean's edge in *From Here to Eternity*—put it down here and allow the image of your perfect trip to take shape. It's only by defining your wishes that you can make them come true, even if your wishes change during the course of the planning stage. And now, together, answer the following questions:

What type of honeymoon are you most interested in?
(Check more than one, if you wish, at this time.)

- ❏ Relaxing and romantic
- ❏ Adventurous
- ❏ Historical
- ❏ Culinary
- ❏ Overseas
- ❏ Beach-oriented
- ❏ Sports-oriented
- ❏ Tourism-oriented
- ❏ Secluded
- ❏ Rustic
- ❏ Five-star luxury
- ❏ Island
- ❏ Continental United States
- ❏ Major city
- ❏ Little-known location
- ❏ Cruise
- ❏ Family vacation with the kids
- ❏ Shopping-centric
- ❏ Wild party atmosphere
- ❏ Nude beaches
- ❏ Lots of nature and scenery
- ❏ Spa

❏ Special event (such as coinciding with Carnivale in Brazil, Mardi Gras in New Orleans, the Super Bowl, the Oscars, an ethnic or a religious festival, etc.)

❏ Country of your heritage

What kind of pace do you wish for your honeymoon?

❏ Ultrarelaxed (i.e., "We want to do little more than lounging on the beach, enjoying utter calm.")

❏ Relaxed (i.e., "We want to lounge on the beach by day but hit the clubs at night.")

❏ Active (i.e., "Forget the beach! We want to fill our days with activities and our nights taking in the sights, sounds, tastes, and customs.")

❏ Always on the go (i.e., "We want lots of traveling from place to place, lots of activities, lots of experiences—only stopping for sex and sleep.")

Do you have any dream destinations in mind?
What is it about these spots that attracts you?

1.

2.

3.

4.

5.

What mode of transportation do you want to take to reach your destination?

❏ Airplane

❏ Auto

❏ Cruise ship

❏ Train

Do you want to travel to a foreign destination that would require passports, visas, immunizations, safety reports, currency exchange, and weather predictions?

- ❏ Travel to another continent
- ❏ Travel to a faraway island or city
- ❏ Travel to a nearby island or city
- ❏ Keep travel to a minimum

Does the length of time you have for your honeymoon allow you enough traveling time to get to and from your destination with plenty of time in between to relax and enjoy your adventure? We have:

- ❏ Less than a week, including travel days
- ❏ 7 to 10 days
- ❏ 11 to 14 days
- ❏ More than two weeks
- ❏ Just one weekend

What kind of climate are you looking for in your destination?

- ❏ Hot and balmy
- ❏ Milder climate
- ❏ Winter weather
- ❏ Mixed weather
- ❏ Doesn't matter

Does your dream vacation revolve around a certain activity (e.g., skiing, golf, a special event, etc.)?

- ❏ Ocean sports (swimming, scuba diving, snorkeling, sailing, surfing, boating, parasailing, etc.)
- ❏ Land sports (tennis, golf, mountain biking, etc.)
- ❏ Winter sports (skiing, snowboarding, skating, etc.)
- ❏ Shopping
- ❏ Sightseeing

❏ Gambling

❏ Food and wine

❏ Historical or cultural events (touring historical estates, museums, cultural centers, etc.)

❏ Other (list here)

Do you have any special connections at any of your ideal honeymoon destinations, such as a cousin who works at a world-renowned resort in Florida, a friend who works at a spa, or a colleague in the travel business?

What are the images of your perfect honeymoon? (Examples include snapshot moments of the two of you on a beach at sunset, scuba diving by a coral reef, biking down the side of a volcano, or reveling at Mardi Gras. Get detailed here, as it is this section that will be most helpful in your planning stages.)

What do you absolutely know that you *don't* want in your honeymoon picture?
(Examples include lots of families with kids around, a wild party atmosphere,
traveling with tour groups, formal attire for meals, sticking to an itinerary,
or just lying around on the beach.)

What other thoughts come to mind as you take your first steps in planning this trip?

Simplify It

Have a picture of your ideal honeymoon vision? Attach it here so you
can flip back and look at it for ideas
and inspiration.

PART I

The Basics

Where to Start

Hen you first started planning your wedding, you gave a lot of thought to the basic foundations of choosing the date, time, and place; the right season for your wedding; and—especially—your budget. All of your plans stemmed from these all-important elements, and you may have even saved a bundle of money by planning your wedding for the off-season, when bridal fees are much, much lower but the weather is still great. All the same principles apply when you're planning your honeymoon.

What Season Is It?

If you read the introduction, you'll remember the story of Julie and Bobby's spontaneous exploration of the Spanish cities and countryside. That trip turned out so well primarily because it was the off-season in Spain, the time when the largest crowds of tourists clear out, prices dip, and hotels everywhere have more availability. "If we had gone in the summertime," says Julie, "we would have been homeless on our honeymoon. We would have had incredible amounts of trouble finding a place to stay, and it would have been extremely frustrating and not fun at all."

While few couples have the courage to plan a by-the-seat-of-the-pants honeymoon, Julie's story is a shining example of how booking a location during its off-season presents so many more opportunities and much lower costs. You won't get the big crowds, you won't get the jacked-up supply-and-demand prices, but you'll still have a new world full of amazing sights, sounds, and tastes to explore. Traveling to a location that will be in its off-season at the time of your honeymoon can be a bright idea for your budget and enjoyment, but there is one little factor you need to keep in mind: Sometimes, the off-season wraps itself around a time of inclement weather. For instance, during the off-season in Europe, it's likely to be cold, rainy, misty, and foggy at times. If your dream honeymoon image includes a bike tour of the Italian countryside, the off-season wouldn't be the best time to go. It's hard to pedal while wearing a parka. In the Florida Keys, the off-season might be unbearably hot and humid. On some islands, the off-season means a hurricane slamming into the shores and blowing the roofs off thatched huts. True, you'll find, after doing a little research, that planning your honeymoon during the off-season can save you as much as 40% off all expenses, but at some locations at the most perilous times of the year, that savings isn't going to give you much comfort—say, if you must be airlifted off the roof of your hotel with minutes to spare before a flash flood is about to drive the entire resort over the edge of a cliff.

For any location you have in mind, find out the months of its in-season and off-season status for your budget, for planning ease, and for your sanity. A quality travel agent will be able to tell you which places are at their best during which times of year, offering you all the benefits and a lower chance of drawbacks.

The Shoulder Season

During your research of these ideal times to visit, whether you're guided by a travel agent or not, be sure to ask about the *most* ideal season at any location, the *shoulder season*. This block of weeks is that gray area between a destination's in-season and off-season, the time when the crowds are starting to thin out, availability is higher, and the weather and attractions are every bit as breathtaking as during high tourist time . . . only it's less expensive because you won't be there right in the middle of peak demand. At some spots, the shoulder season might be right after the kids all go back to school and the majority of family travelers head home to buy those lunch boxes and number-two pencils. You're left with a wide-open, pristine beach more to yourselves, no trouble getting a dinner reservation or a great tee time on the links—and you'll pay some 20% less for eight days at the same resort than the departing family you're crossing paths with on your way into the lobby.

So when's the shoulder season at a particular resort? That's one you'll have to check out on your own, as you do your individual research with a travel agent and as you scan through the weather averages charts I'll discuss in just a few minutes. I can, however, give you a few examples of prime shoulder seasons to whet your appetite. If you've planned your wedding for the peak bridal season of June, you're not doomed to pay top dollar for your honeymoon trip. June is not peak season all over the world. In fact, you're on the receiving end of shoulder season in two of the most popular honeymoon destinations. During the balmy summer months, you may find great deals and nothing's-missing services in Australia and Hawaii. As you toss your bouquet in the summer heat at home, the temperature is cooling off Down Under and on the great islands, the waves are calming down, and the waters are still magnificent for swimming or surfing. And prices have dipped.

In September, just when the summer tourists are packing up and clearing out, head for Mexico to enjoy the milder weather and an enormous lineup of events and activities, tours, and tastes. If you've taken smart budgeting advice and planned your wedding for the off-months of December and January, your reward for this choice could be a fabulous deal in the Caribbean, and you'll hit it right before peak tourist season is about to start later in the winter.

Put the Honeymoon on Hold!

One option that's growing in popularity right now is postponing the big honeymoon for a few months after the wedding and just grabbing a relaxing weekend getaway right after the big day. More and more couples find it smart to wait a few months before going on their big honeymoon trip, which allows them to plan their trip with the wedding money they may have received as gifts. Once they have the cash in hand and know their budget, couples know better what kind of trip they can realistically take. They also might want to wait until the new calendar year, when they have their week or two weeks of vacation available to them. Or perhaps they don't want to run off for an action-packed vacation right after all of those stressful weeks leading up to the wedding. One couple I spoke to said that they wanted to go to Italy for their honeymoon, but they wanted to wait for the off-season, which was six months after their wedding. All of these reasons are valid points, and they make a case for delayed gratification. It's something to think about.

Weather Factors

The weather, obviously, is going to be a big deciding factor for any destination you consider. And not just for its obvious effect on any plans you have to lie out on the beach with a piña colada in your hand. The weather affects so much more than that. Besides the obvious of providing you with a perfect climate in which to enjoy any outdoor activities, you're also looking at the larger picture of safe travel and your own personal safety while on an island or in a foreign country. The weather, after all, is not just rain. It's hurricanes, tornadoes, monsoons, freezing rain, floods, and even dangerously high heat and humidity in some areas. Certain weather conditions bring out the insects in many locations, and in some extremes those swarms of gnats or mosquitoes can make any vacation unbearable.

With these issues in mind—the kinds of issues that you really might not think about at first—you can do some research on the average climate conditions for the list of possible destinations on your list. Ask your travel agent or search the Internet for all the data you need for this very important information.

Watch Out for That Keg!

Unless you really want your honeymoon to take place in the middle of wild and raucous spring break revelry, such as keg parties and wet T-shirt contests, you might want to avoid certain spots around the world in March and April. Or you might really *want* to spend your first week of wedded bliss grabbing bead necklaces on Bourbon Street in New Orleans during Mardi Gras. Whether you want to make a beeline for where the action is or you want to head to the opposite end of the globe from any huge gatherings and public drinking, it's wise to find out if your chosen location will be the site of a big festival. Again, beyond the obvious of streets so jammed with people you can't even drive, be aware that local businesses raise their prices when the festivalgoers come to town ... taking advantage of that all-important supply and demand that keeps the tourism business rolling along. Hotel rates, restaurants, activities, souvenirs, even transportation through town—all are certain to carry higher-than-usual prices at these times. So how do you find out the exact dates of Mardi Gras for your honeymoon weekend? Who do you call to see if the Baja peninsula will be home to a major cultural festival? Start off

Simplify It

To research weather conditions for any destination, at any time of year, check out the following useful Web sites:

AccuWeather
    www.accuweather.com
The Weather Channel
    www.weather.com
World Climate
    www.worldclimate.com (my favorite site for its complete temperature and precipitation charts for thousands of locations across the globe, with links for easy research on in-seasons and off-seasons)

Also check out the major television networks' weather Web sites, like www.cnn.com, for their similar charts and interactive tools.

by calling the tourism department at your destination. (Look at the list in the Resources, or check the Tourism Offices Worldwide Directory Web site at www.towd.com for a link to the tourism office of your choice.) Ask about any scheduled festivals, conferences, and big events that will take place during your stay at their facilities.

If you're a festival chaser—that is, if you're likely to choose a spot *because* it's going to be home to a ton of action, celebrity visits, and non-stop activities, no matter what the price increase—then, again, check with the tourism board. Just for fun, check out www.festivals.com for its month-by-month listings and links to where the parties are all over the world. This site will let you know about the next Sundance Film Festival in Park City (who wouldn't want to run into Robert Redford during their honeymoon?) plus any number of lesser-known and equally captivating festivals that spring up to celebrate anniversaries, holidays, ethnic and religious days of praise, cultural events, and other interesting happenings around the globe.

How Much Time Do You Have?

Remember Shaelynn and Christopher, the couple in the first honey-moon story who planned a quickie getaway to Bermuda because they only had five days for their honeymoon? You too might have a time-crunch facing you, with only a week to devote to a big vacation, and that kind of boundary can limit the destinations you have to choose from. After all, you might not want to lose two days out of the week for travel alone by flying to a faraway continent. Add in a half day to a full day of recovery time when you first get there plus a day to un-wind when you return home from the trip, and that leaves you with only three solid days to enjoy yourself. If, however, you choose a nearby location that's just a short flight or ride away, then you have five days at your disposal.

Distance is a *big* issue with a lot of travelers, not just honeymoon-ers, since some people don't consider the strain, stress, and exhaustion of a long flight or a lot of connecting flights, buses, and ferry rides to be part of the ideal getaway. If distance is an issue for you, find out which exotic cities are closer to you than others. Do some online research on flight departure and arrival times to see just how long that flight to Paris really is.

When you're looking at your available time frame for travel, it's wise to plan ahead with a strategic reservation of your available vacation days off work. You'd be surprised at how many people don't make optimum use of their week or two weeks off. Had Shaelynn and Christopher managed their paid vacation days more wisely throughout the year, they might not have been so limited in their choice of destinations.

Another factor for travel time affects the growing number of couples who plan to bring their kids along on a family honeymoon. For this kind of trip, you'll need to carefully orchestrate your days off, the kids' days off school, and the amount of distance and travel stress you're willing to undergo. Smart advance planning means you can coordinate your calendars for a bigger and better trip.

Simplify It

Forget about getting out the map and measuring out the mileage between your hometown and Borneo. Visit www.indo.com/distance, plug in your hometown and the destination city, and get the exact distance between them in miles and kilometers.

Plane, Train, Boat, or Car?

The issue of transportation—since this is a big, important trip—can also play a part in the kind of honeymoon you plan. Earlier I mentioned that your available amount of time off work might dissuade you from taking a lengthy flight, such as a 24-hour flight to Sydney. For some couples, it's a time constraint thing. For others, it's an aversion to really long airplane or car rides. Whatever your preference, you will need to decide if you're even up for a trans-Atlantic flight or if you'd like your honeymoon to be rather short on certain kinds of transportation.

I recently heard from a couple with a wonderful plan for their honeymoon but a bit of a time-crunch problem. The groom was a New York City firefighter who survived the attacks on September 11. When the couple discussed their ideal honeymoon locations, they thought about the usual tropical spots, but then they realized that although they'd been to many islands and foreign countries together, they really hadn't seen very much of the United States beyond their own home states and Florida. With their own renewed sense of patriotism and a great love for what this country has to offer, they wanted to take a train cross-country in order to see more of the sights in the great stretch between the coasts. However, they only had 12 days for their trip, and that wouldn't be time enough for them to travel by train to California and back. Quite happily, I was able to let them know more about Amtrak's Air Rail program (800-321-8684), which would allow them to take the train one way and then take a quick plane ride the opposite way. This couple chose to fly out to California and then take a leisurely and scenic ride home on the train. Their wish for a great train tour of their country was granted, and the firefighter and his bride will soon see more of the country that means the world to them.

Just the Facts

Bridal Guide magazine asked readers how many days and nights they'd spend on their honeymoon. The results:

Less than 7 nights	39.1%
7 to 10 nights	47.3%
11 to 14 nights	12.4%
15 nights or more	1.2%

The average length of a honeymoon, according to *Bridal Guide,* is 7.7 nights.

How Much Money Do You Have?

Before you can start dreaming of an island getaway or an international jet-set jaunt across the most alluring points on the Riviera, a big question remains: What kind of money are we talking about here?

It's a rare couple who doesn't have to worry about a honeymoon budget at all, but if you're like most, you *do* have to plan your trip according to what you can reasonably afford. The world of travel offers some truly spectacular trips—at some truly spectacular prices—so the best way to keep your feet on solid ground (for now) is to figure out the general range of your own honeymoon budget.

Looking at the sidebar on page 12, you might be surprised to see that the *minority* of couples are blowing the bank, with nearly a quarter spending a relatively modest amount on their trip of a lifetime. Clearly, these money-smart couples have found great deals all over the world, and they're *not* going to start off their married life under a mountain of debt. What lasts after their big getaway are their exciting and romantic memories, not endless credit card charges and interest payments!

> ## Just the Facts
>
> *Bridal Guide* readers planned their transportation mode as:
>
> | | |
> |---|---|
> | Air | 46.9% |
> | Car | 45.8% |
> | Cruise ship | 7.3% |

Wait a Minute! Who's Paying for All of This?

Somewhere out there, brides are picking up the entire tabs for their honeymoons themselves. Sure, the old rules of etiquette listed that the honeymoon was paid for by the groom's parents, but that old etiquette must-do has definitely gone out the window. Now couples and their families are creating their own payment arrangements, with the couple and their families sharing the honeymoon bills as a team. *Bridal Guide* magazine asked readers who was paying for *their* honeymoons, and the results show a big departure from etiquette rules of old:

The bride and groom pay for the honeymoon	60.3%
The couple and their parents share the costs	20.2%
The groom pays for the honeymoon	13.8%
The couple's parents pay for the honeymoon	3.4%

The couple register for their honeymoon	1.2%
The bride pays for the honeymoon	1.0%
Other	0.1%

Chances are you'll either pay for your honeymoon as a couple or you'll pay for it with your parents' help. Whatever the case, it's best to sit down right now to figure out where your honeymoon fund is coming from and when you'll have it to spend. If your parents are kind and generous enough to share the expense with you—or even *really* kind and *really* generous enough to pay for the entire thing—a wise move is to create a special honeymoon fund bank account for their contribution. You might have run into this situation when you started figuring out who would pay for your wedding and how much they'd be able to give. One set of parents might have offered a nice chunk of money, whereas the other couldn't give quite as much. The wisest thing to do, for both your wedding funds *and* your honeymoon funds, is to keep their donations confidential, thereby avoiding any risk of comparison. Just take those checks, give a thank-you kiss, and deposit them in the bank without a word to anyone. That's the way a honeymoon registry works, and it's a solid deal for this type of payment plan as well.

Just the Facts

Bridal Guide magazine recently surveyed readers and found the average honeymoon budgets were:

Less than $2,000	23.9%
$2,000 to $3,499	47.1%
$3,500 to $4,999	18.3%
$5,000 or more	10.7%

The average honeymoon budget of all readers was $2,826.

Where Is This Money Coming From?

Some couples save up for their honeymoons for years, and some use portions of their previous savings. Some set up an automatic deposit plan from their paycheck to a savings account, and others use expected graduation or gift money to finance their once-in-a-lifetime trip. One of the more popular ways to at least partially fund a honeymoon is to use your tax refund check. The Travel Institute of America says that almost 20% of all Americans earmark their upcoming refund checks from Uncle Sam specifically to pay for a big vacation, and what's bigger than your honeymoon? In some cases, if your travel plans are more modest, this one check might pay for your entire trip!

Sign Us Up for Bali!

Honeymoon registries are a growing trend in the travel industry, with more and more couples registering not only for blenders and china patterns but also for their just-married getaways. If you haven't heard of this before, you can now register with a tour operator, a tour company, or even a honeymoon registry travel agency so that your guests can browse your wishes and give you wedding gifts of a portion of

Don't Go Wild with Your Plans!

Clearly, many couples plan to use their wedding gift money, and others depend on their credit cards. Whatever your source of funds for your honeymoon, be sure to keep within the realm of a realistic budget. Even the travel industry knows that honeymooners are extremely likely to go all out and spend exorbitant amounts of money on this all-important trip, with the emotion of it running their spending right up into the stratosphere.

Yes, this is a very important and exciting trip, and you should have the trip of your dreams. But it's an unwise move to act without a set budget, to max out your credit cards and start your married life so deep in debt that your honeymoon winds up costing you almost *twice* its original value once you finally get done paying it off. So keep within your realistic expectations of the amount of money you'll have to spend, make your plans accordingly, and then upgrade your plans with quality activities and experiences on-site.

your total honeymoon expenses—kicking in their contributions so the two of you can go to Hawaii *or* even for wonderful, romantic experiences while you're *on* your honeymoon. I particularly love that your guests can now give you the gift of a romantic dinner in a fine restaurant on the water's edge, his and hers massages in your hotel suite, spa treatments, candlelight midnight cruises, and adventurous outings such as scuba diving or swimming with dolphins. These types of experiences make a honeymoon so much more romantic, magical, and memorable that they become a gift that lasts forever.

One of the most popular honeymoon registries out there right now is HoneyLuna .com, which allows your guests to choose from shares in your trip to exciting individual adventures during your stay. For the more adventurous, activity-oriented couple, there is Backroads.com, where you can register for such full-package trips as biking and hiking tours through Provence, Tuscany, Vermont, California wine country, and the Canadian Rockies.

The time is right for honeymoon registries, since the Travel Institute of America (www.tia.org) reports that 22.6 million experienced travelers gave the gift of travel to others in the past three years. Knowing as they do the joys of getting away, of seeing the world, and of just unwinding in unbelievably beautiful and historical surroundings, these globetrotters love to help others explore the world as well.

Simplify It

Don't use numbers in the starter budget worksheet right now. Instead, use this as a tool to prioritize your honeymoon budget. For instance, if you know you want to stay at a five-star hotel, then mark the "hotel" category with a 10 or five asterisks (*****) or whatever other code you wish to use. If you really don't care about sporting activities, or if the resorts you like offer all activities for free, then you get to write in $0 or FREE or one asterisk (*) to denote that category's low demand on your budget. Create your own system, and start putting together the final stages of the puzzle. Once you get this set, and once you make your decisions on all the particulars mentioned in this chapter, then you get to wander through the vast world of options out there to find the honeymoon that's waiting for you.

Setting Up Your Budget

Once you form an accurate picture of your honeymoon budget's total amount—knowing that you can upgrade your activities and experiences on-site with any extra registry gifts in the future—it's time to create a workable, fluid budget to keep you on track while you research resorts and regions and begin booking your trip. Just as you did with your wedding budget, use this one to keep you within acceptable boundaries, to rule out that "it would be great, but it's just way too much" option. Your budget shouldn't strangle you; it's just a reminder tapping you on the shoulder and reminding you of what you have to work with.

Later in this book, you'll learn more about stretching your budget and perhaps even getting some items and services during the trip for free, and you can shift and change your budget once your smart shopping skills take effect. For now, start off by sketching out a starter budget on the worksheet I've provided here. It certainly won't be your final budget at this point, before you've done a lot of research, but it will help steer you toward a more realistic money picture.

Your Honeymoon Budget Worksheet

Item	Budgeted	Actual
Airfare		
Hotel reservations		
Transportation		
• Rides to and from the airport from home		
• Rides to and from the airport from hotel		
• Transportation during your stay		
• Car rental		

(continues)

(continued from page 15)

Item	Budgeted	Actual
Meals		
Beverages		
Activities and entertainment		
Equipment for activities		
Shopping		
Souvenirs		
Wardrobe		
Beachwear		
Luggage and carry-ons		
Toiletries		
Camera and film		
Communication (cell phone, personal digital assistant, etc.)		
Taxes		
Tips		
Disposable cash		
Emergency cash		
Travelers' checks		
Passport application		
Other ID application		
Immunizations		
Other:		

Doing Your Research

The success of your trip—your ability to create the dream getaway in the ideal location—starts with finding the best information on any resort, cruise, or flight you have in mind. Good researching can turn up great deals and little-known islands or attractions that may be better than anything you originally hoped for, and it can save you from the kinds of travel headaches and nightmares that inexperienced travelers can encounter. You've undoubtedly planned trips before, whether for vacation, business, or family activities, so you're no stranger to the kinds of travel information and Web sites available. But in this case, your honeymoon is very likely to be *unlike any trip you've ever taken before,* so your research tasks might take you in entirely different directions. Before you discover a whole new world on your honeymoon, you'll first have to sort or surf through whole new worlds in your research . . . perhaps lots of them.

Where do you start? The most obvious first step is asking your friends and family where they've gone on the greatest getaways of

Watch Out!

Before we get into the meat of this chapter on researching the best finds out there, I want to remind you that I am not endorsing any Web site or travel program, and at no time am I going to say, "This is the place you should go." I am simply telling you what's out there to check, to subject to your own questions, consumer smarts, and gut instincts. No travel Web site or reservations process is 100% snag-free, and since different people have different needs and preferences, there is no way I can provide a fail-safe resource to meet all individual needs. So make note now that I have simply assembled these resources for you to *explore*. I am setting you on course to research your own trip, using your own smarts.

their lives. If your recently married cousin raves about her week in Costa Rica, then you know that particular adventure trip comes with a big, real-life thumbs-up from someone whose advice you trust. It's just like when you started planning your wedding. Personal recommendations can add a few names to your list of places to investigate further. With those testimonials, your search expands.

Smart research, just like with your wedding, depends on your allowing it enough time and *taking your time* with the process. So start looking and booking early, since that's the best way to sign up for better-priced deals and the best in tour opportunities. Booking more than a year in advance can save you up to 60% off the cost of your trip, whereas booking late can cost you a large percentage more, depending on your choice of location and the length of your trip.

Most of the honeymoon nightmare stories I've heard over the past 10 years have one thing in common: The couples did not spend enough time researching their destinations, and they rushed through the process of booking their trips. They may have snapped up unbelievably low-priced packages without reading the fine print, or they just took the first offer they found. I advise you now to keep an open mind and put as much effort into planning this trip as you surely are into planning your wedding. This is, after all, the trip of a lifetime, and your dedication to doing it right starts right here.

Throughout the course of this chapter, you're going to learn more about the many types of travel resources out there, including some Web sites you've probably never heard of. So even if you've planned plenty of vacations in the past, please do not skip this chapter. Within its pages, you'll learn how to make the most of your research time, and

Where Do You Start Your Search?

Bridal Guide magazine recently polled readers on where they started looking for their honeymoon information, and following is the breakdown of the most popular types of resources consulted. (Please note that survey respondents checked more than one resource, since they researched a wide variety of places to get their honeymoon information.)

Bridal magazines	66.9%
Friends	53.0%
Internet	51.8%
Travel agent	39.1%
Travel books	30.8%
Travel magazines	29.3%
Newspaper travel sections	8.9%
Television/radio ads	8.9%
Newspaper ads	7.7%

Clearly, these numbers show that the vast majority of honeymoon planners cast a wide net for travel information, going to a variety of sources for the latest and greatest in honeymoon travel details.

you may learn how to arrange a far more upscale honeymoon than you originally thought you'd ever have.

Working with a Travel Agent

If you've learned anything while planning your wedding, it's that a top-notch industry professional can make your life and your decisions a *whole* lot easier when you're faced with literally hundreds of options for your very special event. Travel agents can save the day just as well as that "in the know" caterer or cake baker who, during your wedding planning, tipped you off to a great value buy or a truly original possibility you weren't aware of before. If you'd like the initial search process for the perfect honeymoon destination (and the ideal honeymoon package) to go quickly and efficiently—and save you from making any terrible mistakes along the way—consider working with a great travel agent.

Just the Facts

According to the Travel Institute of America's 2002 survey question regarding general vacationers' travel preparation methods, 45% of travelers made their trip plans with the help of a certified travel agent.

Without question, more and more people these days make their travel reservations by themselves over the Internet, but there's something big to be said about the advantages of planning your honeymoon with the help of a travel agent. Make that a *good* travel agent. With the insider knowledge and updated reports that quality travel agents receive, you can quickly and easily find the best and most attractive options out there according to your list of honeymoon criteria. Travel agents can save you money with their own special discounts and deals they receive for moving big volumes of business through the airline and hotel industry. An agent can handle so many aspects of your research and planning, and the real benefit is having a live person answer your questions and make the many necessary shifts and tweaks to your plans for optimum planning in real life.

Again, though, you have to find a *good* travel agent to maximize the benefits.

Finding the Best Travel Agent Out There

As you know from arranging your wedding, you can find quality experts in the business through their membership in a prestigious professional association. Such an affiliation, of course, means that a travel pro has years of experience and a solid reputation, adheres to a set code of high ethics, receives periodic additional training in the field, and subscribes to newsletters or journals for the latest breaking news in the tourism world. To find your own local, top-notch travel agent, check with the following organizations:

> The American Society of Travel Agents: 703-739-2782,
>   www.astanet.com
> Institute of Certified Travel Agents: 800-542-4282, www.icta.com

If you're considering taking a cruise, you can locate a cruise specialist through:

> Cruise Lines International Association: 212-921-0066,
>   www.cruising.org

Questions to Ask Travel Agents

You're putting the fate of your honeymoon, to some degree, into the hands of a travel expert, and that's a big level of trust. In many ways, this pro will share the job of creating your dream trip, so you ought to know that the expert you're dealing with not only has your best interests in mind but also has the skills and knowledge to serve you well. Ask the following questions of any travel agent to be sure you're agreeing to work with the right expert for you:

- How many years of experience in the travel industry do you have?
- Do you belong to any professional travel associations? Which ones, and for how long have you been a member?

- Have you planned many honeymoon trips? A wide variety of honeymoon trips, not just sun and sand vacations?
- Do you specialize in any particular kinds of vacations? Our requested type of trip, perhaps?
- Are you a "preferred supplier" for any particular airline or cruise company? (Answering "yes" to this question means that the travel agent is paid to swing more business to a particular cruise line or airline, perhaps even a hotel. Consider this seriously, since you'll get better deals from an unbiased agent.)
- Do you travel a lot yourself?
- Have you been to the kinds of destinations we have in mind?
- What is the best trip you've ever been on?

Obviously, you'll want to hire a travel agent with a great track record and lots of experience in planning important trips like yours, but the most important information you're looking for here is *not* the number of honeymoons she's ever booked or the number of associations to which he belongs. You're looking for professionalism, pure and simple. When you're talking to the expert, does she seem distracted, not at all interested in being "interviewed"? If so, find another expert. Does he seem rushed, giving you one-word answers so that he can get back on the phone to earn more commission by selling cruises for spring break season? Travel agents work on commission, so they have a vested

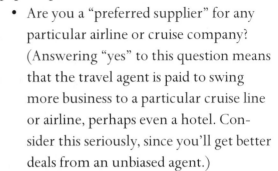

Honeymoon Reflections

We went to our local travel club to have one of their agents book our honeymoon. It's a busy office, and you wait for your name to be called, and then you go to the agent who's available. We wound up with a travel agent who sighed when we couldn't decide between one flight or another, rolled her eyes when we were taken aback at the price she quoted for a cruise, and gave us the old "If you don't book it now, you'll lose the opportunity to take this cruise" pressure job. We were really turned off at her harsh manner and her impatience with us, so we left. When we visited another agent at a different office, we were treated well, and we booked the same cruise offered by the nasty agent for $1,000 less. It really does matter who you go to.

—Sheila and James

interest in closing a large number of deals during the day. A *true* professional will give you plenty of undivided time, answer your questions fully, and be genuinely interested in your explanations of what you're looking for. If a travel agent seems pushy, rude, condescending, or rushed beyond reason, this isn't the expert you want on your team.

Another big issue is personal familiarity with a wide range of destinations. Sure, she may not have been to Bora-Bora, but she should have a good amount of personal experience with different regions, different resorts, and different activities. Would you want to hire a wedding photographer who's only *read* about taking good pictures in a brochure or on a Web site? Of course not. So why would you work with a travel agent who has no actual experience with what she's selling?

When you do make a connection with a great travel agent, work together as a team to find the best deals and possibilities out there, and allow the agent to guide you through all the little extras—like rental cars and additional activities—you need handled. A quality travel agent will also be available to help you *even while you're on the trip.* If a problem arises, you should be able to call your travel agent for some quick help in finding and booking a change to your plane travel or hotel reservations when an unforeseen schedule change forces a twist in your plans. Also, if you're unhappy with your accommodations when you get to your hotel, you should feel free to call your travel agent for speedy work in finding you a new and better place to stay.

Do-It-Yourself Travel Planning

So many people make their own travel reservations via the Internet, they might be just as skilled at finding great deals as a professional travel agent. Whether or not you have vast experience at finding and booking trips, you need to remind yourself that shopping online brings with it a great responsibility to protect your investments, know the pros and cons of shopping at travel Web sites, be willing to read

It's Not Free Anymore!

I thought travel agents offered free service, making their money on commission. But our travel agent charged us $10 to make our plane reservations. Did she rip us off?

No, she didn't rip you off. It *used* to be the case that travel agents received their commissions directly from the airlines and hotels, with reservations coming at no cost to you. Now, however, so many people (preferring to do all the research themselves) are booking their trips on their own through Web sites that airlines and hotels no longer offer the same incentives to travel agents. The travel agency world is experiencing a big shake-up; now these companies need to charge *you* a nominal fee of $10 to $30 for each reservation to cover their costs of printing out your tickets and itineraries. Some services are still offered for free by travel agencies (such as car rentals, printing out maps for you, and the like), but you should expect to pay a small fee for airline, cruise, and train tickets, plus hotel reservations in some cases.

the fine print, and shop smart for the best investment. You'll also do a great deal of research with noncomputer sources such as magazines, books, and even special travel programming you see on television. Whatever your source, always focus on finding the best deal possible, with the least amount of risk and drawbacks.

Travel Web Sites

If you do plan to book your honeymoon yourselves through one or more of the most popular online travel sites out there, keep these little tips at the forefront of your mind, *before* you hit the "Reserve It" button and seal your plans in cyberspace:

- Travelocity.com and Expedia.com are two of the most popular travel-booking Web sites out there, so check through these sites to see

Watch Out!

I can't say it enough—read *all* the fine print when researching and booking any of your travel plans, whether with a travel agent or especially on your own. Triple-check the following:

• Your hotel, airline, and cruise plan specifics should be listed specifically by name and should not be loopholed with a tricky little clause that says that the resources hold no account-ability for changes to your plans in the future, including airline changes, or that they are free to book you in a hotel that's "similar" or "on par" with the resort you've chosen. That's an open in-vitation for switches that will only frustrate you.

• Be sure the airline, hotel, cruise line, or other travel company you're hiring online has a rock-solid cancellation policy. Unfortunately, some of the most popular online travel sites do not have flawless cancellation and refund policies, and many travelers have complained to me that the discount offered originally was not worth the risk and anger of not being able to get refunds.

• Be sure that you're free to switch your flights or room reservations if you need to. Some auto-reservation sites do not let you make a simple shift to a later departure time or even change the size of the bed in your hotel room. Many seasoned travelers enjoy booking their reservations directly through the airlines or hotels themselves because such switches are very often simple with the help of a live attendant at the airline or hotel.

• Look out for anything else that seems restricting or unclear, with the company assuming no responsibility at all.

if they meet your needs. As always, be extra cautious about reading their terms of service so you know what you'll face if you need to change or cancel your booked arrangements.

• Priceline.com is quite popular these days, but you need to be aware that this service does *not* always allow you to make specific plans for your hotel, airline, or other particulars. You can state your requests by region and some conditions, but Priceline.com is going to sign you up for the resort of *its* choosing, for the best fare possible. And you have to accept what this service finds for you. This is a great Web site for regular trips, for business trips, and for some pleasure travel—but for your honeymoon, it may be too risky. The popular site Hotwire.com works in much the same way, offering great fares for available trips but at a price. They too will choose the airline and resorts for you, letting you know what you've agreed to only after you pay.

• SideStep (www.sidestep.com) won't send you back a "Sorry, no availability" notice for the trip you're researching. This site will search almost 100 travel Web sites for available deals on everything from flights to hotel reservations to rental cars and then connect you directly to the site that offers the deal. That means that SideStep does the research for you, and you land right where you need to be to book your reservations.

• Want to find five-star hotels and the best of the best of upscale attractions? If you want to go first-class all the way, Let's Go (www.letsgo.com) is the ultimate guide for you.

• Want to stay off the beaten path and find out-of-the-way destinations? Hidden America (www.hiddenamerica.com) is just the site for you, with its roundup of hidden gems across the country, including bed-and-breakfasts, inns, festivals, and little-known but unforgettable attractions.

• Do you belong to the Triple-A (AAA) in your area? If so, you could be on the receiving end of this travel association's big discounts and special partnership deals on air, plane, and cruise travel, hotel reservations, car rentals, and just about anything else travel related. Check out their packages online at www.aaa.com, or call 800-432-9755 to find a AAA office near you. For a nominal annual membership fee, you get travel scoops plus the inside edge on travel insurance, road maintenance programs, and even partnership discounts with other related companies. I love the vast collections of AAA travel books, which you can pick up for free at your local AAA office or purchase over the Internet.

• Onetravel.com and www.airtreks.com are Web sites that special- ize in international, exotic travel. Sure, the regular travel Web sites can give you the lowdown on trips to South Africa, Hong Kong, and Egypt, but these sites will connect you to specialized travel agents with a laser-focus on specific regions. With a few clicks, you can con- nect with an in-the-know travel professional who can customize your trip, book all of your flights and hotel reservations, and even arrange for your in-city transportation with a legitimate guide or chauffeur. Travel writers love these sites for their time-saving qualities as well as their insider secrets to any destination on the map.

• Check what's available from a travel consolidator, a company that reserves hotel rooms in bulk and then resells them to the con- sumer for 50% to 60% off the regular hotel rates. If you call the hotel directly, you may be told that all rooms have been sold out during a big travel week, but those reserved rooms might be waiting for your call at the travel consolidator's office. Check out the offerings through the Hotel Reservations Network (800-715-7666, www.hoteldiscounts.com) or Cheap Tickets (800-OK-CHEAP, www.cheaptickets.com). One pop- ular consolidator with deals on cruises is MyTravel (www.mytravel co.com). Keep in mind that you still have to check out the fine print for these offerings, research the quality of the resort and the rooms, and make sure you have a money-back guarantee in case of cancella- tions . . . as with *all* of your smart travel planning. And pay with a credit card so your purchase is protected.

• To find further hotel reservations at discount, check out the American Hotel & Lodging Association's site at www.gotrooms.com.

Stressbuster

When you book your flight or hotel reservations through any Web site, always call the airline or hotel to confirm that your reservations are registered with them. If not, contact the Web site with your order number and demand to speak with customer service.

• Great guides to finding hotels have world-famous names. Try Zagat (www.zagat.com) or Fodor's (www.fodors.com) to customize your search, and line up the best plans for any style of trip, particularly upscale vacations.

• To find historic hotels with a colorful past and recently refurbished accommodations to please visitors, visit www.historichotels .nationaltrust.org.

INDIVIDUAL AIRLINE WEB SITES

You'll find a complete list of the major airlines' Web sites and toll-free numbers in the Resources section at the back of this book. Sometimes you can land a better deal and get far better customer service by booking directly through the airline. Plus many airlines offer partnership deals with car rental companies, restaurant chains, and even local attractions at your destination. Taking the time to research through the airlines themselves—doing it the old-fashioned way—can get you great deals and special extras to make more of your trip.

INDIVIDUAL CRUISE WEB SITES

You'll find a complete list of cruise lines and their contact information in the Resources. Several cruise-oriented magazines (and their affiliated namesake Web sites) like *Porthole* magazine and several specialty cruise periodicals are out there for your use as well.

You should know that 95% of all cruises are booked through travel agents, according to the Cruise Lines International Association, because most cruisers like the personal quality of setting up their arrangements one-on-one with a live reservations agent. If you've never cruised before or never cruised on a ship like the one you're considering, it may be a far better move to call up the cruise line or a travel agency and ask all the questions you have about the ship's amenities, the size of the rooms, and the ability to get upgrades and special services for a honeymoon trip. Frequent cruisers also tell me it's easier to find out about special rates and discounts when you talk to a live representative who has access to current specials that aren't posted through online booking sites.

INDIVIDUAL TRAIN WEB SITES

Amtrak offers great package deals at certain times throughout the year. I found fabulous special packages during the winter months, when I booked my train fare for 15% off regular prices, got two nights at a major hotel for the price of one, *and* received five Gold-level passes that allowed me free entrance to some of my destination city's greatest tourist spots. Amtrak information is found at www.amtrak.com or 800-USA-RAIL.

For train travel across the world, check out the Eurailpass for its rates on unlimited train travel in Europe, a golden ticket to go almost anywhere at any time, and do some research on high-style train travel with the Orient Express. All Web sites and contact information are found in the Resources.

INDIVIDUAL RESORT CHAIN WEB SITES

Also in the Resources, I've listed the Web sites and contact phone numbers for some of the major hotel and resort chains so you can easily access their package information and request their honeymoon rates. If you're the type who would rather speak to a reservations associate, this is the list for you.

Tourism Bureaus

For *any* city, state, island, or country you plan to visit, you can do no greater service to yourself than to contact the board of tourism for that area and request a complete tourism package, including brochures, booklets, special package information, and even videos of locales. And be sure to specify that you're planning a honeymoon, since many destinations have special, separate booklets covering top honeymoon attractions and packages. Again, you'll find a complete list of tourism contact information in the Resources.

Magazines, Newspapers, and Television Programs

So many magazines and newspapers run special travel features. This is especially true of bridal magazines, which, as shown in the beginning of this chapter, are *the* most popular sources for initial honeymoon research. Many bridal magazines have their own Web sites in place, and some even provide honeymoon-planning information and booking discounts. Check all deals out thoroughly, of course, and subject even the bridal magazines to the same type of consumer savvy as you would any other online shopping site.

Not just bridal magazines can help you plan your trips. Visit your local library or bookstore and search through the magazines there. You may even discover magazines you never knew existed, like special titles for spas, cruises, food-oriented travel, and sporting activities like biking, surfing, golf, and other outdoor activities.

Some of the top travel magazines offer their own affiliated Web sites. *Travel and Leisure* magazine, a top research choice, can show you a world of options out there; direct links for more information are provided at its site, www.travelandleisure.com. When you pick up a travel magazine, don't forget to search through the magazine's Web site for years' worth of its best and more updated information.

Another great resource is travel channel specials, such as these recent ones: "World's Sexiest Resorts," "10 Great Adventure Getaways," and "Tasting Tours of Italy." Some networks to keep an eye on are the Travel Channel, the Discovery Channel, E! Television, and even the Food Network for its weekly special programming. Don't forget to check the Web sites for these networks as well, as they often feature articles and video streams of recently aired programs. These sites offer Web site and contact information for featured resorts, so be sure to check the networks online if you couldn't write down the resort's name or Web site in time while watching the special.

Penny-Wise

Keep an eye out for budget travel magazines. With the wide range of travel magazines available, you'll find that some are for more upscale trips and others are specifically focused on the budget-conscious consumer. A good one to start with is Frommer's *Budget Travel* magazine.

Your newspaper is sure to offer a world of travel articles and reviews throughout the year, with special travel-only sections running several times a year. Keep an eye out for your newspaper's special features, and keep a clipping file for those great articles that catch your eye.

Also, a granddaddy of the shopping world brings to you a special travel newsletter that's packed with the smartest travel tips and strategies. *Consumer Reports Travel Letter* lets you know the best times of year to make all of your travel plans, the best deals out in the cruise and resort worlds, and smart consumer-savvy tips to help you get more honeymoon for your budget.

Researching the Extras

While you're in an exploring mood, use your time to check out the details on some of the issues you'll face during your travels, such as money exchange rates and local customs in the exotic lands you might visit. As world travelers, you'll be stepping out of your comfort zone and into a whole new culture, so it's best to be aware of these things before you go.

Money Exchange

If you're planning to travel in a foreign country or on an island that's part of a foreign territory, familiarize yourself with that location's currency. You probably know that the peso is used in Mexico and the mark in Germany and that the euro has been established in Europe. But do you know what kind of currency you'll use in Bermuda, on the Cayman Islands, in the Seychelles, or in Brazil? Do you know how many quetzales you can get for your American dollar? You don't need a degree in international finance to figure out global currency names and rates. Just visit X-rates (www.x-rates.com) and use its interactive tool (searchable by country and by currency name) to learn more about the names and exchange rates of almost 40 different currencies across the world. This site's calculator will instantly provide the latest exchange rates between any type of currency so you'll know how your pounds match up to your dollar and how many drachmas you can get for your lira. Don't forget that many islands do run by the dollar, but it's not always the American dollar they accept. The queen of England is on the Bermudian dollar, and Belize has its own individual print of dollar as well.

Local Customs

In chapter 13, you'll read more about finding out the local customs of any foreign destination as a way to keep yourself safe during your travels. When you step into another world, it's best to know the rules of that area so you don't unintentionally offend someone or even make a huge misstep that can put you in legal trouble or even physical danger. That may sound extreme, but there are spots in this world where the simplest move or the simplest phrase can land you in hot water.

For the greater part of your trip, though, you can make your stay far more enjoyable by learning the customs and a bit of the language in that locale, which will help you move around better, interact more comfortably with locals, and generally become part of the experience instead of just an observer. You can find countless resources on the customs and languages of any region by checking the travel section of your local bookstore or library. Flip through some books to get a feel for the culture you'll soon be immersed in, and make yourself a more welcome visitor wherever you go.

PART II

The New Honeymoons

3

Island Honeymoons

The trend in the world of honeymoons may be toward more adventurous destinations and more unique locations. (Think of today's wedding couple showing off colorful and exotic brochures and announcing, "We're going to Hong Kong on our honeymoon!") But the island honeymoon is still *the* hot choice among all types of destinations. According to the Association of Bridal Consultants, 44% of all honeymooners each year will visit a tropical island on their post big day getaway, slathering on that sunscreen, slipping on their shades, and sunning themselves on a flawless white (or pink or black) sandy beach. That's a lot of couples flying or cruising off to the islands of their choice, and if you're among them, you'll be happy to know that you have many, many islands to choose from, including the "usuals" of Hawaii, Bermuda, and the Bahamas, as well as some islands you might not be too familiar with up until now: the Galápagos Islands, Mauritius, St. Lucia, and more.

You might join the tourist scene and stay at a sprawling resort on a big island, favoring its proximity to lots of nightlife, group excursions,

Watch Out for Flying Palm Trees!

One of the top travel must-dos while planning—as a reminder of the tips in the earlier planning chapters—is to pick a destination that's in its best season for visiting. And that doesn't just apply to budget here. Especially with islands, we're talking about your safety! Islands in any region are especially prone to big storm damage during hurricanes and other tropical squalls, so be sure to check out the island's usual good-weather-versus-storm-season forecasts, as well as times of extremely hot and humid weather and even its bug season.

the shopping, and the fun crowds at poolside, or you might want total solitude and intimacy at a private island for two. On your own private isle, reserved for just the two of you, you'll arrive by helicopter or boat; have the beaches, waters, and waterfalls all to yourselves to use as you please; just relax and enjoy one another's company with no distractions or interruptions whatsoever—perfect if your wedding plans, your family, or the demands of your job drove you up a wall during the weeks prior to your wedding day—and retire to an open-air bungalow overlooking the crystal clear waters of the ocean. (If this sounds good to you, check out "Private Island Escapes" later in this chapter.)

You can fly across the globe to an exotic island no one you know has ever heard of, or you can choose from the most popular and well-known tourist destinations in the world. Fly, cruise, even drive to some (connected to the mainland by bridges, of course, like the Florida Keys), and stay for a weekend or for two weeks. You can spend your entire getaway at one resort or island-hop among several in a cluster. You get what I'm saying here, I'm sure. The choices are endless, all up to your personal preferences . . . and your budget.

While I wish I could write about all the exciting, exotic, and beautiful islands in the world here (actually, I wish I could *visit* all of them!), I've included a few spotlights of some of the most popular destinations, as well as some private islands to dream about, to get you started on your own research. Obviously, island resorts have much in common: the beautiful stretches of natural beaches, private lagoons, water sports like scuba diving and windsurfing, great island cuisine and tropical drinks, hot tubs outside overlooking the ocean, and vast stretches of untouched tropical rain forests and natural formations that invite exploration and perhaps a private moment stolen alone. Many island resorts boast incredible nightlife, friendly natives, dinner cruises, and some of the best sunsets you'll ever see in your life. In this section, all of that is assumed for each, and I'll go on to fill you in on some of the other highlights you'll find at each destination. Some special attractions that I found were a complete and enthralling surprise to me, and I hope they spark some curiosity and interest in you as well. Check the Resources for the Web sites of many island tourism departments so you can look at several spots' latest attractions, package deals, and special extras that can make your island honeymoon a truly unforgettable vacation in paradise.

Simplify It

To research any island, from the most obvious to the most obscure, the one closest to you to the one on the other end of the earth, go to *Islands* magazine's Web site at www.islands.com. Here you'll find complete travel information, reviews, features, contact information, and even details on the climate at many of the world's most attractive and exciting island destinations. If you have no idea what Moorea, Taveuni, and Rarotonga are, this is the place to go.

Hawaiian Islands

By far the most popular honeymoon destination of all the islands, Hawaii's "islands in the sun" have it all, from big city nightlife to unspoiled remote beaches, rain forests, and volcanoes to explore, as well as adventure sports and great views from nearly every angle. Recent honeymooners tell me they often awoke to the sight of rainbows arching over the far-off mountains and over the ocean—so often, in fact, that they became a regular sight and no longer called for the honeymooners to whip out their cameras. Other couples spoke of biking down the outside winding trails of volcanoes, bathing in the ritual springwater pools that ancient kings and queens of Hawaii once used during ceremonies and as parts of wedding ceremonies many years ago. Whale sightings are a common phenomenon, and the ocean life under the sea is as exciting and colorful as the plantlife in the rain forests all around. For many, this is the true definition of paradise, as each individual island provides its own level of natural wonder, tourism, celebration, and sensuality to any romantic getaway. According to *Travel and Leisure,* the most highly rated Hawaiian islands are Maui, Kauai, the big island of Hawaii, Oahu, and Lanai. Maui actually took top prize in 2002 as the most highly rated and most enjoyable island destination in the world, so let's take a closer look at some of the most exciting attractions there.

Maui

Maui has wowed the judges of some of the most prestigious travel destination competitions in the world, and it's also wowed countless honeymooners with its romantic tropical resorts, serene beach and mountainous settings, and focus on pure honeymoon bliss. Many of the resorts offer all-inclusive honeymoon packages, complete with spa services, to make your island getaway one you'll be certain to write home about. Another huge plus if your guy is one to hit the links: Maui offers some of the most gorgeous, most challenging, and highest-rated golf courses in the world. That might just be the FYI to put this island at the top of *your* list as well.

When you're not lounging at poolside or ordering a banana daiquiri at the pool's swim-up bar, you might head out for some of the many excursions that make this destination a grand one for couples. On whale-watching cruises and from scenic lookout spots (perhaps your own hotel room's balcony) during the peak times between December and April, you can see the spouting and breaching whales off in the distance, which is always a crowd favorite among visitors to this island. On museum and aquarium jaunts, you might learn more about the whales' mating rituals or walk through underwater, clear-glass tunnels to see a grand array of tropical fish, sharks, sea turtles, and other undersea creatures, all without getting wet or having to rent scuba equipment. When you've had enough of the underwater scene, check out the far aboveground scene with tours on foot or by helicopter of the many volcanoes, some still smoking and smoldering below the earth's surface. As you'll see in greater depth in the next chapter, "Adventure Honeymoons," these types of adventurous outings give an island vacation that extra kick into the new frontier of honeymoon trips: combining the relaxing island getaway with some truly breathtaking adventurous day trips. And few places on earth offer as wide a selection of combinations as Maui.

You might have heard of Maui's famous areas, Lahaina, Kapalua, Makena, and Wailea, and you're likely to hear those names again when your travel agent recommends their grandest resorts. These are the top spots to see or call home while you're in Maui—particularly the landscapes of Wailea, nestled between the majestic Haleakala volcano (which you can tour to the top of and then bike down) and the azure waters of the ocean. It's the epitome of the magic environment of the Hawaiian Islands.

Kathy and Todd, honeymooners from Chicago, recommend the Tour of the Stars at the Hyatt Regency in Maui, which brings you out

Honeymoon Reflections

During our vacation on Maui, we found that so many of the resorts had luxury spas. So there we were, right out on the ocean's edge, getting massages and authentic Hawaiian rose petal and coconut oil treatments, overlooking the ocean at sunset, and just looking over at each other with a "Can you believe this?" expression on our faces. It was truly unbelievable, completely indulgent, and one of the reasons we're going back to Maui on our next big anniversary.

—Marie and Tim

to a scenic spot just before midnight, serves up luscious island strawberries, champagne, and desserts, and treats you to an unbeatable view of the heavenly night sky above the island. Check out the stars, shooting stars, and distant galaxies with the use of binoculars or the resort's high-powered telescope, aided by a constellation guide who will point out the star groupings with the most romantic and applicable histories. For romantic stargazers, according to Kathy and Todd, this evening is a must.

Kauai

Kauai is a snorkeler's dream, with its countless guided and private tours, amazing underwater formations, and seaside attractions. The great resorts and restaurants are here as well, beckoning you out of your room or off the beach and away from those spectacular sunsets, and the scenery perhaps is the best attraction of this island. Often called Hawaii's most romantic destination, with its waterfall tours and horseback riding on the beach, Kauai is a top spot for honeymooners of all ages.

Oahu

Oahu is home to the world-famous Waikiki Beach, well known for its great surfing. The experts are out there riding the big curls, and you might take a tandem lesson in surfboarding on a calmer surf day or at a gentler section of the ocean. One of the most impressive areas on this island for surfing is Waimea (the word you might mutter to yourself after a particularly powerful wave shows you who's boss), where the world's best boarders come to challenge the angry surf, master it, and make it look easy to the many onlookers on shore.

For a less death-defying outing, you might boat out to one of the private islands for snorkeling, go horseback riding on the beach, or enjoy the company of your fellow vacationers of all ages and ethnicities, as this spot is a crowd attracter among the Hawaiian Islands: Oahu is a favorite for couples vacationing with their kids, due to the enormous numbers of museums, aquariums, and swim-with-sealife and kid-friendly ocean sporting opportunities. It's also the home of the Pearl Harbor Museums and the beaches of Diamond Head. And for your sweet tooth (and your diet), this is the home of the famous Dole Plantation, where those sweet pineapples start their journey to your supermarket—and your glazed hams. It's a true taste of the Hawaiian Island flavor, enjoyed right at its origins.

Hawaii

The Big Island of Hawaii is the home of Kona, where that Kona coffee you enjoy at Starbucks comes from, which perhaps tastes even better on the actual island of Hawaii. You can take a helicopter cruise over the vast coffee bean fields or—like on the other islands—simply enjoy the lush tropical surroundings by foot, sea, bike, or air.

Molokai

Molokai is the island for getting back to nature, with the huge resorts and swarming tourism trips kept safely off on the other islands. Many vacationers come to Molokai to escape the built-up portions of Hawaii, step back into time, and enjoy the land as it was before the developers worked their magic with spas and towering hotels. Some at-home attractions of this quieter, gentler island include romantic stops at vistas high atop the mountains, rain forest and waterfall picnics arranged by a tour guide, spiritual shrines maintained to please the gods, true ride-em-cowboy ranches with

Simplify It

To check up on any of the Hawaiian Islands, from the big, bustling tourist-heavy islands to those of the black sand beaches, those with the best golfing or scuba diving, or those where you're more likely to find seclusion, visit the following Web sites:

Hawaii Visitor and Convention Center: 800-GO-HAWAII, www.hawaii.com

Maui Visitors' Bureau: 800-525-MAUI, www.visitmaui.com

Oahu Visitors' Bureau: 877-525-OAHU, www.visit-oahu.com

Big Island Visitors' Bureau: 800-648-2441, www.bigisland.org

Molokai Visitors Association: 800-800-6367, www.molokai-hawaii.com

Lanai Visitors Bureau: 800-947-4774, www.visitlanai.com

wandering cowboys and horseback rides to complete the transformation, and even a natural rock formation called "Phallic Rock" that makes for a "gotta have that" picture and a fun story for your family and friends. Legend has it that if a woman sits too close to this impressive configuration, her fertility skyrockets, so you might want to take pictures from a distance if you're not planning on having kids anytime soon.

Lanai

Lanai is an impressively large island with only two hotels on its shores, which makes it perfect for you if you want a private, untainted island getaway. At the far end of the island, you'll find the Garden of the Gods, an incredible "exterior decorating job" created of massive white and gray boulders and intricate lava formations. Think this island is an attractive option? Get out your wallet because this one's exclusivity means it's extremely upscale. Celebrities, royalty, and even Bill Gates have rented it out for private events, secluded getaways, and weddings.

Bermuda

With its pink sand beaches and irrepressible British charm, the island of Bermuda is a natural draw for honeymooners who want a quiet, relaxing getaway. With all of the benefits of the top-notch resorts, spas, and shopping in its main towns, this little jewel off the East Coast brings in honeymooners by the boatload. Literally. It's one of the top destinations for cruises and an unforgettable vacation for any who set foot on this charming little island's shores. For one thing, just about everything is pastel, from the hotels to the houses you'll pass on your way to your hotel, even to the very few cars allowed on the island (most transportation is by moped or boat). Second, you'll find circular stone archways from point to point along the beach. Legend has it that recently and longtime married couples who kiss under these arches will enjoy a long and fruitful marriage. You have to love islands with built-in romantic legends. Another romantic gesture might be the often-recommended day trip of kissing atop one of the island's most famed lighthouses, the Gibbs' Hill Lighthouse, with an unbeatable view of the island and surrounding ocean. This is the tallest iron lighthouse in the world and will certainly make you feel as if that kiss has you on top of the world.

On your way back from the lighthouse, don't forget to stop and smell the flowers. Bermuda is known for its vast gardens of hibiscus, morning glory, and bougainvillea; it even boasts a wonderful perfumery where you can tour the distilleries and purchase a freshly packaged bottle of perfume—the scent of your honeymoon—as a meaningful and transporting souvenir.

Another day trip, equally view-worthy yet from an entirely different perspective, is the underground crystal caverns, sparkling natural formations of calcium and mineral luminescent stalactites and stalagmites, with guided tours and great photo opportunities. Some of the resorts on this island have made great use of their own underground crystal caverns, turning them into perhaps the most breathtaking nightclubs you'll ever see. Cross a bridge over a seawater-filled cavern as the crystal formations reach up to you from below the water, watch your head as you maneuver through the caves, and then wind up at a slick bar and dance floor where the nightlife, quite literally, *rocks.*

Simplify It

To research the resorts and bungalows of Bermuda's beaches, its cultural heritage, and its crowd-pleasing festivals, contact the Bermuda Tourism Department at 800-BERMUDA, www.bermuda tourism.com.

Jamaica

You've seen the commercials bidding you to "come back to Jamaica," but you might have yet to get there for the first time. This popular

Simplify It

Explore Jamaica through its tourist board at 800-233-4582, www.jamaicatravel.com.

island among honeymooners allows for all the island accoutrements, fine dining, and life by and in the ocean. The spotlight here is the White Suite of the Jamaica Inn on often-recommended Ochos Rios in Jamaica, where the hotel will fill your honeymoon suite with a sea of white roses and candles, setting the mood for those perfect honeymoon nights. On Montego Bay, you'll find many of the most popular honeymoon resorts and a world of honeymooners just like you, enjoying the perfect sunset cruise or diving into the blue waters of the ocean.

The Bahamas

Okay, so you have 700 islands to choose from in the Bahamas, and not one of them is likely to disappoint. Long known as a top spot for water recreation and for its deep clear waters and its abundant sea life, scuba diving and snorkeling are the order of the day. Eleuthera is the place to go for snorkeling and swimming through and around shipwrecks. Andros gives you a fine underwater vantage point of one of the largest barrier reefs in the world, and boating tours among the islands might deliver you to a private cove carpeted with fine pink sand and perfect shells from which to make memento necklaces to commemorate your private afternoon on the secluded shores.

Exotic Islands

Some of the most exotic islands in the world are waiting out in the middle of oceans or just off the coasts of other continents and exciting foreign lands, inviting you to explore their shores and their undersea universes, their rain forests, their waterfalls, their international flavors and personalities, their sunsets and starscapes. Here are some of the most magnificent choice contenders among today's honeymooners who want something just a little bit different, something just a little bit more exotic. I hope you'll include these in your research, and I hope that if you do find yourselves on these sandy shores or showered by their tropical waterfalls, you'll be glad you spent the time finding them:

Simplify It

Seven hundred islands is a lot to choose from. So go "virtual snorkeling" through the Bahamas tourism department's Web site at www .bahamas.com, where you'll find gorgeous underwater pictures and links to many of the top island attractions and resorts.

• St. Lucia (888-4-STLUCIA, www.stlucia .org) has risen in the honeymoon destination standings, bringing couples in record numbers to its shores, as it boasts a true Caribbean atmosphere without the loud throngs of tourists. If you're a boat lover, this is the place to dock the yacht or sign up for a sunrise or sunset sail.

• Bora-Bora (www.gotahiti.com/islands-borabora.htm), a French Polynesian island, features thatched jungle bungalows and more than a few resorts that will bring you a fine, six-course gourmet meal right on the beach. (This island is one of the most rapidly rising stars on the honeymoon horizon, so keep in mind your competition's hunger for those bungalows when you start looking to reserve your space.) This is, after all, on the list of one of the most beautiful places on earth and the supposed inspiration for the classic musical *South Pacific.*

• Fiji (www.bulafiji.com) may be a popular main island, but it's the little-known tiny coral islands within its grouping that offer the utmost in the romantic daily road trip. Rich in culture and one of the most diverse fusions of cuisines of any island grouping, Fiji is the place to be for a variety of experiences both in action and taste. Fiji is known for its resorts' proximity to private cays and coves, where the two of you can be served a lobster picnic on the beach, complete with champagne and hammocks and blankets for your personal use. Few islands offer such a perfect honeymoon outing. Top off your outing with this unique island tradition: taking a midnight snorkeling swim or an au naturel dip in the ocean, whose waters contain a safe, sulphur-tinged quality that makes your skin glow in the moonlit waters below the surface. Now that's magical.

• Tahiti (800-365-4949, www.gototahiti.com), in French Polynesia, is a grouping of 118 islands and atolls with a range of size and attraction. A long-time popular getaway spot for those looking to escape the rush of civilization, Tahiti brings you right out over the water with bungalows near or *over* the ocean, Polynesian spa treatments out in the open air, and rich cultural heritage complete with fine exotic dining to fuel you for all that touring you're bound to do. Don't forget to pick up some Tahitian black pearl jewelry (or dive for your own pearls). This island is famous for the stunning and stunningly valuable pearls available in famous blacks, pastels, and off-whites. Sounds like a great postwedding gift to me.

• Barbados (800-221-9831, www.barbados.org) brings a new level of romance to the Caribbean, with its fragrant plantation tours and underground caves featuring their own waterfalls.

• The Galápagos Islands (www.galapagoschamberoftourism.org) are paradise for animal lovers. Here you can snorkel alongside penguins, play with tortoises and iguanas, and frolic with sea lions, in a land where the animals never grew to fear humans because we've been no danger to them.

• The Cayman Islands (800-346-3313, www.caymanislands.ky or www.divecayman.ky) are rated one of the top destinations for scuba diving and snorkeling.

• Santorini (212-421-5777, www.gnto.gr), the Greek island that so many are talking about, has long been considered a jewel in the Greek islands, and its reputation is growing, thanks to wins in various top travel and world's best competitions. Archaeologists are quietly researching whether this island—with its growing crowds, sizzling nightlife, and charm—was the real Atlantis.

• Nevis, in the West Indies, features the Four Season Resort (the best way to go), where you'll get the ultimate in luxury. This resort brings the outdoors in and the indoors out every-where you turn. With massages, bouquets of flowers, and champagne breakfasts as part of the romantic packages, it doesn't get much more honeymoon-perfect than that. And with history-laden sugar mills as part of your island tours, it doesn't get much sweeter than that.

• Puerto Rico (www.puerto-rico-tourism .com) boasts natural island beauty, some of the best nightlife ever to hit the beaches and nightclubs of any island and some of the finest exports in the world. On this island getaway, it's the music and the dancing that will get your heart pumping. Embark on one of the truly incredible ecological tours on the Caribbean side of the island, through rain forests, up steep hikes, and through much of the indigenous flora, all of which make visitors to this island want to come back.

Professionally Speaking

The Canary Islands are a truly adventurous getaway. Mahe and Praslin in the Seychelles have more of an African feel to their island atmosphere, with rich cultural flavors and great scenery—big boulders spot the beach, and you'll definitely feel like you're in an exotic land.
—Stefanie Michaels
www.adventuregirl.com

• St. Maarten (800-ST-MAARTEN, www.st-maarten.com) combines the cultures of the Caribbean, the French, and the Dutch for a truly multifaceted getaway, complete with livewire casino action at night and plenty of places to spend your winnings throughout the island.

• Bali, the christened "island of the Gods," offers some of the most luxurious resorts and spas featuring exotic international treatments.

• St. Vincent and the Grenadines (212-687-4981, www.svgtourism .com) feature an active volcano, majestic waterfalls, and hikes through the rain forest that seem to transport you to a land before time even started. Known for its ranking as an ecotourist's hot spot, with its unpolluted air and water and its preserved natural land, this South Caribbean island grouping in the Windward Islands is a trip into undiscovered territory—or so you might think.

Professionally Speaking

An island to explore is St. Bart's, which is known as the St. Tropez of the Caribbean. It's a private, 8-mile-long island that attracts the wealthy and the elite, especially during the holiday celebration times of New Year's and Carnivale. Interestingly enough, full-sized cars are not allowed on this island, so during high tourist season, it's quite amusing to see the richest people in the world driving around in little Suzuki Samurais. And the evening party scene is much like that in any upscale resort town: Everyone calls each other to say where the hottest parties are at, and the elite social scene celebrates into the night.

—Stefanie Michaels
www.adventuregirl.com

• Grenada (800-927-9554, www.grenada .org) is known more for its spot in history than for the sweet smell of its shores. This 20-mile island is home to the largest supply of spices in the Western Hemisphere. You can wake up to the soothing scents of cinnamon and nutmeg, both of which are said by some experts to be aphrodisiacs.

• The Seychelles embrace island life off the coast of Africa, with a true taste of noble European style. Nearby Mauritius (www .mauritius.net) is also an island paradise, with fabulous cultural and religious diversity added to the oceanside wonder.

• Isla Cozumel (www.islacozumel.com .mx) is the largest island in the Mexican Caribbean and home to some of the most active and most romantic honeymoon getaways possible. From a veritable fiesta of scuba-diving packages (some just for the dives and some for all-inclusive resort stays featuring a series of exciting dives) to a wide range of honeymoon luxury packages from the basic to the sublimely romantic, from its barrier reef (the world's second largest) to its limestone tunnels and caves to explore as a duo, Cozumel invites you off the shores of Mexico for a honeymoon that's a real splash.

American Islands

Don't forget about the many islands off the shores of the United States. From the Florida Keys to Martha's Vineyard, Nantucket, Catalina Island in California, Hilton Head Island in South Carolina, Sanibel Island in Florida, Sea Island in Georgia, and Mackinac Island in Michigan (where cars are not allowed and the bicycle and the horse and carriage are the way to get around; www .mackinacisland.org)—and some might say even the island of Manhattan—there's plenty of beachside and excursion wonderment just off the U.S. coastline.

• Hayman Island and Lizard Island, both in Australia, put you right at the Great Barrier Reef. Need I say more?

Private Island Escapes

Earlier you read about private islands that you can reserve for your exclusive use, with no other honeymooners, kids, cars, or advertisements in sight. Such an island is your own private oasis, set apart from the world, affording you a level of luxury that you can only imagine. Just picture yourselves waking up in your deluxe suite, with the ocean right in front of you and the gentle ocean breeze bringing in the scent of lilies, gardenias, and hibiscus. Your personal butler brings you your morning coffee, breakfast, and perhaps a fresh bottle of sunscreen before you set out to make the beach and the ocean waters your own. With only the sun's level telling you the time, this is the perfect escape to paradise—or Eden, if you so wish to see it—and you are the only two people on earth. Just as it was when you took your vows.

The rich, the famous, the royal—all have indulged in vacationing on their own private island, where they can frolic in the surf without fear of onlookers, go topless, skinny-dip, or listen to the sounds of the surf or to the fine conversation they're able to have with their ultra-relaxed partner. It's the getaway of your dreams if solitude, privacy, and escape in a natural paradise is on your wish list.

Here are a few private islands that can be rented (hint: cash in your trust fund or win the lottery first) for your preferred length of stay:

• Nekker Island (800-557-4255) is a private resort owned by Richard Branson, owner of Virgin Airways. This is a man who knows indulgence, and his private villa on a sandy island has been visited by an endless list of the rich, famous, and perhaps infamous. You may add your stories to those occurring on Nekker's private beaches, as you may count yourselves among the couples who may have stayed in the 10-bedroom main house or one of the private Balinese villas. And the cost for this? Just $15,000 per *day* for the whole island, or $14,000 per week if you're willing to share the resort with others.

• Turtle Island (800-255-4347, www.turtlefiji.com) in Fiji owns the distinction of setting the backdrop for the movie *The Blue Lagoon.* Those beaches and jungles that Brooke Shields and Christopher Atkins made famous can be yours as well, since Turtle Island rents a private beach to each of the dozen or so couples allowed to stay on the entire island at once. You may not have the entire island to yourself, but your private cove will make you forget about the others and enjoy one another. A few highlights here: outdoor showers, private whirlpools, and the choice of secluded coves or open beaches for your own use.

• Vatulele (800-828-9146, www.vatulele.com), another private island in Fiji, provides many of the same attractions as Turtle Island, only with the distinction of being the only five-star resort in the Fijian islands.

• Cayo Espanto (888-666-4282, www.aprivateisland.com) in Belize affords you one of five private villas, each with its own pool, and meals are always enjoyed ádeux, for the ultimate in private dining.

Of course, other private islands exist, and I do encourage you to seek out your own in the island grouping of your choice. For the discriminating honeymooners who truly want to be left to their own amusement, the importance of this choice cannot be emphasized enough.

The World's Best Islands

Each year the readers of *Travel and Leisure* magazine participate in a world-inclusive survey of the absolute best travel destinations: the gold standard hotels, cities, cruises, and spas across the globe. In the lists that follow, you'll find out which islands grabbed the coveted World's Best awards overall and which earned top honors in specific regional categories. Throughout the next few chapters, you'll discover the winners in other categories, so be on the lookout for *Travel and Leisure*'s World's Best features on pages to come. Please note that these and all other stated results were the most recent ones at press time in early 2002, with the new year's releases on *T&L*'s site right now.

You can find out the current list of World's Best winners at www.travelandleisure.com by clicking on the World's Best icon and choosing your categories.

Now here are the islands that impressed the most experienced and particular travelers—these are the gold standards, the ones most highly recommended to add to your own vacation research list. You'll note that each of the winners' names (here and throughout the book) appear alongside their "scores" as assigned in the competition. I've provided you with these numbers so you can see just how close the ratings are among them:

The Top 10 World's Best Islands, Overall

1.	Maui	78.2
2.	Kauai	77.1

3.	Vancouver Island	76.4
4.	Great Barrier Reef islands	75.5
5.	Hawaii	74.5
6.	Bali	74.2
7.	Santorini	73.7
8.	Sicily	72.0
9.	Capri	71.7
10.	Bora-Bora	71.3

The Top Five Islands of the Caribbean, Bermuda, and the Bahamas

1.	Virgin Gorda	69.4
2.	St. Bart's	69.4
3.	Bermuda	68.9
4.	St. John	67.5
5.	Barbados	67.1

The Top Five Islands of Hawaii

1.	Maui	78.2
2.	Kauai	77.1
3.	Hawaii	74.5
4.	Oahu	71.1
5.	Lanai	69.0

The Top Five Islands of Mexico and Central and South America

1.	Galápagos Islands	64.5
2.	Isla Cozumel	64.1
3.	Ambergris Cay, Belize	59.4
4.	Isla Mujeres, Mexico	56.8
5.	Margarita Island, Venezuela	55.6

The Top Five Islands of Africa and the Middle East

1.	The Seychelles	60.8
2.	Madagascar	59.6
3.	Mauritius	53.9

| 4. | Zanzibar | 57.4 |
| 5. | Réunion | 50.5 |

The Top Five Islands of Asia

1.	Bali	74.2
2.	Phuket	66.0
3.	Java	65.3
4.	The Maldives	59.3
5.	Lombok	55.8

The Top Five Islands of Australia, New Zealand, and the South Pacific

1.	Great Barrier Reef islands	75.5
2.	Bora-Bora	71.3
3.	Fiji	68.8
4.	Moorea	68.3
5.	Tahiti	67.7

Adventure Honeymoons

4

The new honeymoon trend starts right here, with a big departure from the island getaways you just read about. So many couples are looking beyond the tropical experience in favor of a honeymoon that's a true *adventure*. They might climb the pyramids in Egypt and shop the street markets in Morocco. They might sign on for a two-week safari in Africa for a very different interpretation of an extremely wild honeymoon. They might trek through a rain forest, sail down the Amazon, go scuba diving *inside a dormant volcano* (more on that in a minute—and no, lava is not involved). Adventure vacations are the hot choice right now—after all, specialized travel programs on television and various Web sites are dedicated to such journeys!—and honeymooners are eager to add some of those thrills and once-in-a-lifetime encounters to their own great getaways.

So what kinds of thrills are honeymooners after right now? It ranges from the tame, like swimming with dolphins or scuba diving through shipwrecks off the coast of Bermuda, to the "Are you two

Honeymoon Reflections

When it came time to plan our honeymoon, we were fortunate enough to be able to choose any-where in the world we wanted to go. Since this was such a special and important trip, we didn't want to do anything we'd ever done be-fore, like a beach vacation. We wanted our honeymoon to be so unique and so unforgettable—some-thing that we'd talk about forever. You just wouldn't believe the differ-ent types of adventure vacations out there right now, and it was hard to select just one. So we chose a safari that was unlike anything we'd ever seen before—it's a five-star resort right outside of a safari preserve. By day, we did the safari thing, right out there with the lions and giraffes and elephants. By night, we came home to this incredible resort with the best of everything, and we could stand out on our terrace and overlook the African landscape. It was just amazing.

—Brenna and Sam

kidding?!" level of climbing Mount Kiliman-jaro and even venturing down to Antarctica to sleep on an ice floe and helicopter out to see the baby seals and penguins. Your choices are going to depend on what *you* think makes for an incredible adventure. If you're the type of person who has to do some serious carbo-loading and visualizations, just to go to Macy's during the first day of the Memorial Day sales, then the ideas in this section aren't going to be for you. If you're up for climbing the Mayan ruins and rappelling across the top canopies of a rain forest, but your partner gets winded while taking out the trash, then planning an adrenaline-rush honeymoon is going to leave one of you very, very miserable and perhaps strapped to an oxygen tank the whole trip. What I've covered here is the type of getaway for *like-minded* true adventurers. You *both* have to be up for these unique es-capades, or it's not going to work. That is, un-less you consider this . . .

If one or both of you are a little jittery about spending the honeymoon where they don't serve piña coladas and you don't get a Ralph Lauren silk robe in your hotel room, the following suggestion might be an attrac-tive option: You can incorporate adventure elements into any type of honeymoon. You don't have to spend the whole week hiking through rain forests; instead, you can take a day trip during your relaxing island resort va-cation. You can scuba dive, climb the Mayan ruins or castle steps, and even take a mini safari tour as just a small part of any type of vacation. That adventurer in you can be satisfied with just a taste of the wilder part of touring, whether at a resort, on a cruise, or in a big city. And then the rest of the time, just kick back and enjoy that piña colada and that swing in the hammock as the steel drum band plays in the distance.

Throughout this book, you'll see that many different elements can be combined into your honeymoon to make it a multifaceted trip. So read on to see the pure form of adventure honeymoon ideas, and then pick and choose the ventures you'd like to weave into your own trip. As a Jamaican tour guide once said to me, "Now everybody's happy."

Are You Ready for a True Adventure?

To give you a taste of some of the most popular types of adventure honeymoons out there, I've compiled information on just a small sampling of the kinds of trips recent honeymooners and travel experts alike have recommended. You can find out more about all of them and others by visiting the tourist board Web sites in the Resources or by going to the sites of travel magazines for their recent spotlights, features, and top venture picks.

Safaris

If you've never been to Africa or on safari, you have no idea what awaits you on this particular trip of a lifetime. Although you'll certainly find those armed guard–assisted drives through open wildlands in an SUV, where you gaze out at a pack of lions lying in the sun after a fresh kill or baby elephants sticking close to their enormous mother's legs, that stereotypical image of a safari is just a small percentage of what a truly adventurous trip to Africa on safari can bring you. For instance, did you know that some inclusive African tours include trips to wineries and lighthouses, that some of the most popular safari clubs

Adventure Girl

Want to find out about some of the most exciting and adventurous trips in the world from someone who's been there, but you don't know anyone who's even been to Nepal and can give you a first-person account of their trip? Well, now you can get that friend's objective opinion by visiting the Web site of Stefanie Michaels, better known as intrepid vacation journalist Adventure-Girl, who reports on the best- and least-known adventure destinations in the world. She's contributed a few amazing locale suggestions to this chapter and elsewhere throughout the book, and her site describes just the kinds of escapades you're looking for. Visit Stefanie (and perhaps win a trip to accompany her on her next televised vacation!) at www.adventuregirl.com.

were founded by well-known actors of our day, and that many preserves are considered protected ecosystems with strict environmental rules in place? Once you start looking into safaris, you're sure to learn plenty of amazing facts about life across the globe in some of the most beautiful natural land in the world.

Looking at just one tour book for a Kenyan safari and area tour, I immediately added this destination to my own "someday" wish list. Here is what this one tour has to offer: Guided tours through Nairobi bring you into the city (your first stop), where you can shop, check out the museum dedicated to the *Out of Africa* author, visit museums, and pet and feed baby giraffes at the Giraffe Center. Next, travel through lush and fertile lands, past waterfalls, and arrive at your treetop hotel, where you'll embark on a several-day journey of touring some of the most unspoiled and magnificent lands in the world, seeing wildlife of many species in their natural habitat where *you* are something unusual to look at.

Soon after, you might visit the Mount Kenya Safari Club, which was founded by the actor William Holden, and then venture into the

Samburu National Reserve, where grazing gazelles, buffalo, and impalas move about their day as you regard them in awe of their size, grace, and peace at being in their own world. Moving to other areas, you'll see exotic birds, flamingos, cormorants, fish eagles—species you never knew existed and have never seen outside of captivity.

Words can't describe the open-air awe of a safari tour and exactly how it feels to live and travel among the animals, to see how a natural and untouched world looks in relation to our own asphalt kingdoms.

Outside of safari touring, Africa offers a world of culture, history, and tradition, an adventure at every turn. You might visit Cape Town, which has been called "A World in One Country," which attracts you with its city life and cultural centers, museums, botanical gardens, waterfront attractions, and scenic views from lighthouses. One day trip might bring you to the wineries, where you'll learn how early French settlers brought wine making to South Africa, and you'll then be treated to a wine tasting and culinary experience for the utmost in lavish hospitality.

You can combine safari outings with other types of trips, including some cruises that feature safaris as one of their excursions. You can hop over from nearby islands, take this jaunt on your way to Morocco and Egypt, and even make a special stop on your way home from an Asian honeymoon. Or if you're not the international flight type, many zoos and amusement parks across this country have established incredible and authentic safaris and wildlife preserves right on their own grounds. The Disney parks as well have their own African safari adventures, with resorts similar to Ulasaba in their proximity and views of the wildlife. For a truly unique honeymoon, go

Simplify It

Check out the rules for vaccinations in the area where you're going on safari. Many of the popular locations might require you (or just strongly advise you) to get a yellow fever shot and take malaria medication before you embark on this journey. Don't skip this research step. Suffering from malaria does not make for a romantic honeymoon.

where the wild things are—and I'm not talking about Cancún during spring break.

Professionally Speaking

Ulasaba is like the Four Seasons meets a safari. Owned by Richard Branson, who also owns Virgin Airways and the ultraposh Nekker Island, Ulasaba is an elegant resort set right on the edge of the borders between Sabi Sand private game reserve and the Kruger National Park. This rock lodge sits on the boulders at a high view overlooking the valley, where you can see all the animals in their natural habitat. It positively envelops nature, makes you a part of the landscape, all in the most luxuriant of atmospheres with fine dining and Ralph Lauren sheets on the bed. It's the essence of high style, in the essence of an adventurous environment.

–Stefanie Michaels
www.adventuregirl.com

Pyramids and Ruins

Few things are more adventurous than climbing the pyramids in Egypt, taking guided tours of the catacombs below them, and learning the rich history of pharaohs, gods and goddesses, and mummies' curses. The Middle East has long been an adventure traveler's dream destination for its combination of desert oasis treks on camelback, tented villages with authentic regional cuisine, busy street markets, and cultural eye-openers. Visitors to that region tell me of little-known resorts and scenic views overlooking the sparkling star-filled skies and the city lights below, treks to religious holy grounds and blessed water springs. How great a shame that such a land is mired in conflict and essentially blocked from so many who would love to visit the wonders in this ancient land of beauty and opportunity. Perhaps someday the world will change, the conflicts will cease, and the Middle East will once again be able to share its splendor.

Outside of the Middle East's great climbs are the ruins of the Mayan and Incan civilizations, also adventurous journeys and top picks among honeymooners who have spent some time on the Stair-Master at the gym. Beyond the grueling climbs, they say, is the feeling of being very present where a once-great civilization thrived, pausing to picture what that civilization must have looked like, and learning about its riches, its contributions to modern society, and its lifestyle in the surrounds of nature.

Underwater

Your underwater adventures might bring you up close and personal with dolphins, stingrays, or even a barracuda. Scuba-diving tours offer a glimmering view of the undersea universe, and shipwreck dives make you the quintessential explorer. Whale-watching tours can take your breath away when you see a pod of whales migrating to their winter homes, breaching out in the distance, even majestically raising their enormous tails up out of the water to seemingly wave you off on your way. Countless tours and cruises include these amazing aquatic adventures, but by far the one undersea adventure that captures the most buzz among honeymooners is the opportunity to swim with dolphins. At select resorts and aquariums, you might have the opportunity to don a wet suit and swim with the dolphins, allowing these huge and peaceful creatures to approach you, check you out, and play with you. Marine biologists are fascinated by dolphins' innate sense of humor and personality, and some even believe that dolphins can sense emotion in humans. You've probably read stories about dolphins being used in healing ways with sick or traumatized children; some experts believe that swimming with dolphins produces a calming effect on most visitors.

Stefanie Michaels, in her long list of adventure trip standouts, also recommends another once-in-a-lifetime adventure: swimming, scuba diving, and snorkeling inside the crater of a dormant volcano. The location is called Saba, and it's in the Lesser Antilles of the Netherlands. A huge dormant volcano towers before you, and once you get inside, you'll find near perfection in its water sports–friendly world. Hidden from view of the outside world, this natural creation is considered a true ecological system, as the little town inside (called "The Bottom") maintains praiseworthy rules about recycling and the protection of the earth and water. The idea of swimming inside a volcano usually

Swim with Flipper

Dolphin Encounter in the Bahamas, off Paradise Island in Nassau, offers you the chance to learn about and swim with these enormous and playful creatures in their own safe and comfortable environment. Recent honeymooners who have had the experience of frolicking and interacting with these well-trained, kind, and responsive animals call it the adventure of a lifetime.

evokes images of violently churning and spitting lava cauldrons and the sacrifice of a virgin, but in this case the volcano is just a safe, clean, quiet nest for a sparkling underwater adventure of a different sort. No human sacrifices necessary!

River Ventures

If the essence of adventure to you is white-water rafting through the canyons of the western states, you'll be happy to know that you can find tours of every nature, every level of comfort, and every degree of actual danger. With some you may even get first-class service with luxury tents and air beds at your stops along the river, buffet meals cooked by the chef who's been paddling furiously behind you each day, and some of the most beautiful and romantic scenery you can imagine. Deluxe tours even give you the option of sleeping under the stars, providing you with plush and comfy top-of-the-line sleeping bags and sheets. You can go high style or you can rough it. It's all about the adventure of the rafting tour, as the thrill is in the journey, not the destination.

Other river adventures might include cruises down some of the most exotic rivers in the world, river glides through rain forests and preserves, even river jaunts during safari. On each side of you a natural world or a cityscape emerges, and you never know which kinds of water creatures might swim up close to take a look at you.

The Rain Forest

This is the kind of adventure that's grabbed the spotlight on more than one popular reality television competition (if you consider that reality!). Living in a luxury thatched hut with great fabric swags and romantic mosquito netting around the bed, hiking through thick forests and colorful exotic flower fields, skimming across the top canopies of the rain forest trees with monkeys and native songbirds scattering at your approach. Kayaking to a spot in the forest where a luxury spa awaits, having bird-sized butterflies alight on your bare shoulder, cavorting beneath a waterfall and exploring the caves behind it for a little private time to tell your closest friends about later. From the rain forests of Hawaii to Costa Rica to Puerto Rico, and in countless other locations, this is a tropical paradise that not even Tarzan and Jane could ever imagine.

One of the most popular destinations for honeymooners and for all adventure and romance vacationers is Belize. Long known as one of the world's best locations for scuba diving, Belize has risen in the ranks of most-requested honeymoon spots due to its combination of beach and ocean attractions and jungle beauty. Belize itself is in Central America, not an island as some might think, just a bit above Guatemala. You'll find all the above-mentioned benefits of its rain forest atmosphere, with new and luxurious or rustic jungle and beachside resorts springing up all the time. This destination's rising popularity with world travelers means that even more attractions have arrived, or are soon to arrive; this spot is finally getting the attention it has always deserved.

Wake up to an ocean sunrise, take a walk on the beach, and scuba dive along the Belize Barrier Reef, which as the longest barrier reef in the Western Hemisphere was the area's original attraction. Go night snorkeling with an underwater flashlight to catch the deep-sea nightlife of sea turtles, moray eels, lobsters, and alien-looking fish. With both daytime and nighttime ocean attractions, Belize seems to offer more to do in the water than on land.

For a different water experience, you might pack up and head into the jungle for a hike to majestic waterfall areas. Find a pool of water that's been warmed by the sun and sun yourselves like the natural denizens of the jungle. Hop on a raft or boat and float quietly down the waterways and into hidden underground caves that sparkle from their embedded calcium, crystal, and mineral deposits catching the light from a slight crevice in the cave's roof. These natural hideaways seem made just for private moments like the ones you'll most want to share during your honeymoon in paradise.

Lacking the immediate identification punch that Belize has enjoyed in recent days, the Monteverde rain forest (in Costa Rica) is not only elevated among the opinions of adventurers who have made the journey there, but it is also actually elevated, being situated high above sea level. The expected natural rain forest scenery, that of deep green flora and mossy rock trails, with the scents of earth and flowers, takes on a whole new aura with the mists of its cloud cover. The result is an ethereal quality of an edge-softening mist that turns the entire rain forest into something right out of a movie or a dream. As you canopy-tour across the tops of the trees, you're flying through the clouds.

You're Not Going to Get a Tan on This One

Would you believe that for a certain number of months during the year, you can go to the Swedish Arctic Circle city of Jukkasjarvi and stay in a hotel that's made completely of ice? This carved wonder is actually a popular resort spot and a highly booked place for New Year's Eve parties and for beverage companies that want to launch and promote their newest drink served, as expected, on ice.

While staying in a hotel that's made completely of ice perhaps seems a bit extreme (although it might be fun to tell your friends that you melted the bed!), you might be interested in some cold-weather ventures you can heat up on your own, such as skiing in the Alps at Gstaad, Switzerland, or in the hot, hot, hot destination of Whistler Mountain in Canada. Or take to the slopes in Aspen to rub elbows with the rich and famous and try your skills on the four-diamond slopes (or the bunny hill). Other cold-weather adventures of a more adrenaline-soaked degree might include a four-day snowmobile tour through Yellowstone National Park, hiking across glaciers, *climbing* the glaciers, even taking helicopter tours over the most beautiful frozen sections of the earth. Have your picture taken at the famous flag spiked into the North Pole. (How many honeymooners have *that* shot in their photo album?) Tropical sun isn't for everyone—some people love snowbound sports and icy escapades. Tour companies can dogsled you across parts of Alaska on nature and ecological tours, and you can ski your way from Switzerland to Germany, stopping in at your resort to warm up by the fire together with a shared glass of brandy. Or take on "The Last Frontier on Earth" when you head to Antarctica. On this particular tour, you fly in, land on the snow, and pitch a tent on a glacier with expert camp guides who really know how to set up a campsite. Once you're settled in, you can hike out to see the baby seals and penguins, go skiing or hiking, climb the icy mountains and glaciers, and see incredible landscapes that few people besides you will ever get to see. This adventure is an expensive one—from $10,000 to $25,000 per person—but it's so unbelievably worth it from a pure adventure standpoint.

Going to the Pros

Hopefully, I've whetted your appetite for a honeymoon that's at least a little bit more adventurous than finding a different-*colored* frozen drink to sip on by the pool. With some images in your mind of the two of you wandering through a rain forest or waking up in time to see a herd of gazelles racing gracefully by in the distance, you're probably wondering how to make these dreams a reality. Your first step is obviously going to be research—checking travel magazines and Web sites, asking your world-traveler friends and associates for any of their contacts, and talking to travel agents and tour operators. To help you along in your quest, I've compiled a list of some of the top adventure travel and expedition companies that can plan and guide you along during your most exciting getaways. These companies exist to bring you and others like you out into exotic lands and up into the Himalayas, to the edges of volcanoes, on safari, and even out to those sheets of ice in Antarctica. They may be your best sources and one-stop shopping as you sign on to let them lead the way. To give you a solid start to your journey, here is a list of just *some* of the top travel companies out there:

    Abercrombie and Kent: www.abercrombiekent.com
    Adventure Travel Society: www.adventuretravelbusiness.com
        (an association that rates and provides information on various tour companies and expeditions and a great place to research sources listed here as well as additional sources)
    American Society of Travel Agents: www.astanet.com
    Backroads: www.backroads.com
    Expeditions: www.expeditions.com
    General Tours: www.generaltours.com
    Geographic Expeditions: www.geoex.com
    Intrav: www.intrav.com
    Mountain Travel Sobek: www.mtsobek.com
    Quark Expeditions: www.quarkexpeditions.com
    Tauck World Discovery: www.tauck.com
    Travcoa: www.travcoa.com
    Wilderness Travel: www.wildernesstravel.com

When considering any tourism or expedition company, always thoroughly research the company, in addition to the destination. Be sure it's been in business for a long time (you don't want to go on its first tour ever!), and see that it is licensed and insured, it is rated strongly by esteemed travel associations and publications, and it has a strong safety record. On a more personalized note, ask if the company specializes in certain areas of the world or in certain types of tours, and ask for complete, itemized details of your tour. Brochures and

Web sites should explain pricing and travel requirements, the experience of the guides and accompanying experts, any passport or international travel requirements such as visas and immunizations, and details on refund policies.

It's a smart move to tell the tour operator that you're planning your honeymoon so he or she can tell you about special honeymoon offers or opportunities, give you details about private excursions, or even warn you that the close-knit group experience 24 hours a day on this trip might not be the ideal situation for you. If you can't shake the elderly couple from Iowa who have kindheartedly "adopted" you, how will you have any romantic time alone? Most important, as inferred at the beginning of this chapter, be sure that *you* can handle the demands of this trip. If an outing requires a certain level of stamina or fitness, will you be able to participate? Judge your own ability to enjoy each journey so you don't put yourself in harm's way. Let the tour operator know your level of ability, as well as your true wishes for the comforts of home and your level of comfort with the outdoors, so you might work together to find a tour that's perfect for you.

5

Big City Honeymoons

What is it about big cities here in the United States that's pulling countless honeymooners off the pink sand beaches and out of the azure blue waters of the Caribbean and transporting them instead into the middle of a high-energy, fast-paced, hopping metropolis? In a word: excitement. There's always something to do in the city, from dining in world-renowned restaurants to taking in the arts and culture, sporting events, people meeting and people watching, celebrity sightings, dancing at the hottest nightspots, and getting pampered at spas. In many ways, the big city honeymoon can encompass virtually *all* the top elements of each type of honeymoon listed in this book, giving you the best of all worlds in one destination. Call it another interpretation of the term "all-inclusive vacation." It's one-stop shopping for the honeymooning couple who wants it all and the best choice for the couple who's "been there, done that" at beach resort vacations in the past.

As for romance, just think about some of the most romantic movies ever made, and remember the scenes that took place in big cities. Tom Hanks and Meg Ryan meeting atop the Empire State Building—finally!—in *Sleepless in Seattle* (something Cary Grant and Deborah Kerr never got to do in their movie). Audrey Hepburn meandering to the jewel-filled windows of Tiffany's. Clark Gable and Vivien Leigh trading passionate looks in Civil War–era Atlanta. Now think of yourselves in similar big screen moments: dining on the terrace at Tavern on the Green beneath those light-strewn trees, touring the mansions and estates in Atlanta, putting it all on red at the roulette table in Vegas, shopping on Rodeo Drive and getting the *Pretty Woman* treatment as your beloved admires you in that $4,000 hat. Or just stand atop a tall building or scenic lookout point and take in the breathtaking view of the city all around you. No camera can capture that kind of sight and that kind of shared moment quite like real life can.

The big city pulses with energy and diversity, offering you every option your heart desires right when it desires it, and a range of luxury that's right off the silver screen. The couples I've spoken to said that for them, the choice was to experience big city life as a huge de-

The Best of Our Best

Travel and Leisure's World's Best awards for the ultimate destinations in North America include:

1. New York   77.1
2. San Francisco   76.4
3. Chicago   72.3
4. Washington, DC   72.2
5. Montreal   70.8

Again, check out www.travelandleisure.com for their most recent World's Best survey results, and see which big U.S. cities dominate the list this year.

parture from their lifelong small-town existence. Others said they wanted to see the best this country has to offer, since they've already seen so much of the world (Paris, Italy, the islands) and have a renewed sense of homeland pride and patriotism. Others admitted that even though they live less than an hour from a major city hot spot, they'd never actually *vacationed* there and seen the true range of attractions and experiences beyond the usual tourist spots to which they bring their visiting friends and family. They'd actually seen more of the great city right in their backyard on television than in real life! And others pointed to the money factor, saying they could more fully enjoy the best the city had to offer with a wallet loaded with their wedding gift cash—especially since they could save a fortune on airfare by not having to fly to their honeymoon destination. For so many couples, for so many reasons, there's no other choice. It's going to be a big city honeymoon.

It's All About the Culture . . .

You can't beat the level of arts and culture found in big cities. From traveling exhibits in museums to Shakespeare in the park, concerts of every taste in music, and splashy Broadway productions, there's a wealth of selections to suit your deepest and most elevated interests. If you take in even one show, one stroll through a gallery, you've just become a part of a mighty statistic. The Travel Institute of America says that 93 million American travelers included at least one cultural, arts, or heritage event in their annual trips: 53.6 million American travelers have visited a museum or historical site in the past year, and 33 million say their itineraries include ventures to the theater or arts and music festivals. Who says we're all just out at restaurants and clubs and shopping with our gold cards in those big cities? Not at all! Somewhere in between those three-olive martinis and fluorescent cosmopolitans we're swilling in dimly lit and very fashionable lounges

Do Your Homework

While you're researching potential big city destinations, don't stop at just asking the city's tourism board for a list of top cultural attractions. Log on to the city's Web site, check out regional newspapers and magazines (for example, *New York* magazine and *Time Out New York*) for constantly updated, jam-packed calendars of events. The locals read these to get the inside scoop on what's happening where, to find out contact and reservations information, and to learn the experts' reviews of little-known but dazzling displays and performances near them. Not even the concierge at your hotel can know *everything* that's going on in the heart of the city, as well as on the outskirts of town, so go right to the source. Read these fine print columns to load up your honeymoon with the most unforgettable events and tours in town.

and those rides on the double-decker tourist buses, we're taking in the finer parts of life. Because, after all, the finer (and more refined) parts of life are all around you on the big city honeymoon.

The City of Angels or the City That Never Sleeps? Which Will It Be?

To get your big city dreams going, take a look at some of the destinations I've chosen to spotlight here. These are among the most popular big city honeymoon spots, as recommended by travel experts and the couples who participated in a survey on my Web site.

New York City

Of course I'm going to start with the city I love most, the city that never sleeps, the great city that has come back from paralyzing tragedy and terror to grow even stronger, even greater, and even more radiant than ever before. If there was ever a time to visit New York City, it's now.

New York City has been celebrated in film, in song, on television. It's the ideal backdrop for any love story, including your own, with its blend of high-society chic, its worship of diversity, and its still incredible skyline. For pure indulgence, you have a lineup of the best in hotels and romantic enclaves. The city has earned the top spot in *Travel and Leisure* magazine as *the* best location for food *in the world,* and you can't turn a corner without discovering great shopping, every level of entertainment, and something else to get your picture taken in front of. I couldn't begin to explain it all, or praise it all, so I'll send you to the Web site that will take over the info-duties: www.nycvisit.com, the New York City Tourism Board's best collection of attractions by category and must-sees, with complete contact information and rates.

What I will do here is tell you about some of the most romantic and enjoyable spots in the city. As a contributor to a book on the

Penny-Wise

When you're checking out any city's tourism Web site or calling tourism offices to request information, always look at the special packages offered during the summer, holidays, and festival seasons, and especially packages for families if you're one of those couples bringing the kids along. Tourism board Web sites are a hotbed of great deals, freebies, and contact information to help you get so much more out of your trip.

most romantic places in and around New York City, I had the pleasure of touring and reviewing some of the city's top spots for kissing, dancing, hand-holding, and just being in love. (Hard work, but someone had to do it!) In the summer months, if you go to Lincoln Center, you'll wander into a scene that's like a good night's dream. All around that famous water fountain, couples dressed in their finest waltz about in circles under the night sky, to the tunes of live music played just for this dance of a lifetime. At Wollman Park, at what is an ice-skating rink in the winter, you'll find much the same thing, with flowered shrubs surrounding your dance floor, the moon providing a special spotlight, and dinner and drinks served in the round. Aside from your first dance as husband and wife, nothing could be more romantic.

Your next romantic stop might be the New York Botanical Garden, where you will stroll through impossibly perfect indoor and outdoor collections of roses, camellias, orchids, flowering trees, and butterfly gardens, surrounded by nothing but beauty. As one tourist said from behind me as we made our way through the themed areas, "This is what heaven must look like." Another's idea of heaven might be a picnic in Central Park, throwing Frisbees on the mall, wandering over to Strawberry Fields, or lunching at the Boathouse. The zoo in Central Park, a close cousin to the world-famous Bronx Zoo just a short train ride away, brings you face to face with penguins and monkeys. Try not to laugh at their resemblance to your groomsmen on the wedding day.

Romance might come to you in the form of dinner at Tavern on the Green, a walk through the city's many parks, even sharing a hot pretzel from a corner snack cart. It might be having your husband surprise you with tickets to a Yankees game or a Broadway show, the Westminster Dog Show at Madison Square Garden, or a horse-and-carriage ride through Central Park.

From planetariums to subterranean oyster bars, exclusive clubs, open-air performances by the City Opera or the New York Philharmonic Orchestra, there's always room for romance, no matter where you are. New York City knows you're there for pure romance, and it's going to accommodate you. Even the curators of the Empire State Building keep the top floor observation deck open until midnight as an homage to those romantic "I'll meet you there at midnight!" movies so dear to our hearts.

Touring the city isn't only done on foot, by taxi, or by horse-drawn carriage. You might take the slow-speed Circle Line (www.circle line.com) for a tour of the waterways, or you might hop on board The Beast, a top-speed powerboat, for a quicker skim across the harbor's surface. If the view from the water doesn't give you enough of a thrill, even at high speeds, then take to the air for a helicopter ride above the city (Liberty Helicopter: www.libertyhelicopters.com). Circle the Statue of Liberty and the bridges, and ride over the path of the Hudson. This breathtaking airborne view of the city is such a popular romantic outing that it's a top pick among future and hopeful grooms looking for the perfect setting for popping the question. (According to one particular helicopter touring company's spokesperson, there have been more than 150 hovering "Yes!" answers and only one unfortunate "No.") That once-in-a-lifetime adventure ride could be an unforgettable shared memory as well.

New York City has a special place in the heart of the world right now, and that's not surprising to anyone who has spent time there. While you're in New York, be sure to shake the hand of any rescue professional you come across, from the firefighters to police to EMS to horse-mounted patrol and canine dogs. You just might grace your honeymoon with the touch of a hero.

Las Vegas

Another city that has it all, in high style and at a high level of excitement, is Las Vegas. From jaw-dropping shows to ethereal suites in the finest resorts, nonstop action, and special effects at every turn, Vegas is at once satisfying eye candy and an incredibly enjoyable and romantic destination. If it's odds you have on your mind at the gaming tables, just forget the one about the odds of new marriages succeeding. Try your lucky numbers (the date he proposed? your wedding date?), kiss your wedding rings for luck at each roll of the dice, and spin the wheel of fortune to see how lady luck is smiling on you that day. After you've done the casino thing, do the show thing. Take in a performance, a concert, a dance party, even a relaxing few hours at a jazz club or piano bar.

At your resort, reserve a luxury poolside cabana open to honeymooners and high rollers and have a Trojan warrior or a loincloth-wearing servant bring you your drinks. Slather on that SPF 45 and worship the sun that bakes the desert all around that great city. Check in with the Las Vegas tourism board and see what's going on around you that week, and above all else, try your odds at mentioning the magic phrase "We're on our honeymoon." You could just hit the jackpot with offers of free room upgrades, complimentary meals and drinks, VIP tickets to shows, even backstage passes to shake hands and pose for pictures with performing celebrities.

Boston

For the true New England experience, a mix of big city action and the considerably more subdued New England attitude, Boston is a charmer. You have the big hotels and resorts, the nightclubs, a considerable collection of historical and cultural attractions, street festivals, and that great Boston accent all around you. Check out the lighthouses, the craggy coastline, the seagulls hovering over the ocean. Walk the beach at sunset, and stop off at a nearby restaurant for some lobster and clam chowder that's authentic to the area and like nothing you've ever had. Visit the bar that inspired *Cheers*, or visit the grounds of Harvard University. Most of Boston's tourism areas are a walker's paradise, with well-mapped trails available at the tourism bureau (www.bostonusa.com) for your own self-led explorations.

Your Boston honeymoon might just be one stop at the many New England cities that attract huge numbers of tourists. You're less than an hour away from Providence (www.goProvidence.com), with its newly refurbished Renaissance harborfront, where you might take a gondola ride down the river through the middle of the city. At night, catch the weekend festivals of Waterfire, where floating bonfires are lit and sent down the same river in a show of light celebrated by thousands of the city's residents and

Simplify It

For a closer look at the calendar of events in the world of arts and culture, go to www.boston.com and click on the "Going Out" icon; for additional Boston and Massachusetts information, go to www.mass vacations.com.

tourists alike. Walk the promenades of Federal Hill, stopping in at great Italian eateries and bakeries and taking in the shopping. There's a great local accent to hear there as well.

Hop the ferry then to Newport, the diamond of New England, with its opulent mansions and estates, gardens, and yacht clubs. The regattas take place each summer, with the city's tanned and toned high-society vacation crowd coming out in their summer-white capris and Manolos to toast the favorite yacht's victory. As in the Hamptons of New York, the summer beach party and tourism scene in Newport is celebrity-stuffed and camera-ready. In the quiet hours, though, even surrounded by the immense wealth of those estate homes, you'll never forget you're in New England. The mood is just different here than anywhere else in the country. Perhaps it's that sea air, but for the summer honeymoon, your city-hopping trip from Boston to Providence to the Hamptons (and even up to old Cape Cod or out to Martha's Vineyard) will give you the best the Northeast has to offer. So turn on Frank Sinatra's classic song "Summer Wind," get out your sunglasses and bathing suit, and pack your bags for New England. It's big city and small town all wrapped up in one, with the best fudge shops found anywhere outside of Belgium. And chocolate is, after all, a great part of any honeymoon.

Chicago

Okay, so I think we've found a theme here. If Frank Sinatra has sung a song about it, it's a great city to choose for your honeymoon. Think about it: Old Blue Eyes's renditions of "New York, New York," "Summer Wind," and "Chicago" are classics, not to mention top picks in karaoke bars all over the world. Regardless of Sinatra's endorsement, Chicago is a true hot spot in the roster of ideal big city honeymoon getaways. Ranked third on *Travel and Leisure*'s World's Best awards list for the top American cities to visit, this city on the lake is home to the undisputed queen of the media, Oprah Winfrey, and also the location of the Magnificent Mile, which has the most impressive collection of shopping establishments in all the Midwest. From Tiffany & Co. to Ralph Lauren, Saks, Chanel, and Cartier to the Gap, you'd better be ready to lug some heavy shopping bags back to your room.

During the months of ideal weather, you can take a guided gondola ride to tour the center of the city or head out to the beaches where you can participate in most kinds of water sports and adventures. You may not think "beach" when you think of Chicago, but this is definitely a big sparkling benefit to your time spent in the city.

The Best of the Rest

I could fill an entire book with the wonderful charms and exciting attractions pulsing in many U.S. cities, and indeed entire travel books have been written about many hotspots on our country's map. So for now, I encourage you to consider the following list of big cities as your own homegrown honeymoon destinations. (To reach their individual boards of tourism, go to www.towd.com and plug in their states on the main U.S. menu).

- San Francisco, California
- Austin, Texas
- Seattle, Washington
- New Orleans, Louisiana
- Taos, New Mexico
- Los Angeles, California
- Philadelphia, Pennsylvania
- Baltimore, Marlyand
- Washington, DC
- Nashville, Tennessee
- Aspen, Colorado
- Monterey, California, and the coastline linking the major California big cities

On rambling tours, take in the city's rich cultural heritage, experience unforgettable concerts and arts in and around the city, and dine at fabulous eateries and trendy cafés. (Go to www.cityofchicago.org for lists of cultural events and festivals like the Chicago Jazz Festival, a tourism favorite.) If you're an architecture buff, you're in one of the premier cities for the works of Frank Lloyd Wright and Helmut Jahn, not to mention some of the tallest buildings in the world. More of an art person than an architecture person? Some of the city's plazas showcase works by Picasso, Chagall, and Dubuffet, and the nearby museums house even more works of timeless art. Your cab driver can tell you all about the Great Chicago Fire of 1871 that leveled the city, and then you can marvel at the shining and architecturally unique skyline that rose up from those ancient ashes. It's the mix of big city action and *Midwest* charm, this time around, in a city where that middle American ambience is still very much alive.

Recent honeymooners I spoke to gushed and glowed about the city's lively nightlife, the sushi bars, the piano bars, the great weather, and the flower-lined streets in the wealthier and more hotel-studded areas. One couple stayed at the ultraposh Drake hotel (www.thedrake hotel.com), where they reserved an executive suite with access to the members-only executive lounge. While in the lounge, they met celebrities and dignitaries in town for a grand gala, sat down for predinner drinks with politicians and movie stars, and even had a brush with royalty as a princess passed through the lobby, hounded by paparazzi. The Chicago Hilton (www.hilton.com) and many other top names in resort life with Chicago addresses also provide such luxury club amenities, and several, such as the Four Seasons Hotel (www.fourseasons.com /chicagofs/), house world-class spas within their city-view establishments. The Four Seasons' Presidential Suite not only boasts a top-of-the-world corner view of the city, plus every luxury amenity within the room ever dreamed up by a hospitality committee, but also provides child-size plush robes if you're bringing the little ones along on your trip. The Ritz-Carlton hotel (www.fourseasons.com/chicagorc/) in

Honeymoon Reflections

Knowing that we wanted our honeymoon to be within the United States somewhere but already having visited most of the major cities during our business trips and previous vacations, we looked for something very different, very American, and a complete departure from our normal spots. So we chose Montana. Tons of celebrities have homes and ranches out there, and friends of ours who spent college semesters in that state absolutely raved about it, so we looked into the many great cities, hotels, and local events going on. We went to small-town attractions, rode horses with real cowboys, saw some local sights we almost couldn't believe—and that scenery! My parents would call it "God's country" up there, but to us it was just wide-open beauty at every angle you looked. It was a great escape, a purely original honeymoon, and we have the most incredible pictures of us up there. We had an amazing time, and it was the perfect choice for us.

—Beth and Ken

Chicago (which is, by the way, *Travel and Leisure*'s number one hotel on its World's Best list) even has a 24-hour on-call computer expert in case your *computer* suffers from performance problems. Does it get any better than that? *That's* the style and tone of high-life Chicago, one of the best choices possible for your big city honeymoon.

Miami

Jet set with the best of them at Miami's strip of luxury resorts and spas, even if you only have a day to enjoy the city before your honeymoon cruise sails from its port. South Beach is the destination du jour these days for the wild and adventurous couple, with countless nightclubs and a social see-and-be-seen scene you don't want to miss. If people-watching isn't your thing—and this is one of the best places on earth for that particular spectator sport—then hit the restaurants for some authentic Cuban cuisine. Dance the night away at a beach party, join the yachting crowd on a spontaneous sailing trip to Bimini, and keep your eye on the ocean ahead to spot the gently arching swim of dolphins and the slow, lumbering surfacing of manatee. Visit the native undersea residents during scuba dives or snorkeling.

Miami (www.flausa.com) has a hot energy that makes it the perfect place for honeymooners with a hot sense of adventure and plans for a hot honeymoon. But it also has its romantic side, with tropical gardens and museum courtyards set up to give young lovers a place for respite. One such attraction is the Vizcaya Museum and Gardens (www.vizcayamuseum.org), which is a Renaissance mansion set on 10 acres of rambling in-bloom gardens and a favorite spot for strolling hand-in-hand and picture taking.

6

Foreign Honeymoons

Get out your passports! Your dream honeymoon could take you to the top of the Eiffel Tower, the beaches of Monaco, Buckingham Palace, the opera house at Sydney Harbor, or the hot shopping districts of Singapore. If you're planning on an international getaway, you have the world at your fingertips and you have a once-in-a-lifetime adventure ahead of you. For many couples, it's the allure of the foreign experience that beckons them onto long flights and trans-Atlantic cruises, in search of new cultures and cuisines, great vistas, and a personal feeling for the vast and glorious variety of experiences in our world. For some, it's enough to get a small taste of international flavor at a resort spa or ethnic-themed hotel here in the United States. But for the true-blue traveler, there's no replacement for the real thing. And that means a grand trip abroad to some of the most beautiful and exciting countries in the world.

So, Honey, Where Are We Going?

While there's no way I could ever list every single city for ideal foreign honeymoon travel here—bookstores devote *yards* of shelf space just for their travel books and guidebooks on the most popular foreign destinations—I have included a handful of suggestions here to get you thinking and dreaming about where in the world you'll venture for the trip of your lifetime. Where on earth will you begin your married life? Which corner of the globe would you both most like to visit together now, and which will be reserved for your most adventurous getaways in the future, for big anniversary trips, and for places to bring your kids someday? You could throw darts at a map of the world to select a foreign destination— or you could read on here and check the travel Web sites to decide on the setting for your foreign honeymoon and all that it will bring to you.

Simplify It

Of course, when looking at a lineup of foreign destinations, you're likely to do a *lot* of research, asking around among your friends, checking out travel agents. One source to explore for eurovacations is e-vacations.com, which lets you point, click, drag, and create trial itineraries, complete with transportation data and don't-miss sites and excursions. This "create-a-trip" site will help you piece together your most-wanted honeymoon elements and stir up the pot of your destination ideas while you check out the going rates. I recommend that you use this site as a step in your planning process, helping you find your way to the booking stage.

Paris

What could be more romantic than Paris? Monet once used the dazzling pink and purple sunset over the Seine as inspiration for his work, and more than a few honeymooners have used the same sunset as inspiration for a champagne toast, a handheld stroll, or a kiss outside a quaint sidewalk café. Want a preview of that sunset, before you even get there? You'll love this Web site, www.abcparislive.com, for a live camera feed of the changing sky behind the Eiffel Tower and a daily look at the goings-on around that international landmark.

Once that view lures you to the City of Lights (www.paris-touristoffice.com or www.franceguide.com), you might find your-selves checking into one of the many premier hotels and resorts located all around the city, then stepping out to explore the Louvre's great works of art or the collection of equally notable paintings and sculptures at the Musée d'Orsay (www.musee-orsay.fr). For the artisti-cally minded, you don't even have to stand in line or dodge yelping tour guides in these must-see museums. Sidewalk vendors display their watercolors and photographs right along the Champs-Élysées, next to the flower carts and those amazing patisseries that fill the air with the rich scents of freshly baked bread and chocolate delights.

With your artistic appetite satiated, it's time to hit Fashion Central, with stops at many of the world's most famous haute couture hot spots, like Chanel and Yves St. Laurent.

On one of your rambling tourist days, you might cruise down the Seine in a well-appointed tour boat. You might step onto the hallowed ground of Notre Dame Cathedral and take pictures of those incredible stained-glass windows or lay out a picnic blanket for a brunch of champagne, cheese, and red grapes on the Pont des Arts walking path. Ride the enormous Ferris wheel in the Tuileries, and at night hop from one happening nightclub to another.

Penny-Wise

To find great discounts and travel information specifically geared to honeymooners in France, including hotel deals, museum specials, at-tractions, restaurant plugs, and shopping information, check out www.france.com. Another great site for finding the best rates in France, both in- and out-of-season, is www.francevacations.net.

Dine at five-star restaurants like the Restaurant du Palais-Royal, celebrity-watch in some of the most-frequented hotels and eateries, and enjoy a fine French wine served by a fine French sommelier. You're at the heart of the most romantic city in the world, filled with the his-tories of great loves, the inspiration of great art, and some of the best places on earth you'll find to kiss.

Rome

Toss three coins in the Trevi Fountain in Rome to have your greatest wishes come true, and then spend the rest of your days in this fine city knowing that at least one of them was a success—you are having an amazing honeymoon. Rome (www.romaclick.com) is one of those always romantic, always authentic destinations that will steal your heart and give you plenty to tell the folks back home. From a walk past the newly primped Coliseum to a visit to St. Peter's Square, you're sure to hit all the tourism-heavy hot spots, plus discover a few new ones of your own.

Frequent travelers to Rome tell me that with a recent dedication to upping the chic potential of the city, fashionable eateries and celebrity-friendly nightspots have sprung up, plus a few camera crews have visited for the filming of major motion pictures. You've got boutiques and specialty stores to roam through, the Forum and the Baths of Caracalla to admire, step-back-in-time hotels to lounge in, and a bevy of arts and cultural performances to choose from. When it comes to dining, you've come to the right place. Choose from hundreds of cozy cafés to outdoor terrace dining rooms to the utmost in posh and particular that only seem to allow in the famous, the infamous, and people who say they're either one or the other. With the quality of master chef cooking at most of these nontouristy eateries, they can afford to pull a little bit of attitude. If you can get in the door, you're going to have a meal you'll never forget.

It may be a few hundred miles from Rome, closer to Switzerland, actually, than the center of Italy, but Lake Como (www.lakecomo.com) is one spot that's a shooting star in the cosmos of wedding and honeymoon travel. Lake Como in Italy virtually melts from the mountains into the sea, with its villas dotting the cliffsides and its gardens introducing the lakeside villas. Celebrities have honeymooned here. Royalty have vacationed here. The world's most famous fashion designers call it home. Lake Como is *the* hot honeymoon destination for so many couples, and it's no wonder why. Cruises from point to point on the lake showcase glorious natural scenery, and true romance floats on private boats for two. Gardens welcome you at every angle on every shore, from spring blooms to white azaleas to Japanese gardens. Meander among the winding village roads, gaze up in admiration at the churches' statues and carvings of saints and apostles. Hop aboard a seaplane for an unforgettable view of the lake city from above, and sign on for side trips to nearby Lugano in Switzerland or the more city-chic center of Milan, both a day trip away and a nice dash of added flavor. Back in Lake Como, take a carriage ride to the nearest piazza for an incredible sampling of the region's best, homespun meals and wines. And if you're staying at one of the most romantic resorts in town, you just might return to your flower-strewn doorway and flower-filled room to find a mint, a true Italian delicacy, on your pillow. The Lake Como honeymoon is a wonderful escape in a relaxed and enchanted village that doesn't allow you to miss the world outside. While you're there, the question might be "*What* world outside?" Now that's the mark of a great honeymoon destination.

Just the Facts

According to a recent survey run by the American Society of Travel Agents, the top five most popular destinations among all travelers to Italy are:

1. Rome
2. Florence
3. Venice
4. Milan
5. Tuscany

The Riviera

You don't have to be impossibly thin, impossibly rich, and impossibly tan to fit in at the Riviera . . . but all of that couldn't hurt. The Riviera is a catchphrase for the coastal resort towns of such countries as France, Italy, and Spain, and regardless of the language spoken at any, the ambience is the same: pure indulgence.

As the playground for the wealthy, the famous, and royalty, the French Riviera appears like a mirage by boat or by land, with buildings dotted as diamonds into the hillsides and boasting incredible seascapes. Exorbitant private yachts sway at their moorings at each pier, and if you listen carefully enough, you'll hear champagne corks popping all over town. So strap on your bathing suits (make them small to fit in with the thong-wearing and topless crowds) and head out to the beach for some sun and scenery worshiping. This is your immersion into "the good life," so soak it up.

Cannes may turn into a cinema film festival during its annual moment in the sun, but during the rest of the year, this seaside resort town is more laid-back, with a fine sand beach inviting you to the shore and white and pastel sun umbrellas sprung up like a field of flowers. Walk along La Croisette, the walking and shopping and people-gazing promenade that leads past the stately and elegant hotels, upscale shops, and patisseries. Take a ride on the romantic carousel right here on La Croisette and make sure someone takes your picture. Once you get your land legs back, hit the boutiques and ateliers for some serious shopping, or try your negotiating skills *en français* at the many open-air markets.

Not to be left out of any praise, the Italian Riviera stretches along its own length of nature-blessed coastline. Alongside the winding sandy beaches and resulting shore attractions complete with palm trees and pines shading you from that skin-bronzing sun, you'll find olive groves, lemon orchards, vineyards, and fine Italian cuisine like you've never tasted before. Here you'll find Genoa, Cinque Terre, Sestri, Positano, and Portofino—the names alone conjure up images from the most romantic movies and the most romantic real-life moments.

Add in Monaco and Monte Carlo, with their combinations of wealth and splendor—not to mention the tour you *have* to take, the palace currently inhabited by the royal family of Monaco—and you're in the most exquisite surroundings for the most exquisite honeymoon. Take plenty of film with you because you're going to want to capture everything you see and experience.

Greece

From the historically charged city of Athens to the many tiny islands, this foreign getaway combines the best of both worlds if you can't decide between a city or an island honeymoon. Athens is the site of the 2004 Olympics, and even after the Games depart, the many upscale and cosmopolitan additions to this already packed mecca are only going to make it more attractive to tourists.

The Greek islands invite you to their golden sand beaches and their blend of Old World roots and New World tourism intensity. Mykonos, for example, has developed a fine reputation of being another extension of the Riviera, with its rich and lovely visitors, its chic waterfront restaurants, and its trendy shopping centers all within close proximity to its preserved traditions of small-town villas, exquisitely maintained churches, and windmills. On Santorini, you're actually walking along streets and cliffsides that have been formed by a volcano, with a fine resort town built on the sculptures and moldings of that natural formation. Skiathos and Skopelos, two of the natives' most favored islands, provide unspoiled beach relaxation and activities, added to local flavors and a never-ending vista of that crystal blue sea and the islands peering out of it. Once you're sun drenched, tour the big city of Athens itself for a few days.

Enjoy and experiment with Greek cuisine and your strong beverage of choice, and take in one of the arts, cultural, or religious festivals that abound during the high seasons of even the smallest villages. This is why the big Mediterranean cruise ships make it a point to stop in Greece, and this is also why so many filmmakers have brought their crews here to shoot the cliff- and landscapes, the clear blue ocean, and the soul-filled and beautiful eyes of the locals. When you come to Greece, now or in the future, you'll understand as well.

London

On your wedding day, you're going to be a fairy-tale princess: regal, elegant, bejeweled, and beautiful, with all of your ladies-in-waiting surrounding you at every turn. So after peeling off the ballgown, and perhaps even removing the tiara from your upswept hair, what better place to honeymoon than the land of princesses and queens, royalty and nobility? London seems to revolve around the pageantry and delicious antics of its royal family, and its resulting tourism factor brings you right up close and into the various castles, palaces, and favorite stops of the crowned elite. A close second to *your* wedding, of course, would be any royal wedding, so drop by Buckingham Palace. With special arrangements, you may be allowed into Buckingham's State Rooms, where today's royal family meets and greets visiting dignitaries and royals alike. Look around while you're in there, and you'll see authentic Rembrandts and Rubens paintings, the same familiar view your favorite real-life princes and princesses view on an almost daily basis.

Windsor Castle is, of course, one of the residential palaces and the setting for Prince Andrew and Sophie Rhys-Jones's wedding as well as many of the royals' state and family functions. Additional tours of the site might bring you into the state apartments, where you can touch the doorknobs Diana might have touched and view the valuable artwork she might have admired. At Eltham Palace, you can walk the grounds of the palace and even enjoy high tea in the palace's kitchen or sitting rooms. Just such proximity to the British royals is enough to give some visitors a thrill. Others would rather delve further into London's nonroyal lineup.

On your tours, you might go to the Houses of Parliament, Westminster Hall, the Tower of London where the Crown Jewels are safely stored, or various churches and cathedrals of note. There is even a fun themed Jack the Ripper walking tour in the East End of London, where the famous murderer made, shall we say, a name for himself. For a less bone-chilling look at London's rich history, you have your choice of some 300 museums and art galleries within the city and vicinity, the oldest of which is the British Museum, the home to the Rosetta Stone and countless other jaw-droppers.

For a romantic swirl around the scenic cityscapes of London, sign up for day cruises and river tours along the Thames, where your guide will point out the most fascinating tidbits about Big Ben in the distance, Westminster, and the Tower Bridge. Some cruises or catamarans will deliver you to and from the shopping districts or simply take you for a ride in style to lunch along the river's edge. Dress for high tea at your hotel, munch on a crumpet or scone, and then head back out to explore London's rich history, high society, and cinema-familiar backdrops, as well as perhaps a royal sighting or two.

Penny-Wise

For complete touring information and discounted or even *free* entrance tickets to many of London's most popular attractions, go to www.londontown.com and click your way into saving a few pounds (that's British currency, not weight you'll lose during your trip).

Australia

It's a *looooong* flight, but anyone who takes it says it's worth the time—twice the time, actually—for the pleasures of visiting Australia. Any country that can produce such beautiful treasures as Mel Gibson and Nicole Kidman has to be great, right? The lure of Australia may have come to the forefront during telecasts of the Olympics, but as any traveler to the land Down Under can tell you, those expertly edited and network-produced tourism segments just couldn't do justice to the natural beauty and sheer energy of Sydney and the surrounding communities of Australia. You just have to be there.

On your Australian getaway, you might sail around Sydney Harbor or perhaps jet-ski or water-ski alongside the famously active locals. You might ride some curls on Australia's finest surfing beaches and hang out with the pro surfing crowd that gravitates to this country at certain times of the year. Or you might flex your adventure muscles with a professionally guided climb up the Harbour Bridge, as some locals are wont to do.

At the Sydney Opera House, that instantly recognizable piece of modern architecture that looks like something out of mythical Atlantis, you might don your finest formalwear and take in *La Traviata* or another cultural production, then sign up for a tour behind the scenes and even a moment's stance on stage.

If you have no idea what a kookaburra is, then you should visit one of the nearby wildlife sanctuaries or go on a wildlife tour, where you'll see native kookaburras, koalas, and wallabies frolicking about and then conducting the serious and productive parts of their day. At the Australian Museum, you can take in the wide range of local art and cultural customs and also learn the incredible history of Australia's native Aboriginal people and the rise to greatness of the land itself.

Head out into the Outback, the vast center of the continent, far from the developed cities on the coastline. Guided tours will take you out into nature, show you the land of existing Aborigines, and perhaps allow you to participate in native rituals and games.

Speaking of wildlife, head out to the local pubs and nightclubs to throw back a few with a rowdy party crowd, perhaps those professional surfers from the beaches. Take in the local cuisine, from Vegemite to a big juicy steak, and simply enjoy that unmistakably charming Australian accent that surrounds you at every turn.

Just a short hop away from Australia is New Zealand (www.tourism info.govt.nz), a collection of South Pacific islands that have been preserved in their natural splendor (almost a third of the land falls under the protected umbrella of national parks). A mark of New Zealand's culture is the natives' propensity for active and adventurous (sometimes adrenaline-soaking) outdoor interests. Here you can sign up for kayaking or cross-country hiking that leads you in one trek up through lush green hills and gradually into icy snow-capped peaks. A short distance from there are rain forests, hot sulfur springs, sports-inviting beaches, and world-famous hiking tours that are so popular you need to make reservations a few months in advance (www .ultimatehikes.co.nz). New Zealanders are notoriously friendly to tourists, and you might follow their penchant for extreme sports, such as bungee jumping from the top expanse of a bridge, mountain biking, rock climbing, and skydiving. Whatever *your* penchants, New Zealand is a stop to schedule.

Mexico

After Hawaii, Mexico is the leading spot for honeymoon destinations, according to a recent survey by the Association of Bridal Consultants. With hot towns like Cancún and Cabo on the map, it's no wonder that newlyweds from near and far have made this foreign country one of the most popular options out there.

It's not just spring-break-wild things on vacation in Cancún. With their wedding rings shining brightly under the hot Mexico sun, couples flock to the wide and wonderful beaches of this resort city, diving into the ocean as excitedly as they dive into Cancún's famous poolside parties and tequila-soaked nightclub scenes. It may be the social scene, and it may simply be the cuisine scene, but Cancún will always rank high among Mexican locations, simply because of its lineup of premier resorts and proximity to where the action is.

Where to Go in Mexico

The American Society of Travel Agents' recent survey says that the top choices among vacationers heading off to Mexico are:

1. Cancún
2. Puerto Vallarta
3. Cabo San Lucas
4. Mazatlan
5. Cozumel

In slight contrast to the hopping resort mecca of Cancún is Puerto Vallarta, with its collection of beaches perfect for snorkeling or horseback riding, just a short ride to the more cultural centers with galleries, musical performances, ethnic dance showcases, outdoor art displays, and plenty of shopping to keep those pesos flowing swiftly out of your hands.

On your more adventurous days in Puerto Vallarta, you might hike and tour the Sierra Madres, look in on an in-progress archaeological dig, rise above the countryside in a hot-air balloon or attached to an off-boat parasail, or even cruise the sapphire waters along the coast in a replica of Christopher Columbus's *Santa Maria.* From history to ethnicity, cuisine to craft, Puerto Vallarta has incorporated the best of Mexico's substance and style for a must in your Mexican itinerary.

Simplify It

Take your pick from among Mexico's many levels of resorts, cities, attractions, and activities by contacting the Mexican Board of Tourism at 800-44-MEXICO, www.visitmexico.com.

The Mexican Riviera is often called the "Gold Coast" of Mexico, perhaps because it incorporates the gold standard of ideal attractions in a long strip of beaches and resort cities including Mazatlan and Acapulco. Cliff diving? Golf? Jungle jaunts? Nightlife? It has all of these—and more. The playground for the celebratory vacationer alongside the on-hiatus movie star, the Mexican Riviera offers the full range of choices for any honeymoon mood, combining the attraction of island getaways with international flavor, adventure sports with culture, fine food that's *nothing* like any Mexican food you can get at home, and nonstop nightlife to thoroughly exhaust you and still get you to call it fun.

The top resorts in any of these resort areas, from Cancún to the Riviera to Cabo to the Yucatan Peninsula, have pulled off the impossible. They've created hotels with built-in attractions to rival the designs of Mother Nature. Whether it's a swimming pool that seems to have no end before the ocean starts to lead into the horizon, hotel rooms with individual swimming pools on their terraces, a spa with distinct Mexican flair, or music that stirs your soul and gets you on the dance floor, the Mexican honeymoon experience has earned its high ranking among honeymooners and will continue to do so for a long time to come.

Asia

You can't get much more removed from the sights, sounds, and tastes of your regular, everyday world than you can in the Far East. Frequent travelers and travel agents tell me that Asia is the choice du jour of "been there, done that" vacationers who are looking for the trip of a lifetime and a showering of all new senses. From taking an inspirational climb up to a Buddhist temple, where you can make offerings of flowers and incense at a shrine, to passing through working rice paddy villages that time seems to have forgotten to experiencing the ultramodern and futuristic city attractions in Japan, the Asia honeymoon is a choice to consider strongly.

One of my favorite all-encompassing tours through Asia is the illustrious Orient Express combination tour of rail and boat travel

Top Picks in the Far East

The American Society of Travel Agents says that the top five choices in Far Eastern destinations are:

1. Hong Kong
2. Beijing
3. Bangkok
4. Shanghai
5. Tokyo

through more than 1,200 miles of the greatest sites and experiences in the Far East. Starting at Singapore, you'll ride the elegant Orient Express (with all of its fine accommodations and well-appointed serving cars) to Bangkok in Thailand. Once in Thailand, you'll hop a riverboat through hypnotic riverside scenery to Mandalay and through countless notable shoreline villages along your route. It's an upscale tour through some of the most incredible scenery you'll ever glimpse in person, and you'll want to take in every aspect of each of the five senses.

During your walking tours of the Asian cities and countryside stops, look around you at the street markets and try out the unusual findings there for just a nominal amount of change. Look to the left and see an orange-robed monk emanating inner peace as he makes his journey to a far-off temple. Up in the hills, once you've made the self-rewarding journey, you might happen upon a number of such shrines and temples, where you can set a garland of flowers at the feet of a bronze god statue, or you might be invited as a once-in-a-lifetime honor to ring the prayer bell. Stick around and observe the customs of these spiritual people, perhaps learn a few rituals to add to your own spirit-minded or yoga practices, and have your marriage blessed at the feet of a wise master or spiritual guru. For many, it's these types of interactions and finds, most unexpected and stumbled upon along the way, that make this journey one of both outward and inward enjoyment. In very few places in the world will you find such an authentic atmosphere, and it may be that you'll never chance upon a sight quite like this one again, which makes this honeymoon very special indeed.

In Hong Kong, it's a return to the action and intensity of big city living. Called "The City of Life," Hong Kong blends old Asian customs (and architecture) with the sprawling spread of a major metropolis, complete with nightlife and shopping to make even the most city-bred feel right at home . . . but with something just a little bit different. Museums abound, with the Hong Kong Heritage Museum a tour leader's favorite. This site's 12 separate galleries are joined by an open-air courtyard that reminds one of a castle layout. Nearby, you can visit the flower markets, shopping centers, and open-air markets, where the greatest attraction of all seems to be the plethora of fish—not dead-eyed fish sitting in vats of ice, ready to be carved into dinner, but puffy little baggies of brightly colored goldfish, which are considered possessions of good luck and fortune in many Asian homes. These in-demand little guys are *everywhere,* so bring a few back to the room to swim in your ice bucket and give your honeymoon home base a good dose of luck for your future.

Hong Kong isn't just a bustling city. You'll also find a beach center where the most surprising things await you. On one chartered tour, you might spot one of the very rare pink dolphins that live in the open waters. For this foreign city filled with everything from A to Z, you'll definitely need a complete tourism guide; www.discover hongkong.com is a good bet, as is a travel agent with a specialty in Asian tourism.

Something to See: The Wonders of the World

You've probably heard about the Seven Wonders of the World, and you might even know where most of them are. But did you know that there have been *many* attractions that have been classified as wonders of this world, both man-made marvels and natural masterpieces, span-ning from ancient times right up to the present? With the gracious permission of Alaa Ashmawy, the creator of the Seven Wonders of the Ancient World Web site (ce.eng.usf.edu/pharos/wonders/other.html), I've provided the following lists of some of the most remarkable sites around the globe. Your honeymoon might lead you to several, so you can add a wonder of the world to your list of must-sees on your trip.

Structural Wonders
- The Aztec Temple in Tenochtitlán (Mexico City), Mexico
- The Colosseum in Rome, Italy
- The Great Wall of China

The Top Foreign Spots

Travel and Leisure's rankings for the World's Best:

Europe

1.	Florence	81.4
2.	Rome	80.4
3.	Paris	77.4
4.	Venice	76.3
5.	London	74.6

Asia

1.	Hong Kong	74.1
2.	Bangkok	72.8
3.	Singapore	68.0
4.	Kyoto	65.8
5.	Beijing	64.1

Australia, New Zealand, and the South Pacific

1.	Sydney	74.5
2.	Christchurch, New Zealand	66.8
3.	Melbourne	66.3
4.	Queenstown, New Zealand	65.0
5.	Auckland	64.3

Mexico and Central and South America

1.	Buenos Aires	66.3
2.	Rio de Janeiro	65.5
3.	Mexico City	63.6
4.	San Miguel de Allende, Mexico	63.4
5.	Santiago	61.1

For this year's World's Best in foreign city travel and awards in the best international hotels, cruises, food, service, and other related categories, go to www.travelandleisure.com and click on the World's Best icon.

- The Leaning Tower of Pisa, Italy
- The Mayan Temples of Tikal in northern Guatemala
- The Moai Statues in Rapa Nui (Easter Island), Chile
- Mont-Saint-Michel in Normandy, France
- The Parthenon in Athens, Greece
- Stonehenge in England
- Taj Mahal in Agra, India

Natural Wonders

- Angel Falls in Venezuela
- The Bay of Fundy in Nova Scotia, Canada
- The Grand Canyon in Arizona, United States
- The Great Barrier Reef in Australia
- Iguaçú Falls in Brazil/Argentina
- Krakatoa Island in Indonesia
- Mount Everest in Nepal
- Mount Fuji in Japan
- Mount Kilimanjaro in Tanzania
- Niagara Falls in Ontario (Canada) and New York State (United States)
- Paricutin Volcano in Mexico
- Victoria Falls in Zambia/Zimbabwe

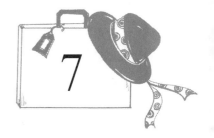

Food and Drink Honeymoons

So what makes a honeymoon truly great? Besides the obvious romantic elements, besides the great scenery and shopping and scuba diving and sailing, there's one big element that for many couples can make or break the trip of their lifetime . . . the food! You've given a lot of thought to the menu for your wedding, wanting those hors d'oeuvres to be just right and that cake to be gorgeous and delectable. Now it's time to think about what you'll be eating (and drinking) on your honeymoon getaway.

I asked hundreds of couples who'd just returned from their post-wedding trips to tell me about the cuisine on their journey, and the stories I heard made my mouth water. From butter-soft filet mignon to oysters topped with caviar and chilled vodka granita to pan-seared tilapia, abalone, maki shark, and crème brûlée, the list sounded like Emeril's corner of heaven. As for drinks, champagne flowed, creatively named frozen margaritas in rainbow colors lined the bartops, and my survey respondents cooed over an endless list of wine vintages, liqueurs, and especially those limit-of-three Hurricanes in New

Orleans. It's not surprising, of course, that couples think ahead about the kinds of local and exotic cuisines on a destination's menu or that they actually plan ahead for the exciting new tastes they're about to experience. What *was* surprising to me was the huge number of couples who planned their honeymoons *around* culinary and wine tours, making the adventures of food and drink a large focus of their trips! From vineyard jaunts in Napa and Sonoma Counties in California, complete with bike tours and private tastings in the darkened and romantic wine cellars of the vineyard elite, to culinary tours of Provence and Normandy with celebrity chefs providing a taste of that region's best, clearly many couples are letting their palates (and their stomachs!) lead the way in their planning. If food and drink is not the sole purpose of their visit, then it's at least a large, large factor in determining wherever they plan to go.

Just take a look at *Travel and Leisure*'s latest World's Best awards (www.travelandleisure.com) in the categories of best food served at resorts, on cruises, at spas, and in cities all over the world (along with their scores in the competition). For this prestigious traveler's magazine to survey readers about the tops in cuisine, you know the top criteria for a fabulous vacation spot rests strongly in the chefs' and sommeliers' hands.

Fine Foods

Your appetite for the indulgent, exotic, and authentic of the world's cuisine might take you to the culinary epicenters of Tuscany, Florence, and Normandy in Europe, or you might prefer an Asian flavor on a tour of the Far East, with stops in Singapore, Vietnam, or Osaka. Perhaps you'd like a freshly baked baguette and a sampling of cheeses as you sit at an outdoor café in Paris overlooking the Eiffel Tower. In Chicago, your first stop might be for a world-famous deep-dish pizza, while in New Orleans it's going to be shrimp étoufée and beignets. If

A Five-Star Meal Is Closer Than You Think

Think the best eateries in the world are in Paris, Milan, and Florence? Think again! American resorts, hotels, and restaurants have beaten out the crème de la crème of years past to snag many of the top spots in this international survey. New York City has emerged as the leading culinary center of the universe, with more than 18,000 restaurants, in every size, style, and level of formality, ranking number one in the world as of the 2002 awards ceremony. For the most current awards and ideas for a few delicious destinations to add to your honeymoon hunting list, go to the World's Best awards link at www.travelandleisure.com.

The Top Cities for Food: Overall

1.	New York	91.3
2.	Paris	90.3
3.	New Orleans	89.9
4.	San Francisco	88.7
5.	Rome	83.6
6.	Chicago	82.5
7.	Florence	81.5
8.	Boston	77.7
9.	Venice	77.6
10.	Montreal	77.4

great eats are on your dream honeymoon wish list, you can search out the best places to go for the kinds of food you desire. The best magazine and Web site sources to check first are the Food Network (www.foodtv.com) for its lineup of culinary destinations and recommendations, *Epicurious, Travel and Leisure, Conde Nast Traveler, Gourmet, Williams Sonoma's Taste,* and other resources that spotlight food-based travel. Even wine magazines and sites like *Wine Spectator* (www.wine spectator.com) profile the best in culinary getaways that tie in with the top names in wineries and vineyards.

On a fine culinary tour, you might enjoy an itinerary full of shopping at open-air markets where the scent of freshly picked peppers fills the air with an aroma you've never smelled before. You might estate-hop from one well-known vintner to another, swirling a fine port or brandy in your glass as you talk with the owner about the estate's champion breed horse farm nearby. An outing during your culinary trip through Normandy might bring you to the scenes of historic battlefields like Omaha Beach, or you might find yourself winding through the vineyard trails where American soldiers once marched. It's precisely these kinds of extras that make culinary and arts tours through Europe so exciting for many, especially those with long family ancestry and histories in the area. Returning to your fam-

Welcome to Cooking 101

When you start researching culinary-based vacations, you're going to find two different types of tours. One is an expert-led tasting excursion to the finest restaurants and wineries across the globe, with five-star meals served to you in style at some of the most breathtaking resorts (and even castles) you can imagine. The second type is significantly educational, where you're taking lessons from these expert chefs. You'll go on shopping trips and learn the difference between a good batch of arugula and a bad one, then you'll tie on your apron and discover various cooking techniques from the masters. Many couples love culinary class–type trips and even incorporate a day or two of such lessons into the first-described culinary trip, whereas others don't want to work so hard and learn so much during their trip. So be *sure* to read all Web site descriptions of culinary tours very carefully . . . so you don't wind up doing homework on your honeymoon.

ily's heritage homeland; walking through the piazzas and markets where your grandmother played as a young girl; boating in the lake where your great-grandparents once met in a secret and scandalous fashion, ignoring their fathers' refusal of right to marry and eloping with more love in their hearts than money in their pockets—how much more tied to your family roots can you get than that? Clearly, the satisfaction of culinary tours runs much deeper than what's on the silver platter before you. Culinary tours hold history, of a region and culture and of your family's beginnings.

So where is everyone going for this fine food and a walk back into history? Some of the more popular destinations for those embarking on culinary tours are:

- Provence
- Normandy
- Tuscany
- Paris
- St. Remy, France
- Basque Coast (the French and Spanish Rivieras)
- Nova Scotia
- Costa Rica
- Mexico
- Thailand
- Vietnam
- New York City
- New Orleans

CARRIE AND TIM'S NEW ORLEANS FOOD FANTASY

We'd been to New Orleans before during Mardi Gras, but we mainly did the parade and Bourbon Street thing during all that revelry at the celebration. Still, we'd seen enough of the restaurants and the jazz bars to know that this was definitely the place we wanted to go for our honeymoon. Hearing that New Orleans has also been ranked as one of the most romantic cities in the country and "America's European Masterpiece" only made it better . . . and New Orleans definitely proved that it deserves its spot on that list.

We went to relaxed and smoky jazz clubs, had predinner martinis at the Polo Lounge in the Windsor Court Hotel, ate at the finest restaurants in town and spared no expense to dig into desserts as well, took a carriage ride to the French Market, walked along the Moonwalk path down by the river . . . it was just so incredibly romantic, every minute of it. But *the food!* We promised not to worry about calories and fat grams during this trip, and it's a good thing because we feasted on every kind of seafood imaginable, from jambalaya to shrimp gumbo. Also, we ate at Bella Luna (which was rated by *Glamour* magazine as one of the most romantic places to kiss), where we had dinner and then ice cream smothered with Jack Daniels. And we ate at the Court of Two Sisters, which we'd also seen on Food Network; this place seems like something out of a fairy tale with its flower-filled courtyard and vines making it look like "The Secret Garden." We even had a five-star meal specially catered for us and served to us on the veranda of our hotel room. Talk about indulgence! It truly was the most magical, most romantic, and most delicious trip we'd ever been on.

Wine, Anyone?

Picture the two of you biking along a country road with rows and rows of grape arbors surrounding you on both sides, a clear blue sky overhead, and a half dozen or so brightly colored hot-air balloons floating by in the far distance overhead. The air smells of fresh green trees and sweet fruit, your floral dress is flapping in the breeze, and you turn onto the cobblestone path leading to a sprawling estate where they make the best wine in the country. Inside the winery, you're led down a candlelit curved stairway to a stone-walled tasting room where a waiting buffet of grapes, cheeses, and finger sandwiches invite you to nibble while your host brings out crystal glass after crystal glass of Merlots, Petit Sirahs, Cabernets, and Chardonnays as you sip and taste your way through a lineup of award-winning vintages. After your afternoon at the winery, you walk your bikes to the nearby charming country cottage inn, where you climb into your feather bed and dream of tomorrow's antique shopping, horseback riding, and art gallery browsing.

Such is the delight of the wine country honeymoon. It's romantic, relaxing, and indulgent, a fine break from the big city life you may be used to, and one of the biggest trends in American travel today. I spoke to many travel agents and proprietors of wine country bed-and-breakfast villas, and all said the same thing: In today's travel industry, couples long for an escape from their real world. They want the simplicity of olden days, a slowed-down pace, and a return to nature but still with the spoilings of five-star food and drink—all of this without the flight to Europe. Simply put, it's the wine regions of *this* country that are attracting more and more couples who want a tasteful and tasty honeymoon.

So where are the winery hot spots? Of course, the first names that come to mind are the Napa Valley and Sonoma Valley of California. Napa is the granddaddy of the wine region, with among the largest number of wineries and volume of tourism throughout the peak summer months. In this region, you'll find the more commercially oriented, big-name hotels and resorts, spas, restaurants, and tourist attractions surrounding the better-known wineries such as Mondavi. This is where the action is, which is why Napa has such a grand name in the world of wine. With some 250 different wineries to choose from, you have an almost overwhelming selection of the kinds of tours you can take. Choose from simple group or private tastings to witnessing the harvesting and selection of grapes, where you can

Honeymoon Reflections

We stayed in Napa at Maison Fleurie, one of the Four Sisters Inns (www.foursisters.com), as part of its Vintage Nights package that we found through the tourism board. When we arrived there, we felt like we'd just pulled up in front of an estate in the French countryside, with its brick exterior and trailing vines, flowers, and fences. Our room was like a French provincial stateroom with antiques and a fireplace, and the gardens were unbelievably in bloom. As part of the Vintage Nights package, we were whisked away by limousine to a wonderful restaurant, and we enjoyed winery tours all over the area. The city where this hotel is happens to be a bit outside of Napa, so it was much less crowded, a great atmosphere for us to just relax together and take in the scenery.

—Anne and Mike

watch the impressive wine technology and techniques as the grapes are pressed, combined, and filtered into the great casks that will hold them for years to come. You might be allowed to wander among certain sections of the winery's vineyards and arbors, where you can have a picnic lunch and enjoy a glass of wine under the shade of a tree overlooking the vast landscape of hills and horse farms. Some vineyards will create an open-air luncheon complete with fully set tables of bread, wine, and fruit and strolling musicians for a very Shakespearean picnic scene. All you need is a Victorian-era dress, a parasol, and Gwyneth Paltrow's expertise with a British accent, and you're all set.

Whereas Napa gets a lot more attention for its size, number of wineries, and sheer tourism factor, nearby Sonoma County has kept its focus on the business of producing fabulous, award-winning wines. You'll find fewer wineries here, but you'll recognize the names of the best ones, such as Kendall Jackson and Korbel. The area isn't crowded with hotels, spas, and countless wineries, so the experience of Sonoma is a pure one, with smaller crowds and more relaxed tours (some for free!) than you'll find in the tourist hub of Napa. For many couples, this is a great escape and a truer experience of wine country. Quaint bed-and-breakfasts dot the hillsides, observation decks over the greenest and lushest of hills allow for great picture-taking opportunities, and the smaller, family-owned wineries welcome tourists into their homes and inner workings, such as providing hillside dinners and insider secrets to the best hot-air balloon tours in town. Bring your camera and get ready to ride through some of the most beautiful wine country untouched by urban sprawl (Sonoma County Tourism: 888-842-2684, www.sonoma-county.com).

Napa and Sonoma are, of course, not the only wine country areas in the United States. Take California's Mendocino County (www.gomendo.com), which combines all the attractions of wineries and the related wine-tasting lifestyle, food festivals, and the natural attractions of the Redwood coast: whale-watching expeditions nearby, horseback riding on the beach, lighthouse tours, botanical gardens, and the like. Outside of California, you'll find lush wine country in New York and New Jersey's green hills areas, in New England (including the upscale Newport, Rhode Island), and in many other states and regions. It just takes a little bit of looking around.

> ## Simplify It
>
> One of my all-time favorite resources for anything having to do with wine—and that includes finding the best wineries and restaurants with incredible wine cellars and tastings—is *Wine Spectator,* both the magazine and the Web site (www.winespectator.com).

Food and Culture Festivals

Great food and wine seem to go hand in hand with the many different festivals that take place across the country and the world. They might be food festivals, arts and cultural festivals, heritage festivals, even patriotic festivals, but all spotlight great area cuisine accented by a flurry of action, crowds, entertainment, and perhaps even enlightenment. According to the Travel Institute of America, 31 million Americans attended festivals during their vacations last year, seeing them as a way to visit other cultures and enjoy more of their *own* culture in a great and exciting environment. Arts and music festivals were among the most popular, with country fairs and food festivals following closely behind in the rankings. Again, check those food travel Web sites for mentions of any wine, seafood, or ethnic food festivals on the horizon, or go right to the source at www.festivals.com for a more-than-complete listing of well-known and barely known festivals planned for around the world.

Family Honeymoons

If you're one of the many couples who will become an insta-family when your marriage brings your children from previous relationships into the mix, you might consider using your honeymoon as a bonding vacation for all of you. Bringing kids along on the honeymoon might seem like an odd notion if you've never heard of it before, but so many couples say it's a great way to start the marriage off on the right foot all the way around.

> I have two kids from a previous marriage, and my fiancé has one child from his. We worried a lot about the kids accepting each other as stepsisters and also the kids accepting both of us as a parental team. They've spent time together in the past, but we really think that spending a week together in Hawaii, having fun together, will help them bond further with one another and really make a statement that we are a complete family. We just didn't think it would be good if the two of us went off together to the islands and left the kids at home.
>
> —TERRY AND PETE

We took our kids on our honeymoon cruise, and they had a great time together all day at the kids' activity group while we spent some romantic quality time together on board, in the room, and on excursions. In the evening, we spent time together as a family, going to shows and movies, eating dinner together, and just hanging out and talking on deck. At the end of the week, my new husband's son asked if he could call me Mom, so that made the trip that much more special.

—JANICE AND TOM

Surely, honeymooning with the kids gives you plenty of bonding time for the kids and a fabulous entry to a new level of parenthood, in the most relaxing and enjoyable of environments. For many couples, this trip is the beginning of a beautiful future in more ways than one.

So where will you take this family trip of a lifetime? Where will you laugh together, play together, watch your kids grow closer to one another? Will it be a Club Med–type getaway with sand, surf, and sun? A week at the Disney resorts, where adults have just as much fun as the kids? A return to nature, where you'll camp under the stars and kayak down a river surrounded by majestic cliffs? A cruise to Alaska, where the kids will get perhaps their first wide-eyed glimpse of whales, bear, caribou, and bald eagles outside of captivity, in their natural, clean, and untouched environments? The choices are endless, as the travel industry provides a wealth of family-friendly getaways to please all individual tastes and budgets.

I've collected just a few of the most popular family honeymoon options here to get you thinking of your ideal trip style, and I encourage you to make use of the "Tips for Traveling with Kids" at the end of this chapter before you start calling travel agents. Since you have more people to please, and since this trip is such an important one, starting off on the right foot is essential. Now, read on and imagine yourselves on the following honeymoon trips.

Island Honeymoons with Kids

You're probably already dreaming about that island getaway, the crystal clear blue waters, warm tropical sun, miles and miles of endless beaches, steel drum music playing by the pool, slow dancing on the beach at sunset—it's a honeymoon paradise. When you have kids along on your island vacation, the dream can still be yours. Countless resorts on the islands open their arms to families like yours, enticing you with a honeymooner package with all the right romantic elements *and* incredible island activity programs for your kids.

For instance, take a look at Club Med's Villages for Families (www.clubmed.com) in such far-flung destinations as the Bahamas, Ixtapa, St. Lucia, and several other top vacation spots. While you and your new husband are off riding white horses on the beach at sunrise or indulging in couples' spa treatments at the resort, breakfasting on your balcony together or dancing at the nightclub, your kids have an itinerary of their own. In the safe and capable hands of the resort's adult GOs (for "gracious organizers"), the kids will spend their days and nights frolicking on the beach, snorkeling among iridescent schools of fish, taking tennis lessons, body-boarding, or even swinging from a flying trapeze on the beach (safely harnessed, of course). Add in daily group activities, shows, and family excursions and cruises, and you all can have shared family fun time as well.

Simplify It

To find the perfect family resort on any island, visit www.travelwithkids.about.com and search through the many articles and listings of special all-inclusive family deals in the Caribbean, or go to www.frommers.com for outstanding choices on a budget.

Club Med may have a big name in family traveling, but it's not the only island resort chain with a hospitality program for kids of all ages. Here is just a small smattering of the kinds of highlights at other resorts:

- At Sandals' Beaches resorts in Negril and in Turks and Caicos, the kids can while away their days at the Sega game center and the kids-only pools and beach areas.

- At SuperClubs' Starfish resorts in Jamaica, your little ones can fly and flip during their own trampoline lessons while you stand on sandy ground with the camera clicking.

- At Pebbles resort in Jamaica, your children will be paired with a nanny, who will keep a watchful eye on them during all the kids' activities outside your presence.

Cruising with Kids

In chapter 9, you'll read all about cruise honeymoons, from the various exotic island and international destinations to choosing the right size and type of cruise that's perfect for you. If you're bringing kids along, you don't need to fear that your preschoolers or teenagers will be doomed to a week of bingo and shuffleboard. Today's cruises feature action-packed kids' clubs with planned activities such as dances, scuba diving, first-run movies, swimming, volleyball, arts and crafts, scavenger hunts and other competitions, and even trips to the kid-sized buffet complete with hot dogs, pizza, and an ice cream sundae bar. On deck, kids have access to several different pools, and even a spiral waterslide, to keep them splashing through your warm-weather getaway.

From the Disney Cruise Line to the more family-friendly theme cruises among many of the top-name cruise lines, there's a sailing that's perfect for kids of any age. So talk to your travel agency's cruise specialist, comb through the cruise Web sites listed in the back of this book, pick up *Porthole* magazine (dedicated solely to cruising vacations), and go to *Porthole*'s Web site www.porthole.com to find out what the cruise industry has planned for your family getaway and how the two of you can spend your days and nights while the kids are off having the time of their lives (and maybe even a teenage shipboard romance!). Look for special family rates, theme week cruises, and especially child-appropriate ports of call and excursions that you can all enjoy together.

Disney Honeymoons with Kids

Few places on earth are as family-friendly and make for a better group getaway than the Disney Resorts in Orlando and Anaheim, plus the Disney cruise on the Disney Cruise Line. Step into their magical land and you're transported back to childhood, where wonder and beauty surround you and you can't wipe the smile from your face. Talk about an escape from the real world! The pros at Disney make a lifetime focus out of predicting your needs, giving you the royal treatment, and filling your plate with nothing but enjoyment.

Disney is a top choice among family honeymooners, not just because of the theme parks' reputation for fun for all ages but also because Disney has now prepared special services for honeymooners. While the kids are priming themselves for a romp in the park, the honeymoon specialists at Disney are preparing you for a romp of another kind. Honeymooning parents and couples are VIPs in the Disney universe; a Disney honeymoon consultant will give you a call a month before your visit to map out your plans; confirm all of your travel, hotel, and activity arrangements; and make sure the red carpet is rolled out for you upon your arrival (figuratively, of course). Your consultant can sign you up for champagne cruises, couples' massages, spa treatments, even rose petals scattered on your bed, making this "small world" quite a romantic one for the two of you while the kids are off playing with Goofy or participating in the many kids' camp activities.

On shared days roaming the parks, you can visit several different theme areas within the span of your week's stay: the Animal Kingdom takes you on a safe and inspiring safari; the House of Blues brings you right to Bourbon Street with jazz performances and Cajun cuisine;

Epcot takes you on an unforgettable tour around the world without the need for a passport—and that nighttime water and light show will give you time to snuggle up, hold hands, and watch the magic unfold before you.

Aside from the attractions and rides of the theme park itself—the ones you remember from when you were a small child and all of the new ones built and perfected up until now—your hotel can be a main attraction. Both inside and outside the park, you can choose from the step-back-in-time Grand Floridian (a favorite of visiting celebrities), the right-in-the-middle-of-it-all Polynesian, and rustic campsites and truly livable treehouse bungalows for a touch of the Robinson Crusoe experience. In Florida, check out the new resort at the Animal Kingdom, which features African-style decor and a view overlooking the safari park. You'll swear you've been transported to the African plains on an adventure that's right here at home.

If you haven't been to Disney's worlds, it's time to check out the possibilities for a fun family honeymoon, delighting family members of all ages and making for a lifetime of family memories. Talk to your travel agent about the wide range of resorts, activities, and special deals both in and around the Disney parks, and get ready to see the kids cheer and dance around the house when you say, "We're going to Disney World!"

Theme Parks Across the Country

Disney isn't the only theme park or alternate universe out there with plenty for kids and adults to do together. Among the thousands of individual theme parks, animal parks, nature parks, marine parks, and waterparks in the United States, Canada, and overseas, you're sure to find just the right mix of play and adventure you're looking for at one great Web site: www.amusementpark.com. I spent a few hours surfing through the site's many listings and spotlighted daily specials, and I found parks that I never knew existed, special exhibits at Sea World and the San Diego Zoo (including a display of new baby polar bear cubs!), and even extreme sports for the whole family. In Kissimmee, Florida, for instance, you can line up for Sky Venture, which is a ride that allows you to experience skydiving at 85 miles an hour with up to three family members or friends, without jumping from a plane. Talk about a thrill and long-lasting memories!

Penny-Wise

At www.amusementpark.com, you'll find click-and-buy discount passes for entry into theme parks, with tickets delivered right to your home.

Ask your travel agent for the best ideas in and around theme parks, or check out www.amusementpark.com and www.waterparks.com for focused research on exciting attractions near any major city or resort you plan to visit.

Big City Honeymoons with Kids

In chapter 5, you read about big city honeymoons, where the two of you would take in all the action and culture of the great metropolis, dining in style, swinging by tourist attractions, and absorbing the palpable energy of the big city scene. Well, the big city honeymoon is also a great plan for those bringing kids along. Our nation's big cities' tourism departments will map out all the best attractions for kids and teenagers, great theme eateries, historical sites, and hotels with fabulous children's activity and discount programs. Countless travel guides and books out there specifically focus on the best places in the city for kids, and even travel Web sites have special sections for child-appropriate attractions in any destination you have in mind.

For instance, if you're headed to New York City, you've got a world of culture at your fingertips, from the ballet to Broadway plays like *The Lion King* and sports meccas like Yankee or Shea Stadiums and

Madison Square Garden. In the fun but slightly cheesy category, there are tourist traps like Mars 2110 close to Times Square, where you take a virtual space shuttle ride to the red planet, where costumed Martians serve you dinner. And for the toy-happy, don't miss the new Toys"R"Us with its indoor Ferris wheel and heaven-on-earth collection of toys and games for the shopping spree of a lifetime. After that, head on over to Central Park for a day in the sun, playing Frisbee and maybe even catching the FDNY softball team in action. Keep an eye out for celebrity sightings, and keep that autograph book handy.

With one call to the Greater Boston Convention and Visitors Bureau (888-SEE-BOSTON, www.bostonusa.com), I received a packet filled with maps and information on the city's Summer for Kids programs, including an attraction- and trivia-filled booklet titled *Kids Love Boston,* which outlines historical walking trails, museums, great restaurants with kid menus, water sport and boat ride locators, and even the exact location of the Boston Marathon finish line. Add in the World's Narrowest House (10 feet wide and, as legend has it, built only to annoy the neighbor behind it), a 40-foot-tall milk bottle, and Niketown, and you have some fun and quirky asides for the kids before you all enjoy your clam chowder by the wharfside.

Obviously, the big city trip affords some of the most memorable tourist stops possible for families. In St. Louis, check out the Boeing Space Station (www.slsc.org), a new, high-tech science center that features an in-depth look at the universe of space travel, more than 100 interactive hands-on exhibits, and what has been called the most realistic and impressive planetarium out there. Your little future astronaut will love this particular stop, making your family honeymoon trip something she'll remember for a lifetime . . . and maybe even think back to when she works for NASA someday. Other great one-day touring stops in big cities: the Rock and Roll Hall of Fame in Cleveland, the NFL Hall of Fame in Canton, Ohio, the Smithsonian in

Washington, DC, and other thrilling sites you just have to experience in person rather than over the Internet.

Camping and Taking It Outside with Kids

If your group is the outdoorsy type, or if you're just in the mood for a vacation unlike any you've ever had before, then take it outside and go camping with your new family. This type of trip is gaining in popularity among families who don't want to spend thousands on a posh resort vacation or don't have a lot of time to spend traveling, flying across the world, or touring. A camping getaway is a step out of your normal world, a great way to spend quality time with the kids (without a television turning them into glassy-eyed zombies), and also a fine adventure for those who have never spent extended time in the great outdoors.

From hiking to boating to fishing to roasting marshmallows over a fire you built yourself, the family camping trip can be a fun return to simpler days and a great way to see and learn about nature and wildlife. You can choose your level of comfort individually, booking a rustic or fully equipped cabin or roughing it in tents you construct yourself. Or rent an RV (found through www.cruise america.com or www.rvra.org, among others listed in the Resources) and sleep in the well-appointed trailer, stepping out into the morning sunshine for a dip in the river or a clean breath of fresh air. While the kids are off trying their hand at fly-fishing, the two of you can spend some time alone in the beauty of the wild.

Simplify It

Looking for a great family camping trip, an organized outing that provides planned activities, meals, and tours? Go right to the source and browse among 500 different family camps across the country at the American Camping Association's site, www.acacamps.org.

For complete information on national parks such as Yosemite and Yellowstone and other sanctioned camping areas, as well as specific contact information and details on campsites, lodges, and expert-run tours and activities during your camping trip, visit the following Web sites:

U.S. Parks System: www.us-parks.com
E.S.C.A.P.E.: www.park-escape.com
GORP: www.gorp.com

The best of these sites will give you links and all the information you need to plan the camping trip you'll never forget, plus printout-worthy primers on local plants, animals, and scenic spots along the way. One family I spoke to said they supplemented their nature trivia with a toystore-bought constellation finder chart so that they and the kids could spend a clear night looking up into the heavens and searching for Orion, Andromeda, Perseus, and Hercules. "Back home in the city, we're lucky if we see the Big Dipper or any other stars through all of that smog," says the proud new stepfather. "But out in the national

…And You Just Might Learn Something Too!

If stargazing will be part of your family's nighttime ritual, why not make it an educational game as well? The Hawaiian Astronomical Society offers a site, www.hawastsoc.org/deepsky/and/index .html, where you'll find a complete listing of constellations, plus fascinating write-ups of each constellation's own particular mythology and printable maps of where each cluster is visible in the night sky. Or go to your local bookstore and pick up a complete guide to the stars and planets for even more educational tidbits.

park, the sky is incredibly clear. We worked together as a team to find the constellations that were supposed to be visible to us at that time of year, and we all got excited when we saw a shooting star. You can't plan a family moment like that. It was a highlight of our trip, and the kids started to really take in the whole camping experience."

Another tip from experienced family campers: Bring plenty of good toilet paper and toiletries the family can use in the RV or lodge. Providing some of the comforts of home can help keep all of you in better spirits so your week or weekend in the outdoors doesn't become a complaint fest simply because your kids are uncomfortable. It's the trip leader who insists on roughing it to the extreme that invites mutiny.

Tips for Traveling with Kids

So what makes for a great family honeymoon? Quite simply, it's step one: smart planning right from the start. Here are some road-tested tips for planning your family honeymoon in all the best ways:

1. It's not a good idea to simply announce to the kids where you'll all be spending a week on vacation. At this highly sensitive time for both you and the kids, I can't recommend highly enough the obvious basics of making sure the honeymoon you plan works for every member of your family. Think about the right kind of location and the right activities to suit each family member's style. Think about the kids' personalities and preferences. Think about where both you and the kids would *love* to go.

2. Make the choice of family honeymoon destination a *group decision*. Gather up some brochures or tour guidebooks, call the kids in for a family meeting, and talk about the kind of trip you all want to plan.

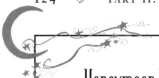

Honeymoon Reflections

I was really surprised that Tammy (my dad's new wife-to-be) asked for my opinion on where I wanted to go for this trip. She pulled out a bunch of brochures and said that she really wanted my opinion and that any trip I didn't want to go on was off the list. I think that's the point where I really felt comfortable with her, knowing that she wasn't going to come in and shake up our lives, wanting everything her way. She listened to me, let me choose which trip I preferred, and that felt really great, to be listened to like that. I said "no" to the trip to Europe and the cruise and "yes" to the island vacation or the trip to LA.

—Lisa, age 15

The kids get to contribute their ideas and wishes, vote down a camping trip if they're not the outdoorsy type, and take a good look at what they can expect from their week on a tropical island.

3. Think about everyone's schedules. If your wedding and honeymoon will take place during the popular summer months, check into the kids' schedules. Some may have plans for cheerleading or sports camps, and requiring the kids to miss those important trips with their peer groups could leave you with one sullen preteen who's determined not to have a good time on this trip, nor to let you have a good time. I'm not advocating that you hand all the planning power over to the kids, but I am suggesting that it's a good idea to avoid potential catastrophes simply by taking the kids' schedules into consideration. Outside the summer months, think about the kids' school schedules. Will you have to pull them from school for a few days in order to go on the trip? According to the Travel Institute of America, 22% of parents—that's 16 million adults last year—let their kids miss a few days of school in order to join them on a fabulous family getaway.

4. Find out where other families have taken their kids on their own family adventures of a lifetime. You might be surprised to hear just how great the kids' programs are at a particular resort on Aruba, and you might hear from the kids themselves how much they loved their trip to New York City. It's exactly these kinds of firsthand family travel success stories that can open up new worlds of opportunity for you.

5. Think about the hassles of long-distance or foreign travels when it comes to the kids. Will you have to get passports for them? Will the kids need shots for some of the more exotic lands you hope to visit? Sometimes it's these extra headaches that can knock exotic travel off the possibilities list.

6. Think about the activities available to kids at the destination you'll be visiting. While you may know that the cruise has kids' programs, will your teenager find the activities too juvenile? Will the arcade provide a week's worth of entertainment for your 10-year-old boy? This is an important one, since kids need to have plenty of options.

7. Choose a resort that is kid-friendly—not just in the activities department but also one that has a great chance of attracting other families with kids. Specify to your travel agent that you're bringing your kids on your honeymoon and that you want to go to a family resort. She'll help you choose the best options so your kids aren't surrounded by romantic honeymooners all week and so they can make some vacation friends to spend time with. According to travel agents, many of the top-name resorts in the Caribbean and Hawaii, as well as in the continental United States, offer supervised child programs at their hotels. Hyatt, for instance, runs its Camp Hyatt program with activities planned for kids ages 3 through 12. And select Holiday Inns now offer Kid-suites stocked with video games, activity tables, and even bunk beds for the little ones. So many hotels and resorts now offer child-friendly attributes that you'll actually find it hard to

Just the Facts

According to the Travel Institute of America, 60% of families who travel with kids make use of children's clubs, programs, and services while on their vacation. To break it down, 41% arrange for special kids' meals at their destination, 30% use a resort's children's discounts, 22% let their kids enjoy video games provided in hotel rooms and on resort grounds, 13% sign their kids up for supervised activities, and 6% use a destination's on-call babysitting services during their stay. The TIA says 71% of couples aged 35 to 44 used children's services during their trips.

find lodging that *doesn't* offer some sort of special deals and attractions for kids.

8. Check out the prices and discounts for family packages. Some resorts surely welcome you and your crew, but their advertised "kids stay free and eat free" deal might only apply to one or two of your children, not all three or four. While you're reading the fine print on these perks, see if the resort has a maximum capacity per room. Will you, your husband, and the four kids be able to sleep in one efficiency suite, or does the resort have a four-person-max-per-room clause? While many hotels and resorts are more than happy to accommodate your larger-sized group in a suite or villa on the beach, you really need to specify the number of kids you're bringing along so you get no unwelcome surprises upon arrival.

9. Lighten your load. Instead of lugging that dual stroller, a baby monitoring system, car seats, room gates, and other kid-gear onto the plane, you can arrange to have these necessities delivered right to your room! If your hotel doesn't offer these items for free or for a nominal rental fee, check out www.babysaway.com to see what you can order for the duration of your stay in many national cities and Hawaiian islands.

Simplify It

Many travel Web sites will categorize lists of great family-friendly resorts and destinations, so be sure to do some checking around online. A few top-notch sites to check out are www.vacationtogether.com, which not only lists its choices in top-rated family resorts but will also connect you with a family travel specialist via a toll-free call, and www.travelwith-kids .about.com, which lists top desti-nations as well as a collection of the best family travel discount packages and deals offered through many dif-ferent Internet travel-planning sites.

In Transit

Traveling with kids, especially on a long and involved trip with many connecting flights, overseas destinations, customs, and long waits, can seem like a qualifying round for sainthood. Most travelers get stressed out in crowded airports to begin with—add a fussy three-year-old and battling teenage stepsisters to the equation and you have the makings of a Calgon "take me away" commercial. But with the right preplanning and knowledge of the airport's available help, you can make that travel time tantrum- and hassle-free.

In chapter 13, I've listed the many attractions within airports that can absorb your child's attention and make the wait more enjoyable. From the great chain restaurants in the terminal to the kiosks where you can rent a DVD player during your wait (www.inmotionpictures.com) so the kids can watch a movie in the airport or even on board the plane, you'll find plenty of ways to make traveling more peaceful. Flip to chapter 13 for even more smart practices while in transit with kids.

Simplify It

If your new blended family makes you a visiting "party of five" or six or eight, supplement your questions to the travel agent or the resort reservations agent with a quick visit to the VacationKids site at www.travelwithkids.about.com. This section lines up suggestions for resorts catering to larger family groups.

During Your Vacation

The potential kid hassles might not end the moment you walk through those sliding doors into the resort's lobby. When you're bringing children of any age along on your honeymoon trip, keep the following tips in mind so the whole family can make the most of this important getaway:

1. Of course you'll want time alone for just the two of you, as well as time together with the kids. So when you do plan shared activities, make them enjoyable ones. It may be having meals together, taking a few excursions around the island, sharing a fun activity like scuba diving or windsurfing, or even participating in a resort-run family competition like a scavenger hunt or a volleyball tournament. Whatever you decide to do, be flexible, invite the kids' ideas, and make the shared time memorable.

2. Be sure to allow each family member some *alone* time as well as all that shared bonding time. Packing the kids' schedules and forcing shy or unfamiliar new siblings to spend 24/7 with each other is just loading too much powder into the keg. If any family member wants a few hours on his or her own, that's not necessarily a sign that your dreams of a blissful blended family are never going to work. It just means the kid needs a little breathing room, a little downtime, and a chance to rest up or think. *You* might even want to grab a little alone time as well, which is perfectly fine. Recharging now and then is a good way to enjoy your trip as a whole.

3. Take plenty of pictures! Make good use of underwater or panoramic one-time-use cameras to catch the kids—and yourselves—during some of the most unforgettable moments of your trip.

Just the Facts

The Travel Institute of America surveyed frequent family travelers and found that the activities they most often planned with their kids included:

Shopping	36%
Outdoor activities	22%
Visiting museums and historical places	15%
Visiting theme parks	14%

4. Stay in contact. Some resorts give the kids in their daytime activity groups and kids' clubs special beepers so parents can call them out of playtime to enjoy lunch or a planned tour together. Some couples give their kids handheld two-way radios so they can keep track of them during theme park visits or beach outings that separate parents from kids for a while. Your kids' safety is paramount, and no parent should put the responsibility into the hands of a camp counselor or resort employee. Staying in touch with your kids during a trip helps give you peace of mind and also reminds the child that he or she is missed during the day, not just dumped off at playgroup.

5. Plan for bumps and bruises. Kids get hurt, and kids get sick. It's a fact of life. Besides bringing along a good first-aid kit while traveling with little ones, look into the services of Express Doctors (800-324-8922), a service that will send a qualified doctor to your hotel for a fee that is often covered by many insurance plans.

Cruises

Sail away from the real world for a week or two on board a veritable floating city, where the nightclubs, casinos, indoor and outdoor pools, Broadway-style shows, and lavish feasts are just a few steps away from your room. Cruise ships bring the best of any vacation right to your doorstep, combining adventure, food and drink, and tropical island and cultural city tours all in one price. Honeymooners from all over the country tell me that they loved the ease and simplicity of a cruise vacation, where they had plenty to do on board and they woke up in a new port of call each day. No travel exhaustion, no confusing road maps and train schedules in faraway places, no having to pack and unpack several times during the trip. As a pure escape, they say, you can't beat a good cruise honeymoon. So convinced that this is an ideal choice for a honeymoon, most couples are absolutely shocked when I tell them that the Association of Bridal Consultants says that only 9% of all marrying couples choose to go on cruises for their big trip. "Nine percent?" said one incredulous recent honeymoon cruise-goer.

"Well, then all of those other couples are—pardon the pun—*missing the boat,* because a cruise gives you all angles of a great honeymoon."

Forget about those old *Love Boat* episodes. Today's cruise is an adventure at every turn, pure indulgence in service and culinary artistry, fitness, spa service, and ports of call at exotic islands and cultural meccas. You might bathe under a waterfall in Dominica one day, snorkel among stingrays and luminescent fish the next day, tour historical ruins the next day, then shop in a big city the next. On board, you can take in a concert, slow dance at the piano bar, try your luck at the roulette table, get a massage, show your good sport side when the ship's comedian singles you out of the crowd, and work your way through the buffet line with a free drink in your hand and a smile on your face.

KAREN AND GREG'S HONEYMOON CRUISE

We decided on a seven-day Carnival cruise through the western Caribbean because I'd sailed on Carnival once before and loved the trip immensely. Greg and I are the type who like to relax but not be bored, and I knew that this particular cruise line offered something for every mood. So we spent our week with plenty to choose from: lying out at poolside one day, bathing in a waterfall on one of the tropical islands we stopped at, shopping, dancing, meeting other honeymooners. But by far the most notable part of our trip, the most romantic part, was walking out on the ship's deck at night. Out in the middle of the sea, with so little air pollution and being at a different area of the hemisphere from home, we just couldn't believe how beautiful the stars were. Millions of them, incredibly bright, in constellations we had never seen before. It was absolutely breathtaking and something we'll never forget. I've been to over 50 countries during my world travels, and I've never seen a sky that gorgeous, except perhaps for in the middle of the Australian Outback. We couldn't have asked for better scenery, and we couldn't have asked for a better honeymoon.

Check Out These Destinations!

Quick! Which islands do you think of when you imagine a cruise? The Bahamas? Jamaica? Bermuda? The Florida Keys? Sure, these are popular ports of call for many cruise lines, but you're going to be surprised when you start looking into cruises and discover just how vast is the selection of destinations *all over the world.* Cruise ships aren't limited to the Caribbean or the Mediterranean, and their expanded list of stops delivers you to lands even more exotic than the islands off the tip of Florida. I can barely just scratch the surface here of the thousands of stops a large, small, or private cruise line can make. Following are some lists of typical cruise line stops by region all over the world, just to get your mouth watering for the types of floating tours you can select:

Just the Facts

Caribbean destinations are the number one destination of choice for couples planning seven-day cruises.

- The Bahamas: Nassau, Freeport

- Western Caribbean: Key West, Playa del Carmen, Cozumel, Grand Cayman, Calica, Ocho Rios (Jamaica), Costa Rica, Panama

In Grand Cayman, don't miss the seven-mile beach, the Turtle Farm, and Stingray City, where you can swim with stingrays. The snorkeling and scuba here is top-notch as well, a real underwater adventure. In Ocho Rios, you'll wander upon breathtaking waterfalls that have been immortalized in famous paintings and posters in the art world—except you'll be there, ready to dive on into an almost ethereal pool of cascading water. It's pure heaven.

• Eastern Caribbean: Bahamas, St. Thomas, St. John, St. Maarten, Key West, Belize, Cozumel, Playa del Carmen, Progreso/Méerida, San Juan, St. Croix

In Playa del Carmen, you'll find beautiful botanical gardens to tour, as well as some of the most fascinating Mexican ruins to climb through and tour.

• Southern Caribbean: San Juan, St. Thomas, St. John, Martinique, Barbados, Aruba

Martinique is an enigma. Long the playground of the Parisian elite, this French island gives you the sophistication of Paris shopping, rainforests, a dormant volcano, crystal clear ocean waters with a wealth of undersea sights and activities, and nightlife like you wouldn't believe. Martinique is one of my most memorable vacation stops, if only for the diverse crowd and the many interesting fellow vacationers and European "names" we met along the way. At one brunch, we dined with French commandos on shore leave and a British family watching over two choir boys from Westminster Abbey. Quite the crowd and a fun touring group.

• Baja Mexico: Catalina Island, Ensenada

• Mexican Riviera: Puerto Vallarta, Mazatlan, Cabo San Lucas

• Bermuda: Major port cities in Bermuda

• Northern Europe: London, Copenhagen, Berlin, Helsinki, St. Petersburg, Estonia, Amsterdam, Paris (shore excursion), Ireland, Scotland, Iceland

• The Mediterranean: Italy, Monaco, Monte Carlo, Greece, Turkey, Spain

If I could return anywhere in the world, it would be Monaco. From the impossibly perfect yachts lined up at the piers to the stony pebble beaches, the pristine hotel fronts, and the beauty of the city as it appears from out of nowhere dotting the side of a mountain, this is one of my favorite destinations on earth.

• Alaska: Vancouver, the Inside Passage, Ketchikan, Juneau, Endicott Arm, Skagway, Sitka, Prince William Sound, Seward, Glacier Bay, Valdez, Anchorage

Alaskan cruises spotlight the beauty of untouched nature, from magnificent glaciers to protected national parks, bald eagles flying overhead, caribou and bears on the shoreline going about their hunting and fishing with barely a glance at the humans floating by, humpback whales breaching out in the open ocean, it's nice to know such a place still exists relatively undisturbed, and you have to be there to appreciate how clean the air is and how vast is the landscape.

• Hawaii: Maui, Kauai, Oahu, Honolulu, Molokai, Kona, Hilo, Lahaina, Nawiliwili

Rainbows arching over the ocean after a misting, smoking volcanoes in the distance, the sweet smell of hibiscus flowers all around you, tropical rainforests, and a dip in the seven sacred pools of Hana where ancient Hawaiian royalty once bathed their kings.

• Panama Canal: Cartagena, Panama Canal, Puntarenas (Costa Rica), Acapulco, Ixtapa, Puerto Vallarta, Mazatlan, Cabo San Lucas

• The Grenadines: Grenada, St. Vincent, Petit Nevis, Mustique, Canouan Island, Tobago Cays, Carriacou, Bequia

• Canada and New England: Halifax (Nova Scotia), Newfoundland, Newport (Rhode Island), Boston, Cape Cod

• Africa: Cape Town, Namibia, Jamestown, Walvis Bay

• Rio de Janeiro: Rio de Janeiro, Salvador de Bahia (Brazil), Fortaleza (Brazil), Barbados, San Juan

• Additional options: Asia, South Pacific islands, Australia, Antarctica, Morocco, Madagascar

Again, I haven't even come close to the true, complete list of cruise ports of call, but these are some of the most popular stops for the vast selection of itineraries out there. It's a wide-open world, accessible by water, and the sights you sail past are only part of the adventure when you add in the shore excursions where you're delivered to exciting cities, islands, tourist stops, and off-the-beaten-path finds that only the locals could point out to you. Combine the bliss of an island stay with the high-energy action of the big city, add in your most-wanted honeymoon romance moments, and you'll see why so many couples consider a cruise to be the perfect getaway for those who want it all.

Ships with a Reputation

Carnival may be touted as "The Fun Ship" and Disney's Big Red Boat may feature costumed characters and lots of kids running around, but they're not the only cruise lines with a so-called specialty. Depending on your preferences for the *type* of cruise you'd like to go on, whether it's action and adventure, leisurely, or one focused on food and wine, you should know that certain cruise lines have a reputation for the particular type of trip you have in mind. Although any cruise line can offer a great mix of food, fun, sports, shows, excursions, and gambling, certain ships are targeted as the place to be if you have certain activities or modes in mind. Consider the following:

- Adventure: Carnival Triumph, Grand Princess, Explorer, Voyager of the Sea
- Sports: Carnival, Princess, Royal Caribbean, Norwegian
- Casinos: Holland America, Crystal Cruises
- Romance: Princess, Radisson Seven Seas Cruises, Silversea Cruises
- Broadway-type shows: Carnival, Celebrity, Princess
- Culinary Arts: Celebrity, Princess, Crystal Cruises, Windstar

Again, these cruise lines have made a name for themselves with their particular offerings, such as rock-climbing walls, fabulous five-star dining rooms, or a replica of a big-name Las Vegas casino. So if you're set on a certain type of cruise with a particular focus, include these choices in your research, and ask your cruise specialist for even more, targeted cruise lines for the activities and type of crowd you seek.

Ports Close to Home

Thankfully, the cruise industry has made it infinitely easier for many people to hop on board their floating resorts, just by planning for new and different ports where their cruises depart. Now you don't *have* to fly to Florida for a great Caribbean cruise. You can book your trip for a ship that sails from New York City, New Orleans, Baltimore, and many other major cities. Here are some additional, relatively new departure points to ask your travel agent about:

- Boston
- Seattle
- Galveston, Texas
- Philadelphia
- Charleston, South Carolina
- Houston
- Los Angeles
- Mobile, Alabama
- San Diego
- San Francisco
- Tampa, Florida

Penny-Wise

The joy of these new departure points is that you might not have to *fly* anywhere to get to the cruise ship of your choice. That means hundreds of dollars saved in airfare, not to mention the savings of a half-day of extra travel you would otherwise have used in getting yourself to Miami!

Finding Your Perfect Cruise

You've seen the commercials on television, with those handsome men and women jet-skiing together past a stately cruise ship in the background, dancing in the nightclub, and helping themselves to a crème brûlée at the buffet table. Looks enticing, so how do you start your search for the perfect cruise? Where do you go to get not only the best deal but also a flawless trip aboard a new, state-of-the-art cruise ship as part of a well-rated cruise line? How do you know which cruises are best for honeymooners and which will be hosting the American Legion, a time-share sales convention, or a loud, cheesy singles theme week? There's a lot to look into, so let's get started on the best ways to research the offerings, which Web sites to rummage through, and which experts can help you best.

Starting Off: What Do You Want?

Take some time right now to brainstorm your wishes for the perfect cruise vacation so you know what you're looking for. Cruises come in all shapes and sizes, so if you narrow your choices down with your wishes, you'll save a lot of time and aggravation when you're ready to make your choices. Following are some questions you should consider:

• When will you be going on your honeymoon? With hurricane season making some destinations risky propositions for a cruise vacation in the summer months, or the weather making for some extra-chilly prospects in winter months, you might find that some locations are not ideal for your time frame. So keep the magic date in mind when you start talking to cruise experts.

• Do you want to go on a large cruise ship or a small one? The larger cruise ships offer much in the way of activities and amenities both on board and off, whereas the smaller ones might be better for you if you're cruising just to relax. A large cruise ship might surround you with thousands of people on a daily basis, which is great if your idea of the perfect getaway includes mingling with different travelers and other honeymooners. A smaller ship or even a private yacht could give you more of the privacy you crave, in true celebrity or royalty fashion.

• Which are your most wished-for destinations? Hawaiian Islands? Caribbean islands? The Mediterranean? If you can narrow down your touring choices, the process of finding the right cruise line will be infinitely easier.

• Do you want a summery, tropical island vacation, or are you more into touring cities, ruins, museums, and other notable stops? If you're not the piña colada types, you'll be best served looking at cooler weather spots or city-type destination cruises.

• Are you bringing the kids with you? If you're among the percentage of honeymooners who are blending your family and bringing the kids along (see chapter 8), you'll need to select a cruise that's both kid- *and* adult-friendly.

• What's your budget? This might be the most important question for you, and it will certainly help you separate the high-end packages from the more moderately priced ones.

• How long will you have to travel? If you only have a week off of work for your entire wedding weekend, then you'll be narrowing down your choices to seven-day, five-day, or even three-day trips. Those two-week jaunts to Alaska or Europe are out the window. Many couples who have a week or more of open vacation time still do choose the four-day packages, saving a bundle, still enjoying a fun getaway but giving themselves a few days at home after the trip to unwind, visit with friends, open those wedding gifts, and get ready for the workweek ahead. Consider now if you like this option or if you want the full week of sailing time.

• Which activities do you want to enjoy during your cruise? Think ahead of time about whether or not it matters to you that the cruise ship has a casino, four nightclubs, seven restaurants, a health club, an on-site spa, and a movie theater. Knowing which activities are on your must-do list can help you find the ship of your dreams. Keep in mind that some cruises are known for their theme focus: for instance, Crystal Cruises hosts more than 20 wine-and-food-themed cruises, attracting chefs and culinary artists from around the world to delight their fine-palated guests. Crazy about golf? Some cruises run special golf packages, giving you passes to golf courses at some of Hawaii's best links.

• Do you both have passports? The ship itself may sail from the United States, but you might need a passport to gain entry into some exotic ports of call. This issue alone makes some couples think twice about booking trips to foreign destinations and go, instead, to Alaska or Hawaii.

• Are you a comfortable cruiser? If you've cruised before, you know that the big ships have stabilizers that cut down on the boat's rocking motion, and you know that safety and security is taken very seriously by the ship's staff. But if you've never cruised before, you might want to ask friends about the comfort level, whether or not you need to work to get your sea legs, and just how claustrophobic they were in the staterooms. Thinking about this now allows you to address your concerns, ask the right questions of the travel agent or cruise specialist, and plan ahead to allay any fears or trepidation you might have about cruise travel. That way, you can look forward to your trip, not add to your stress level.

Surfing Through Cruise Reviews

Like most people planning vacations, you'll no doubt spend a fair amount of time on the Internet or huddled in front of the newspaper travel section and magazines, looking at cruise specials and reviews of the top cruise lines out there. Aided by suggestions from friends and family who have gone on fabulous cruises all over the world, you'll visit Web sites they've recommended and stumble upon great sites you discover using a search engine. I'd like to recommend a few great Web sites to add to your initial research:

• www.porthole.com. *Porthole Cruise* magazine devotes itself to the cruise industry as a whole, and its Web site and magazine are filled with reviews, travelogues, photo features of popular and little-known cruise destinations, and countless insider tips on finding and enjoying the perfect floating getaway. Look at recent surveys, or look back at past issues to find recommendations and secrets for your honeymoon trip.

• www.travelandleisure.com. *Travel and Leisure* is one of the gold standards for travel reporting. On its site (and within the pages of its magazine) you'll find many features on cruise lines and cruise destinations that are currently on your radar. At the end of this chapter, you'll find just two recent lists of *Travel and Leisure* World's Best awards in the cruise line categories, and I highly encourage you to visit the *Travel and Leisure* site for additional cruise line rankings in other categories.

• www.islands.com. While this magazine and Web site focus specifically on islands, you'll find detailed reviews of the art, culture, sights, sounds, and tastes of many of the islands you might wish to cruise to. It's a great way to find out where Mauritius is and what you can expect to do while you're stopping in at Molokai.

• www.caribbeantravelmag.com. *Caribbean Travel and Life* magazine and Web site give you an in-depth look at the high life in the Caribbean, the Bahamas, and Bermuda. As with most respected travel magazines, this one serves up travelogues, destination reports, and tasty reviews of the local culture, best restaurants, and cuisine of the area.

• www.frommers.com. If you're looking for the best cruises on a budget, make sure you stop in at the site of *Arthur Frommer's Budget Travel* or pick up copies of this magazine at the bookstore. Dedicated to the low-cost vacation but still focused on flawless quality of service and accommodations, this company scours the earth for the best finds out there and the best insider secrets for getting twice the honeymoon on half the budget. It's a favorite of frequent travelers, and I'm confident that you'll return to this resource for your future trips and travel plans.

• www.cruisesonly.com. This popular cruise-booking site offers customer reviews of the top destinations and cruise lines, plus access to steep discounts of 20% to 50% off your reservations.

Talking with the Experts

Of course, you can certainly research and book your honeymoon cruise over the Internet, especially if you're a big-time traveler with plenty of experience, but for this trip (especially if you've never cruised before) it's a wise idea to get some input from a cruise specialist. Notice I said a *cruise specialist,* not simply a travel agent. I'm sure the vast majority of travel agents are extremely well versed at explaining and booking terrific cruises, but when the option is there, go for the cruise specialist. This experience came to me from a couple in New York City, who went to their local AAA office in order to book their honeymoon trip. They waited in line at the busy shop and were then escorted to the desk of a friendly faced travel agent who launched into "the big sell." At a hurried pace and without much explanation, this particular travel agent urged the couple to book a $2,000 cruise *right now!* Flustered by this agent's lack of knowledge about other cruise lines and not wanting to book the first cruise the agent recommended with great urgency, the couple left that office and talked to the bride-to-be's mother. Turns out that the mother always booked her cruises through that AAA office's resident cruise expert, who wasn't the travel agent this couple had seen. A few days later, the couple returned to the office (walking past the sheepish hard-sell travel agent) and relaxed into the great guidance of the cruise specialist, and they booked their seven-day cruise aboard a different cruise line with a great honeymoon package for less than $1,000. Needless to say, it's very important to get your information from the right cruise specialist, someone who hears your needs and allows *you* to make the decision for yourselves.

Penny-Wise

With the right research done ahead of time, you might find a great deal by booking your cruise through a travel consolidator, a company that buys cruise stays in bulk and then sells them at discount to individual travelers. One popular cruise consolidator is www.mytravelco.com, so check out their offerings and see about the restrictions of booking in such a manner. As always, read that fine print so your savings of several hundred dollars doesn't cost you in the long run.

When you find the right travel agency expert, walk through your wish list and ask specific questions about the cruise lines and individual cruise ships she recommends. There are as many different cruise ships in each line's fleet as there are desserts in a ship's buffet line, so you'll have a lot to explore. Your cruise specialist will certainly show you detailed booklets and brochures with complete descriptions of the boat and its offerings, dates and times of departure, and a layout of the rooms available within. You might also get to watch a video of the cruise ship as enjoyed by smiling, tan, and well-dressed guests, as well as footage of some of the shore excursions you might enjoy on a particular cruise. It will be a wealth of information, enhanced by the cruise specialist's own travel experiences; many travel agents get to enjoy free cruises as a job perk, so they can fully recommend the best cruises they've enjoyed. Ask your specialist which cruise lines made the biggest impression, adding his or her subjective opinion to your list of criteria.

When booking your trip through a cruise specialist *as employed by a particular cruise line,* the subjectivity won't quite be there, but you're very likely to get the latest information and a full description of the ships within the cruise line's registry. Ask plenty of questions when chatting with this expert, and look at all the cruise line's fine print before handing over your credit card and booking your trip. As you'll see in just a few moments, that fine print on most cruise lines' brochures and tickets can reveal some tricky considerations. Be a good consumer, as always, and look fully into all of your travel details, arrangements, and agreements before making your final choice.

Watch Those Extra Expenses!

When you look at those colorful brochures and line up your room level choices with the price tag, you need to know that this is just the baseline of what your cruise will cost you. Adding in onboard tips, the price of drinks (through the roof on some cruises!), shore excursion fees, and other charges, your grand total might go up a few hundred dollars or more. Be informed and know that cruise travel carries with it some inherent expenses during your trip, and be prepared to pay for the elements that will make your honeymoon more special. Here are some of the extras you need to be aware of:

• *Gratuities.* Some cruise ships automatically include tips in your bill, freeing you from having to carry a wad of singles around with you, and others give you the *choice* of whether or not you want to register for auto-tipping, or whether you'd like to choose for yourself the percentage you'll leave on the bar or table. Remember that tips are expected for your waiter, the bell captain, bartenders, maid service, room service, any specialty therapists like massage experts, and spa employees.

• *Food.* Sure, that buffet may be a delectable freebie, but your additional meals might not be included in your package. So if you want a burger on the pool terrace or some shrimp cocktail and oysters delivered to your room at night, be prepared to pay a sizable extra charge plus tips for these snacks and additional meals.

• *Drinks.* Here's where the cruise line makes some money. On some cruises, certain kinds of drinks are part of your all-inclusive package, but others are considered for-pay. Check in specifically with your waiter or bartender to see which kinds of liquors are on the freebie list, which drinks are on special that day, what soft drinks cost, and the exact dollar amounts for those pretty, brightly colored frozen drinks you see in everyone's hands. If you have kids traveling with you, some cruise ships offer debit cards for the kids' use in getting soft drinks or water on board.

• *Activities.* Whereas many classes and activities are part of standard cruise life, others are in the pay category. Check ahead of time with the social director to see which sports and activities are on the expense roster and how much the cruise is charging for the pleasure.

• *Spa treatments.* These are not cheap, so pick and choose for your most-wanted treatments, whether it's a massage, a pedicure, a steam, or a trip to the sauna. Be aware that many cruise lines actively try to sell you on the spa treatments, sending out their hawkers with special coupons and a sales pitch by the pool at lunchtime. Don't be taken in by another hard sell; make your decision on spa treatments ahead of time, or save $75 by massaging each other back in your room, which is infinitely more enjoyable.

• *Shore excursions.* When the ship docks in Cozumel, you're likely to want to step off the boat and enjoy the attractions, scenery, and tourism spots this destination has to offer. You can sign up for the cruise ship's guided excursion at a fee, or you can hop off the boat and explore on your own without paying an excursion fee. (Frequent travelers tell me that the guided, for-pay shore excursion winds up being three times the expense of going it alone.) Some excursions will run you from $25 to $50 for a half-day tour and up to $250 for a full-day tour, including meals and elaborate outings such as helicopter tours, river rafting, and winery tours. This one is a matter of personal choice. If you'd rather not worry about finding a taxi or finding the exact location of the Mayan ruins or botanical gardens and hurriedly get back to the boat again before departure time, then by all means sign up for the excursion. If you'll go it alone, you can be your own tour guide by requesting free copies of location maps and tourist information from your own travel agent before the trip or from the island's tourist board via e-mail or a phone call (see the Resources for an extensive list).

> ## Honeymoon Reflections
>
> We beat the system during our cruise honeymoon. At happy hour, they had a "buy one drink, get one for free" deal, so we both ordered two drinks each, got two more for free, and then just carried the free ones with us to dinner.
>
> –Karen and Greg

• *Port charges.* Don't be shocked, but at some locations you may have to pay just to get off the boat at the port of call.

• *Taxes.* The list is endless and quite surprising. Government taxes, *fuel surcharges?* There's a tax for everything in this world, and cruise ships are not exempt. So read the fine print in the back of the cruise booklets or brochures and educate yourself as to where your money will be going.

• *Tourist money traps.* The drink served in the souvenir glasses at $12 a pop; the roving photographer who snaps a picture of you at your table with the other guests, just like at the prom; the Eliza Doolittle hawking single, long-stemmed roses on the ship's deck—all of these common money suckers are meant to capitalize on the sentimentality of your trip and separate you from your cash. Skip 'em.

• *Special bon voyage packages.* Even I can't believe some of the special going-away arrangements that you, your spouse-to-be, or your family members can arrange to make your stay more special. The most common packages include flowers, champagne, fruit and cheese platters, and gift certificates for pictures on deck or free drinks, at a hefty price. Other packages might include a free throwaway camera, coupons for the bar, souvenir T-shirts and visors, engraved champagne flutes or brandy snifters, and a bottle of sparkling wine. One cruise ship will even decorate your room with garlands, streamers, and balloons (in case you've forgotten you're on your honeymoon and need a printed balloon to remind you), topping that off with a special cake baked just for you. If your honeymoon registry includes these things, that's great. It's something your family might choose to do to send you off in style. But paying for this yourself? Save the cash.

• *Formalwear.* Yes, it's true. You can rent a ballgown and tuxedo on some cruise ships for the grand gesture evening of a lifetime. But be prepared to pay.

• *Souvenir shopping.* Don't shop on the boat. Buy your souvenirs at ports of call, where trinkets and T-shirts cost a fraction of those big-time gift shop prices.

As always, ask about all extra charges and hidden fees so your dreamy honeymoon doesn't end up in a stressful argument when you

A Look at the Difference in Room Prices

You're going to see a huge difference in price between the spacious and elegant presidential suite with the oversized balcony, the king-sized bed, and the dining area and the interior state-rooms with a bit of space to move around in, no windows, and little more than the essentials. The key is to choose somewhere in the middle if price is an object.

get the final bill tally and discover that you've been *paying* for all those piña coladas all along!

When you're choosing your stateroom, your home away from home for the duration of your journey, know the differences between the categories of rooms. Suites and penthouses will come, of course, at top dollar, and you'll be paying for the extra space and perhaps even butler service. "We came back from dinner one night, and the butler had, for some reason, taken my lingerie that I had laid out on the bed for that night and actually shaped it into the form of an anchor," says one tickled bride after returning from her cruise through the Caribbean. "After that, I left out my lingerie every night to see what he would do with it, and he made a seahorse, the moon, and what we think was a doughnut when he was running out of ideas. It cracked us up to think that the extra $1,000 for the top-of-the-line room got us Godivas on our pillows and my nighties twisted up into different shapes!"

When you're offered the choice of a balcony, that one is up to you. For some couples, it's a must, since they wanted to eat breakfast alone out on their terrace, overlooking the ocean at sunrise. Others couldn't care less and spent so little time in their room that not having a window didn't matter.

One issue to definitely bring up is your wishes regarding your beds. If you don't ask for a double bed, or a queen- or king-sized one (should your room allow), you might be given a room with two twin beds. How romantic!

Some Tips from Frequent Cruisers

I interviewed many recent cruisers, both honeymoon and nonhoneymoon, and here are their tips to help you make the most of your own cruise getaway:

• "When choosing your room, know that inside rooms with no windows or balconies are far less expensive than the outside, well-lit rooms. Sure, it's nice to have a balcony, but when you think about how much you're paying for it, it's certainly not worth it. Besides, you'll probably have better things to do than look out the window in your room, right?"

• "Rooms closer to the water level will give you far less of a sensation of the boat rocking than those rooms that are higher up or on the outside edge of the boat, rooms that by their position are going to get more swaying from the boat's movement."

• "Don't skip the travel insurance! If a hurricane cancels or cuts your trip short, prevents the boat from going to half of its planned ports of call, or otherwise ruins your trip, that insurance will save you a mountain of headaches. Considering how much can go wrong when sailing across an ocean or hopping among islands during storm season, this is one investment you should make."

• "Look at your tickets to see all the fine print. Some cruise lines reserve the right to change the itinerary, *not* hold your wedding ceremony on board due to any scheduling errors, or pretty much do anything they'd like, and it's all in the fine print. One couple tried to sue the cruise line for canceled stops but got nowhere because the fine print stated that the area of jurisdiction was in Liberia, not the state in which they lived and had filed the suit. Fine print is all-important."

• "Get special insurance for kids if you're bringing them along. With sea and sports activities on their rosters, it's good to have them protected in case of any accidents. Many cruise ships offer special insurance rates for kids younger than 17 years of age, for under $100."

• "Comparison shop for the airline-cruise partnership deals. If your cruise line has a special deal for partnered airfare to bring you to the departure city, don't forget to figure in the cruise line's offer of free shuttles and transfers because it really can be quite a distance between the airport and where the cruise ship is docked."

• "Pack well, and include every type of toiletry and medication you think you might need during your trip because the prices at the cruise ship gift shop can be outrageous if you have to buy something during your sail."

• "Find out the dress code for the ship. Some cruises require more formal attire for their dress-up dinner nights, and some won't even let you in the dining room if you're wearing shorts and a T-shirt. Check ahead of time and pack the right type of clothing, ties, dress shoes—whatever you'll need for those one or two nights where casualwear is not appropriate."

• "Ask for a smoke-free cruise ship if you're sensitive to cigarette or cigar smoke. Many cruise lines run completely smoke-free ships now for their guests' comfort and preferences. If you're a smoker, ask about smoking areas because you might have a long hike ahead of you to the right deck or lounge where smoking is allowed."

• "Bring motion sickness bands and medications, just in case. Even if you've cruised a dozen times, the water may be choppier than you're used to, especially if the weather is rough. In addition, you may be fine on the big boat but not so fine on any smaller seacraft you board during your adventurous outings. It's better to be safe than to miss one night of your trip with seasickness or nausea."

Travel and Leisure's World's Best Cruises Awards

Large Cruise Lines

1.	Crystal Cruises	80.6
2.	Holland America Line	77.4
3.	Renaissance Cruises	75.7
4.	Royal Caribbean International	74.9
5.	Princess Cruises	74.7
6.	Cunard Line	74.7
7.	Celebrity Cruises	74.7
8.	Norwegian Cruise Line	71.6
9.	Orient Lines	70.6
10.	Disney Cruise Line	70.4

Majority of ships in fleet carry more than 400 passengers.

Small Cruise Lines

1.	Radisson Seven Seas Cruises	78.7
2.	Seabourn Cruise Line	77.6
3.	Silversea Cruises	76.4
4.	Windstar Cruises	73.8
5.	Abercrombie & Kent	73.6

Survey results appear courtesy of *Travel and Leisure* magazine, www.travelandleisure.com. Check their most current World's Best lists to find out their newest top choices in cruiselines.

• "Bring a higher level of sunscreen and plenty of it. Out in the middle of the sea, with the sun reflecting off the water, and even while you're touring, you're catching some serious rays. If you normally wear an SPF 12, increase the level to SPF 20 or SPF 30. The same goes for wearing a hat and good ultraviolet ray-blocking sunglasses."

• "Don't gag and splatter when you dive into the shipboard pool. Many cruise lines fill their pools with filtered salt water, so be prepared, and rinse off after a swim to protect your skin, eyes, and swimwear from salt damage."

• "Don't get trapped by the casino. Sure, it's exciting and may be a change of pace for you, but don't get suckered out of your honeymoon money. Set a limit of cash you'll spend at the casino, walk out while you're winning, and explore the rest of the ship as well."

• "Be prepared to gain some weight. With all of those buffets and amazing food, and all of those drinks, you might pack on a few pounds during your stay. Bring a pair of shorts that are a little expandable so you can wear something in comfort without having to go to the gift shop for the depressing task of buying a larger-sized outfit to wear at the end of your trip."

• "Get the details on your special diet restrictions. Most cruise lines will take your requests if you give them enough notice, but some cruise lines do not do kosher meals. This is something to check out so you won't be in a food quandary during the trip."

• "Take plenty of pictures. You're going to have an unforgettable time."

Private Yachts and Charter Cruises

When Grace Kelly married Monaco's Prince Rainier, they spent their honeymoon aboard his ultraluxury yacht, sailing in and out of various ports of call in the Mediterranean. You don't have to be royalty to arrange a private yacht or charter cruise, but you might need a jewel-encrusted tiara or two to pay for a trip as exorbitant as Princess Grace's. Fear not, commoner. You may not be aware of it just yet, but there are many, many private yachts for hire out there, complete with full staff and cooks, private luxury staterooms, and even helicopters and hover-craft for a jaunt to the mainland.

Or imagine yourself on a beautiful charter sailboat, slicing through the azure waters before Monaco and Monte Carlo. This too is a possibility for the right price and is certainly something to research through your travel agent. To get you started and to entice you into the world of private charters, here are some Web sites to check out, if only for the drool factor and something to envision when you buy your next lottery ticket:

www.catamaranco.com
www.metanicharters.com
www.moorings.com
www.stardustplatinum.com

Spotlight on Out-of-This-World Cruise Offerings

While researching the many different types of cruises out there for your selection, I came across a few that made my jaw drop. Chances are, you don't have 105 days to spend on the Radisson's Seven Seas cruise that features having dinner with the royal family of Bali and taking in a performance at the Sydney Opera House (this one costs a mere $40,000 per person, double-occupancy), but you might get a glimmer of interest in some of these other "Who knew?" cruises out there:

• Seaborne Cruise Lines can deliver you to a sand-boarding excursion in the Sinai Desert and then to a Bedoin campsite for an up-close and personal look at a whole different lifestyle.

• Windstar Cruises will deliver you to New Zealand, where you can watch enormous whales nurse their newborn calves.

• Star Princess will take you on a tour of the Far East without that incredibly long airplane ride. Sail through Singapore, Taiwan, Bangkok, Okinawa, Osaka, and Kyoto, take in the culture and tastes of the Orient, and then sail on home.

• Royal Caribbean Brilliance of the Sea doesn't allow you to miss one second of the fabulous views as you sail among more than eight Caribbean islands. The ship features a nine-story glass atrium, more outside cabins than you'll find practically anywhere else, and—so you don't miss a thing—even glass-fronted elevators that look out over the ocean.

Spa Honeymoons

Finally . . . a chance to relax! After all that wedding stress, you might choose to go to a destination that's all about relaxation, pampering, and living the good life as your escape from the real world. It's just the two of you getting massaged, lying side by side as a team of relaxation therapists work every kink out of your neck, engage your senses, and get your shoulders down from up around your ears. For some couples, there's no better way to start off married life.

Before we start talking about spas here, I want you to get a very important point: There's a *big* difference between a spa and a resort spa. A spa (commonly called a "destination spa") focuses itself on health and wellness, with many fitness, yoga, and sports classes available and healthy food and beverages on the menu. Some don't serve alcohol at all (no champagne toasts, that means!), and the menu can be a bit restrictive in some locations. Delicious, by all means, but still healthy fare. Some examples of destination spas are Canyon Ranch, Cal a Vie, and the Golden Door, all locations focused on the pure spa experience. A resort spa, on the other hand, is a resort with all its amenities and activities, swim-up bars and nightclubs, wine cellars and gourmet restaurants for true indulgence, sports and activities, *plus* an on-location spa or the offering of spa treatments at the hotel. You need to make that distinction clear when you're researching spa locations because if what you're looking for is a relaxing getaway, you don't want to end up at a place that's more like a fitness boot camp and weight-loss academy. Once you know the difference, you'll know better what to look for. During your research, you can check out a location for its list of activities, menus, restrictions, and ratings.

For the ultimate in researching spas and resort spas, browse through the listings at www.spafinder.com. This site and its related print magazine are dedicated solely to the spa experience, and you'll find everything you need to know about spas right there. To further your research, go to www.traveland leisure.com for reviews of the most popular spa getaways in the world. If you're interested in a resort spa and you wish to stick with a well-known hotel, the Marriott (www.marriott .com) has incorporated spas into many hotels both in the United States and overseas. In fact, Marriott International boasts spas in more than 20 countries, giving you that great spa experience combined with the thrill and adventures of overseas touring.

Simplify It

Confused by all the different types of spas out there? Do you lack time to check the Web sites of 50 different spas to find the one that fits your wishes? With more than 300 spas to choose from, you probably could use a little help sorting out the many destinations and packages available. Just call 800-ALL-SPAS and let the experts at *Spa Finder* magazine find the perfect place for you according to what you're looking for.

International Treatments Right Here at Home

Thai massage. Indian Ayurvedic treatments. Flower-strewn baths reminiscent of a Javanese wedding ritual. Balinese massage. Finnish saunas. Italian mud baths. Eastern medita-tion in a replica Buddhist garden. It's exactly these types of exotic and international treat-ments that allow the spa-goer to feel like he or she has gone to an exotic land without even leaving the country. Those who are hes-itant to fly to another continent, or those who don't want to bother with getting a pass-port, can transport themselves to another world with a visit to the right spa.

Would you have ever thought that you could enjoy a Japanese bathing ritual, right down to wearing luxurious silk kimonos and sipping green tea before stepping into a *furo*, or deep-seated tub, and then enjoying several body treatments incorporating ginseng, gin-ger, and cucumber without taking that long flight to Japan? If you'd like an Australian Aboriginal ritual, all you have to do is go to the right spa in . . . *Florida!* No long flight, no time zone confusion. Going to a spa that features a wide array of in-ternational and exotic treatments can give you a veritable trip around the world, stress-free.

Professionally Speaking

Spas are re-creating a vast array of treatments that have previously been available only to those who travel extensively. Ultimately, this is about the spa industry going global, gathering the best of what's out there and translating it into some-thing that is appealing to American spa-goers while still retaining the flavor of each distinct country and culture.

—Susie Ellis, vice president of industry development
Spa Finder Magazine
www.spafinder.com

Finding Your Perfect Spa Resort

So what are the main criteria in searching for the perfect spa getaway? It goes way beyond what packages cost and delves more into what the environment will be like. Susie Ellis, Vice President of Industry Devel-opment at *Spa Finder* magazine, provides the following hot topics to consider when choosing the perfect blend of relaxing or romantic ele-ments at the spa of your choice:

Will My Man Like It?

I love the idea of going to a spa for our honeymoon. I've heard that some places have couples' massage rooms and other great treatments that we both would enjoy. But I'm having trouble deciding if my fiancé would like this type of trip or if this is something that would be better as a trip with my girlfriends. What do other couples say?

Susie Ellis from *Spa Finder* says that men are initially hesitant to go to a spa at first, but once they go, they love it and go back again. If you're nervous about putting your man in a spa environment, seeing this as too great a risk for a trip as important as your honeymoon, then choose a spa that's part of a bigger resort so he has other options besides spa treatments to make his week enjoyable.

- "Check to see if it's a destination spa or a resort spa so that you know if you'll have access to the kinds of resort amenities you might wish to enjoy."

- "Look at the size of the facility. Some spas limit their numbers of guests so that the place isn't crowded, affording the visitor more of a sense of peace and privacy on an uncrowded beach or pool deck."

- "Find out where the spa is located. You might be surprised to find out that a highly praised spa is in a state closer to you than where you might expect, cutting down on your travel time and expenses."

- "Look at who else is likely to be there. Is this a spa or resort that attracts a lot of women? Couples? Families? If, for instance, the spa and all of its activities are filled with women, will your fiancé really enjoy this as a trip of a lifetime? Look for a place that attracts more couples if that is the crowd you wish to experience on your honeymoon."

- "Look at what the resort offers. Is there a beach you can relax on? Is it quiet? What kind of food is offered? Be sure that the spa or spa resort provides the rest of what you're looking for, beyond the pampering aspects."

• "Request a menu of the resort's services from the hotel manager so you can see what is offered and at what price. Remember, most treatments you'll have to pay extra for, so it's a wise idea to see what they charge for a massage or pedicure."

One of the most important things you're looking for is the opportunity for couples' treatments. And that goes beyond his-and-hers massages. At many of the newer resorts, you might find wonderful couples' experiences, such as the option of his-and-hers gentle exfoliation or massage treatments, after which the massage therapists leave you to your own private villa where you can enjoy the sauna, steamroom, showers, and Jacuzzi together, uninterrupted. This kind of romance and sensual mentality in a resort's offerings can make for some wonderful time together and some unforgettable memories.

Travel and Leisure's World's Best Spas

Travel and Leisure magazine named the best spas and best hotel spas in the United States and around the world in a recent issue. Here is the *Travel and Leisure* list of the 2002 Best of the Best plus scores according to an index of ambience, accommodations, treatments, service, food, and value. For this year's newest and most up-to-date lists of new award-winning spas, go to the World's Best awards section at www .travelandleisure.com.

Best Spas in the United States

1.	Canyon Ranch Health Resort, Tucson	80.4
2.	Golden Door, Escondido, California	76.2
3.	Canyon Ranch in the Berkshires, Lenox, Massachusetts	74.0

What About Tipping?

Don't forget about those tips! Each time you enjoy a great treatment, tip the therapist from 15% to 20% of the bill, even if a service is included as part of your spa resort stay.

4.	Miraval Life in Balance Resort & Spa, Catalina, Arizona	70.1
5.	Greenhouse Spa, Arlington, Texas	70.1
6.	Nemacolin Woodlands, Farmington, Pennsylvania	68.8
7.	Lake Austin Spa Resort, Austin, Texas	66.9
8.	The Ashram, Calabasas, California	66.7
9.	Cal-a-Vie, the Spa Havens, Vista, California	66.7
10.	Green Valley Spa, St. George, Utah	66.5

Best Hotel Spas in the United States

1.	Ritz-Carlton, Naples, Florida	85.1
2.	Four Seasons Resort Maui at Wailea, Maui	82.1
3.	Lodge at Pebble Beach, California	81.5
4.	The Phoenician, Scottsdale	81.3
5.	The Greenbrier, White Sulphur Springs, West Virginia	81.1
6.	Arizona Biltmore Resort & Spa, Phoenix	80.6
7.	Grand Wailea Resort, Hotel & Spa, Maui	79.8
8.	Hyatt Regency Kauai Resort & Spa	79.6
9.	Four Seasons Resort Hualalai, Hawaii	79.1
10.	The Breakers, Palm Beach	78.8

Best Spas Abroad

1.	Clinique la Prairie, Clarens-Montreux, Switzerland	79.7
2.	Thermes Marins de Monte Carlo, Monaco	79.2

3. Royal Parc Evian Better Living Institute,
   Evian-les-Bains, France   76.2
4. Hotel Terme di Saturnia, Saturnia, Italy   73.5
5. Hôtel les Sources des Alpes, Leukerbad, Switzerland   73.3
6. Therme Vals, Vals, Switzerland   72.6
7. Grotta Giusti Terme, Monsummano Terme, Italy   72.5
8. Villa Paradiso, Fasano del Garda, Italy   72.1
9. Les Sources de Caudalie, Martillac, France   72.0
10. Ferme Thermale d'Eugénie,
    Eugénie-les-Bains, France   71.3

Best Hotel Spas Abroad

1. The Oriental, Bangkok   83.4
2. Four Seasons Resort Bali at Jimbaran Bay   82.2
3. The Ritz, Paris   82.0
4. Ritz-Carlton Bali Resort & Spa   81.6
5. Four Seasons Hotel George V, Paris   80.7 (tie)
6. Four Seasons Resort Bali at Sayan   80.7 (tie)
7. Mandarin Oriental, Hong Kong   80.2
8. Grand Hotel Park, Gstaad, Switzerland   79.5
9. Fairmont Banff Springs, Alberta, Canada   78.1
10. Fairmont Chateau Lake Louise, Alberta, Canada   77.7

PART III

The Details

Passports, Visas, and Proper Documentation

J ust like your marriage license is a must-have for your wedding day, so too are passports, visas, shot certificates, and any other valid legal document you'll need to travel anywhere outside the United States. You might already have a valid passport from your previous travels, in which case you can cross that little item off your to-do list. But is it still valid? Have you checked into whether or not you'll need a visa to visit some of the international sites you have in mind? Do you know if you'll need any immunizations before jetting off on your wild safari or rainforest adventure? In this chapter, you'll learn how to find out the exact steps to take so you're not turned away at the airport or the border, having to dial your hotel to cancel your reservations.

Passports

If you don't have a passport, or if your passport has expired (or will expire by the time of your honeymoon), you'll need to apply for a new one. Apply as early as possible. The entire process can take six to eight weeks from application to receipt, and any number of snafus can occur along the way. Consider this *the* most important part of your preparations if you're planning to travel overseas, and this *does* include Bermuda, the islands, cruises, and other sites that aren't quite clear-cut as foreign destinations.

Sign by the X

To apply for your passport—or for passports for your children if you'll be taking them along on your trip; even infants need their own passports!—start at square one by obtaining an application from any of the accredited passport agency stations. There are some 45,000 of them in this country, so it shouldn't be too hard to find one of the following locations:

- Select U.S. post offices.
- Select federal, state, and probate courts.
- Select libraries.

No Need to Go to the Passport Office

You can download passport application forms online at travel.state.gov, or you can call the National Passport Information Center at 900-225-5674 (*not* a toll-free call) to have forms sent to you. If you have a valid passport that just needs to be renewed, go to the same Web site just mentioned and read the directions for passport renewal. If your existing passport is in good shape, you should be able to download Form DS-82 and send it along with your expired passport, two new passport photos, and your fees to the address indicated in the instructions. This site does provide a street address in case you wisely choose to send your packet via a registered mail delivery service.

• Select municipal offices.

• By appointment at one of the 13 main passport agencies in Boston, Chicago, Connecticut, Honolulu, Houston, Los Angeles, Miami, New Orleans, New York, Philadelphia, San Francisco, Seattle, and Washington, DC (which has two agencies, one being for special circumstance issues). See the Resources for direct contact information for each of these offices, or check the Web site travel.state.gov/agencies _list.html for details. Please note that these are the places to go if you need your passport in a hurry.

• To find out quickly and conveniently the closest passport facility near you, for ease of application, log on to the U.S. Department of State's passport finder page at iafdb.travel .state.gov and enter your city, state, and ZIP code. Be sure to call the recommended facility to ask for its hours and requirements before you hop in the car. Although the state makes every attempt to keep its records up-to-date, things do change daily.

Penny-Wise

Keep an eye on the calendar! A rush order to the passport agency to get your renewed passport booklets via next-day processing service or one-week delivery might cost you an extra $35 to $50. Avoid this unnecessary expense and ensure your passport's validity as early as possible.

The forms themselves will lead you through the process, directing you as to how to submit your application and how to submit accompanying identification forms. Follow the directions carefully, and submit your forms into the system. Following are some questions you might wonder about:

1. *What happens if we need to rush-order our passports?*

For so many reasons, whether you lost your passport on a trip taken a few weeks before the wedding or you just didn't notice the approaching expiration date in that little blue passport booklet, with all the craziness of the wedding plans, you might find yourself in urgent need of a new passport. If this potential nightmare happens, just make an appointment to go in person to your nearest passport agency. You'll need to show the clerk your airline tickets and travel confirmations as proof of your urgent need for a new document. You'll pay a fee, but it will be worth the expense to get your passport in hand.

And if you don't live within easy distance of any of the main passport agencies? Call in to arrange for reliable overnight mail delivery service, protecting what you send by certified mail with return receipt.

Simplify It

Go to the Web site for the Centers for Disease Control and Prevention (www.cdc.gov) and click on the link for accessing vital records. Find your state, and then follow the directions to locate the agency at which you'll apply for a copy of your birth certificate. Start this process as early as possible, as it could take weeks to receive this vital document before you even step into the weeks it might take to get your passport!

2. *What proofs of identification are needed?*

You'll certainly need a copy of your birth certificate as authentic proof of who you are. Without fail, you'll need to obtain a certified copy of your birth certificate stamped with a raised, embossed seal, along with the registrar's signature and the date it was registered. Right now you might be wondering where your birth certificate is. Like many people, you might not have a copy ready, or you might not even be sure you ever had one in the house. If this is the case, then you can submit a request for an official, certified copy of your birth certificate.

3. *How do we apply for our kids' passports?*

If you're a parent, you can apply in person for your child's passport. One or both parents must be present with the child for the application process, and the parents must submit identification for themselves as well as for the child. (Clearly, the government has rules about protecting children.) You'll need to sign your consent and continue the process for your child's passport application.

Smile and Say "Cheese!"

Every passport, without fail, includes a photograph of the bearer. For the passport application process, you'll need two copies of the same picture. In some instances, you'll have your photo taken at the passport issuance agency where you turn in your applications, and in others you might be able to get a passport picture taken at a camera shop or travel club office.

The standard size of a passport photo is 2 inches by 2 inches, and professional camera shops and travel clubs know just how to produce passport-appropriate pictures. Yes, you may be able to submit your passport application online in the state where you live, but at that point you still need to submit a photograph of yourself *that fits the passport office's requirements.* This means your picture needs to be deemed of high enough quality—of a certain resolution, not grainy, not a poor image—before it can be used on your passport. Since technology isn't always reliable, I advise you to take a real photo to a passport application facility and submit it the old-fashioned way. Your odds of the process going more smoothly and efficiently are a bit better this way.

Photos must be clear, black and white or color, taken within the past six months, with you face-front. For your own safety while abroad, do *not* wear any civil service or other type of uniform while getting your picture taken. Wear regular street clothes that would not identify you as any kind of threat in case of trouble on the road. Take off tinted glasses, but wear your regular glasses if they're a normal part of your daily appearance. This isn't a model portfolio

Penny-Wise

If you are a card-carrying member of a travel club, such as AAA, you might receive, as a perk, a high discount on taking and developing your regulation passport photos. In renewing my own passport just under the 15-year validity wire, I price-checked the costs of passport photo processing and found that a local camera shop charged me nearly double the going rate at the travel club.

you're posing for; it's a document for your identification *and your safety* while overseas.

Once you get your passports, treat these little booklets like gold. A very smart move is to make a photocopy or two of the information page of your passports. Tuck one away in a safe place in your home (perhaps a lockbox or safe), and pack the other copy among your luggage for the trip. If, by some stroke of crisis, your passport is lost or stolen during your trip, you will have that copy of your information to at least help you get back home.

Visas

A visa is a special stamp on one's passport that allows him or her to legally remain within a country's borders. Each country has its own rules and requirements for granting visas to any travelers, and I can't

What About My Medications?

I'll need to bring along a sizeable amount of prescription drugs that I'm on. What do I need to know?

You can protect yourself by keeping your prescriptions in their original prescription vials and *not* transferring the pills to a pretty container. The authorities will certainly check out anyone who steps on or off a plane with a bag full of pills, so you'd better be able to provide documentation that you have them for a purpose. Bring along a copy of a letter from your physician, stating that you're on these medications for a particular reason, just for backup proof. For more information, contact the Food and Drug Administration at 202-307-2414.

emphasize enough that the process ranges from ultrastrict fraught with red tape to the laughably simple. Some countries require that your passport be legal for six months prior to applying for a visa, and fees range wildly as well. In the Resources, you'll find a list of many countries' consulates and Web sites for your research needs.

It'll Only Hurt for a Second

If your honeymoon plans will take you way off the beaten path or even just to a seemingly harmless foreign country, you might face a requirement for several immunizations. World travel means that so many people are landing in regions they've never been to before, and their bodies may not be used to the kinds of conditions in their destination. Thus some destinations make it mandatory for all visitors to be immunized against such unwelcome souvenirs as malaria, diphtheria, cholera, yellow fever, and other infectious diseases. Your certificate of vaccination might then be just as important as your passport to be allowed into the country!

While we're on the subject of vaccinations, even though we'll talk more in chapter 13 (on safety and well-being) about protecting your health during your travels, another good source for learning more about the kinds of vaccinations and health risks of certain destinations is available through Frommer's Travel Health Center at (www.frommers.com/tips/health).

Simplify It

For any specific passport concerns or answers, or to check the status of your passport application during its processing time, call the National Passport Information Center at 900-225-5674 (for a per-minute charge to speak to an operator or receive automated assistance) or 888-362-8668 (for a flat rate to get assistance).

Customs Forms

Forget taking home those Cuban cigars or maybe even a coconut from your Hawaiian adventures. The U.S. Customs Agency has *strict* rules about what you can bring home from your travels. During your return trip, you'll most likely receive a customs claim form before your plane even lands back home. On these forms, you'll declare the value of any items you bought while on your trip, and depending on the country you visited, you may be granted an exemption of from $200 to $1,200. After that amount, you may have to pay 10% duty taxes on the rest of your new purchases.

To make this process easier, and to speed your way through customs just a bit more quickly, be sure you pack all of your new goodies in one bag, all together, with their receipts easily accessible. Be honest on your claim form, since the authorities are extra-vigilant about checking all items in customs.

Customs agents are also checking your bags for any items that you aren't allowed to bring into the country from a safety point of view. You don't have to have a degree in botany or be on the board of an ecological committee to know that some plants, fruits, flowers, and even foods can harbor dangerous insects, bacteria, and soil-implanted dangers that can transport a disease from one country back home to your own. The folks at U.S. Customs take this *very* seriously, so check out the list of no-no's at www.aphis.usda.gov/travel for complete information. Here you'll find out if you can take home a small vial of pink sand from your Bermuda getaway (usually, you can) or if you can keep the shells and starfish you collected on the ocean's edge (only if they're clean). But you'll also find

Simplify It

To find out complete information on obtaining a visa for entry to select foreign destinations, log on to travel.state.gov/foreignentryreqs.html. One you've done that, be sure to *call* the consulate of your location to double-check the validity of the site's advice. Laws change every day, so it's best to get live authenticity of your requirements and steps.

out about the strict penalties for importing anything from ivory statuettes to tobacco products to plants, bulbs, or seedlings.

For specific information on import rules from Canada, Mexico, Hawaii, Puerto Rico, and the U.S. Virgin Islands, check out the U.S. Department of Agriculture's special pamphlets on just these destinations, order the pamphlets and get more general information on customs allowances at www.aphis.usda.gov /travel/pub.html.

Take this part seriously. Violating any customs or import rule, even unintentionally, can land you in a world of trouble. The new security measures at airports, and the new vigilance on importing, means that your illegal souvenirs might be sniffed out by canine customs officials or detected by X-ray machines and scans. Fines range from $250 and up, and if the violation is severe enough, you're going to jail.

Simplify It

The Centers for Disease Control (www.cdc.gov/travel /index.htm) can provide you with the official list of immunizations that you'll need for your intended travels, plus any warnings on active epidemics and outbreaks across the globe. So too can the Citizens Emergency Center of the U.S. Department of State (202-647-5225). I, for one, would want to know if that dreamy little remote island destination of mine is currently quarantined for dengue fever before I take two planes, three buses, and a kayak to get there.

Travel Insurance

You might be wondering if you should purchase travel insurance for your honeymoon, since this is a trip of momentous importance. The issue might seem a bit more important to you, especially if you're planning a lengthy trip through exotic areas, some of which may be a bit more risky to visit. Whatever your decision, research travel insurance plans well, and see if your own existing insurance plans will cover you for your world adventures.

If you need to find new travel insurance coverage, you'll have plenty of options to research. Several respected travel experts and publications have recommended an insurance company called Travel Guard International (800-826-1300, www.travel-guard.com), which offers plans to cover such expenses as credit card theft or fraud during your trip, damage to or loss of your valuables, emergency assistance, medical fees, and expenses related to lost passports and travel tickets, among other unforeseen circumstances. Travel insurance packages are also offered as part of membership benefits in some travel clubs, such as AAA. As with any plan, research well and read the fine print.

Have a Safe Trip!

12

$\mathbf{A}$nytime you travel, you're certainly careful about your own safety. You lock your luggage, avoid the dangerous parts of a city, and check where the emergency exits are on the plane. For your honeymoon, you might want to be extra cautious because any kind of trouble or injury can completely ruin your trip of a lifetime or even put your life in danger. Especially when you travel to foreign destinations that aren't as free or as patrolled as your own hometown, you could court disaster if you don't practice safe traveling smarts.

Although some of the tips here might seem elementary to you if you're a seasoned traveler, you should remind yourself of these steps no matter how security-savvy you are. Your dream trip probably doesn't include a four-day stay in the local hospital or hours in a police department filling out reports on the thief who lifted your bags from the hotel lobby. And I must warn you that some popular destinations have put out legitimate warnings that their visitors not venture off the resort compound for fear of criminal activity by the locals.

176 • PART III: THE DETAILS

No destination comes without its own inherent dangers, and sometimes we forget that there are legitimate reasons why we're warned about dangerous conditions in some regions of the world. Certainly, these days you may be extra-vigilant about any warnings of civil or criminal unrest in an area, and that's a very smart way to think. If at this time you're still shopping around for a great, exotic honeymoon destination, check out the State Department's updated list of travel warnings (travel.state.gov), a register of locations that are currently experiencing dangers, if not outright battle. *Not* wanting American tourists to visit these areas, the State Department puts out this list to protect citizens from any sizable threats. If you are looking globally for your ideal honeymoon spot, I urge you to check out this Web site now at the time of your planning, and—if you do book a foreign destination—check the site again right before you leave for your trip. Better to cancel your trip and lose your deposits than fly into a war zone.

Honeymoon Reflections

We were warned when we were checking in to our hotel on a popular island in the Caribbean that we should never leave the resort without being driven by one of the hotel's cabbies. Apparently, a couple of honeymooners had ventured off the grounds on their own, not wanting to take a group tour of the island. Off on their own, they got lost and wound up in a really seedy part of town where they were robbed at knifepoint and the woman was raped. Upon closer inspection, we saw that the entire resort was surrounded by a tall wall with razor-wire coils on top. Definitely not something we saw in the brochure.

—Jennifer and Evan

Before You Go

Following is a checklist of things to take care of before you leave:

- ❏ Be sure you both have valid passports (and visas, if necessary) ready to go. Be sure to fill in all the emergency identification and notification blocks within the booklet and sign where necessary so your passport can serve you in case of a crisis.

❏ Make two copies of your passport data pages, and leave one with a relative back home, just in case.

❏ Keep the extra copies of your passports in your luggage or in another place separate from your original passports.

❏ Write up a complete copy of your itinerary, and leave it with a family member back home. This move is for your own safety and also so your relatives can get in touch with you in case of any emergency at home.

❏ Leave photocopies of your airline tickets and hotel reservations with a reliable family member as well.

❏ When you're making your travel reservations, ask the travel agent for any and all information related to safety at that location.

❏ Look up the phone numbers of the American consulates and embassies in the regions you will visit, and record them on a card to keep in your wallet. It's better to be safe and have the numbers on hand than to go through the hassle of trying to find out while on the road.

❏ Record the serial numbers, denominations, bank name, and date of issue for all travelers' checks on a separate card, and pack that card in your luggage. This vital information written down ahead of time and stored efficiently can help you replace lost or stolen travelers' checks more easily and in much less time.

❏ Record your credit card numbers, the customer service phone number for each card, and your credit limit for each card on a paper that you'll carry with you in a separate place from your actual cards. I advise you to keep careful track of your credit limits. This is important not only because it would hurt your credit—or at the very least embarrass you—if you were to exceed your limit with an excited string of purchases but also because in some countries, trying to pay with a credit card that is denied because it's over the limit can actually get you arrested.

❏ Since you can't dial 800-numbers in some foreign countries, look up your credit card number's regional customer service number (the non-800-number) and record that for your use while on your trip.

❏ Stop your mail and newspaper delivery services so an overflowing mailbox doesn't announce to would-be robbers that you're not around to protect your belongings. You can submit a stop-mail request through the U.S. Postal Service Web site (www.usps.gov) or by writing out and submitting a form at your local post office. These forms do have a box you can check for all of your held mail to be delivered to you on a day after you return, which can save you a trip to the post office.

❏ Sign up for a calling card or purchase individual preprogrammed calling cards for your communications and emergency contact use. Be sure, though, to check if a particular calling card will work in the region where you will be; some calling cards are not valid for use overseas.

❏ Find out if your cellular phone will work in the region you'll be visiting. Call your cell phone company and inquire about long-distance usage, access, and perhaps even temporary plans to expand your territory.

❏ Ask a reliable friend to occupy your house or to make it look occupied, by coming in to turn on lights at night, open shades and close them throughout the day, water the lawn, and generally make your place less of a glaring target for thieves.

❏ Read up on any travel warnings and traveler advisories as posted by the State Department to check the safety status of your destination *and surrounding areas.* Remember that it's a small

What If We Don't Have E-Mail?

If you can't access the State Department's Web site to get copies of these all-important travelers' advisory notices or "Consular Information Sheets," you can send a self-addressed, stamped envelope with a request for the particular reports you need to Overseas Citizens Services, Room 4811, Department of State, Washington, DC 20520-4818. To receive a fax of your forms, call 202-647-5225 and follow the automated directions. You can also ask your travel agent for these reports when you make any international travel reservations.

world we're living in, and one country's civil unrest can affect treatment of Americans in nearby regions as well. Intolerance doesn't stop at country borders.

❑ Read up on local customs so you are familiar with any gestures or practices that can be offensive to the locals. In some lands, a simple wave with your hand facing the wrong way can get you attacked. Read up on dress codes and be prepared to follow the rules of local custom so you'll blend in. Now's not the time to "make a statement" or refuse to honor social codes where you'll be staying. In some cases, knowledge can save you from hardship.

❑ Invest in quality luggage and carry-ons, complete with locks and reliable identification tags. (For ease of bag identification, consider a brightly colored elastic strap that you can wrap around your bags on the outside.) Be sure your luggage and carry-ons feature covered or flapped identification tags that hide your personal identification and proof of your nationality.

❑ Insert a copy of your identification information and the hotel name and number where you'll be staying inside your luggage so your lost bag can be delivered to you if the outside identification tag is knocked off or damaged.

❏ If you will remain at a foreign destination for more than two weeks, the State Department recommends that you call to check in with the American consulate in that country, providing your name and contact information in case you must be located or notified for any reason.

❏ When making your travel reservations, choose to travel into and out of the larger airports having more updated and modernized security systems.

❏ I know this is creepy, but you should make sure all of your legal affairs are in order before you go on a major trip. Make sure your wills are up-to-date and your insurance documents and power of attorney forms are marked and set for easy discovery by your family members in case of the worst. Check your insurance policy for its coverage of loss or death while you're overseas, and ask your insurance handler if you need to purchase an additional rider for your trip. Also, check with your health insurance company for your plan's rules on coverage for any overseas or even out-of-state medical care or hospitalization. Some health insurance companies will reimburse you for medical fees incurred on any trip, and some have strict (or even ridiculous) rules about not covering you when you travel to Third World or remote areas where medical care is barely available. Ask about the availability of special traveler's health insurance riders or buffer plans that will prevent any insurance nightmares during or after your trip.

Tips for Preventing Robbery

• Never let your bags—any of them—out of your sight for even a moment.

• Never carry too many bags or overstuffed, heavy bags. Keeping your burdens light means you can move around more easily, and you'll be less likely to keep setting your bags down for a rest, leaving them open for a quick swipe.

• Try to avoid using fanny packs or purses that have way-too-easy-to-open zippers or even always-open flaps. A talented thief knows just how to gain access to these common travelers' accessories. Instead, conceal your belongings in inside pockets or inner-waist pouches worn under clothing.

• When you're in a restaurant or bar, don't hang your purse on the back of your chair. This is a common setup for a quick and undetected robbery right behind your back. Instead, place it on the table, to the side of your place setting, and always in sight.

• Don't keep all of your money in one pocket. Seasoned city travelers shared this tip with me, and I've heard it since in many safety lectures: Keep some money in your pocket, some perhaps in a waist bag, and even some in your sock. Splitting up your money like this means you won't be completely wiped out if your pocket is picked or your wallet lifted.

• Keep your passport on you at all times while traveling, whether in your handbag, carry-on, or waist pouch. When you're at your hotel or out on the town, keep it in the room safe. If, by chance, your passport is stolen or lost, use the photocopy you've made of your information to get you through the last legs of your trip (and pack two extra passport photos of each of you, just in case you need replacement passports made on the spot during your travels). When you return home, you'll need to report the loss or theft of your passport, and you can request the appropriate forms (Form DS-46) with complete directions online at travel.state.gov/lost_stolen.html.

• When planning your honeymoon wardrobe, think beyond what will be comfortable and what will make you look amazing on the beach. The State Department recommends that if you're traveling to any foreign destination, you should avoid wearing any clothing that marks you as a wealthy (and therefore vulnerable) traveler. Leave the diamond earrings home, and scale down your look to fit in more wherever you go.

• Get travelers' checks, and plan to bring along only one or two credit cards. Walking around any destination with a big wallet, a fat roll of cash, or a lineup of credit cards can mark you as easy prey for any well-handed pickpocket, seasoned thief, or even street urchin with a great distraction and an easy reach into your bag.

• When you're exchanging money into local currency, do so only at established, reputable agencies, like banks or your hotel. Street vendors aren't as likely to give you the fair market value.

Safety Tips for Travel Time

• Adhere to all airport and airline security requests. Expect long delays due to increased security measures, and prepare for delays so you don't get frustrated by them.

• Book a nonstop flight between home and your destination so there are fewer takeoffs and landings to worry about. These are the most dangerous parts of your flight, in most instances, so eliminate extra risks by just taking one flight each way, if possible.

• Do some research into the safety records of different airlines or cruise ships. When asked in surveys, most future honeymooners said that an airline's record of safety was one of the most important factors in their decision to fly with them. Most would pay extra to fly on a safer airline with a newer fleet of aircraft and well-trained professionals manning them.

• Don't spend a lot of time in the public areas of airports that anyone can access. When you check in, move right through security into the more secure areas for passengers.

• Check the Consular Information Sheets for any reports that say tourists are being targeted while on public transportation at your destination. Recent crime sprees in the subways are often shown on these reports, so know if you need to avoid public transportation and take a cab.

• Never get into an unmarked taxi. Ideally, ask if your hotel offers its own shuttles for anywhere you need to go.

• When traveling on buses or trains, be sure your passports and money are safely tucked in inside pockets and impossible to reach by pickpockets. It's a common traveling target for pickpockets to use crowded buses or trains as a way to get close enough to grab your wallet.

• When traveling on trains, especially for long treks or overnight stays, lock your compartment doors. Some trains are designed so you can hook your bunk bed ladder over the doorway to completely restrict access by outsiders.

• Rather than risk your bags disappearing and your pockets being picked, stay awake while traveling, or take turns sleeping so that someone is always awake and able to watch your valuables.

• Don't get drunk and pass out on trains or buses. That's a welcome mat for criminals.

• If you rent a car, don't get a flashy sports car. Choose a model that blends in, and drive conservatively, according to the rules of the road. Make sure the car has good safety features, like auto locks and air bags. Keep the doors locked at all times.

Honeymoon Reflections

We were warned that criminals in the area were actually drugging the people on the trains so that they could rob them while they were passed out and snoring. We never considered ourselves the ultrasuspicious types, but hearing a story like that from other travelers really made us open our eyes. We won't accept a drink from anyone while we're on vacation, and we'll keep our eyes open.

—Cindy and Steve

• Drive with the windows closed so thieves can't just reach in and grab your valuables.

• Keep in mind the kinds of criminal ploys you've heard about here at home, and use your intuition to avoid any dangerous situation on the road or during your travels.

Safety Tips During Your Stay

• Again, don't dress to stand out but to blend in. In some regions, you might want to avoid anything bearing slogans that identify you with your home country or state. Leave the valuable jewelry and watches at home (who needs a watch on your honeymoon, anyway?), and keep your cash and credit card hidden in an inside pocket.

• Stay in a larger hotel that offers greater security, either by the development and safety of its grounds borders or its hotel staff's ability to monitor who enters and exits the grounds. The better-known resorts have outstanding security systems for your protection, so do keep that in mind when looking for your reservations.

• When looking at hotels, if possible, consider booking a room that offers access only from an inside hallway and not from the street or beach levels. This setup can lessen the chance of someone breaking into your room.

• When booking your rooms with your safety in mind, request a room on the second to seventh or eighth levels, which is the height that most fire department rescue trucks can reach with a ladder.

• When you arrive at your location, participate in any safety lectures or drills, especially on cruises.

• When you're in the room, keep the door bolted and chain-locked at all times, especially when you're sleeping. That's just basic hotel safety smarts.

• If you have sliding doors in your hotel room, be sure they are closed securely and locked. If a hotel has provided a dowel for security reasons, lay it in the track behind the closed door so robbers cannot gain entry.

• Don't leave cameras and other valuables out in your hotel room. Always use the hotel safe for such important items. My family found this one out the hard way on our first night at an island hotel when we went out for dinner and came back to the room to find that *all* of our cameras had been stolen . . . on the first day. The hotel did nothing to help us, so we checked out and found a better place to stay. And we dealt with that first hotel later.

• Check out your fire safety escape route when you first get to your hotel room, and do this for every stop you make while on your trip.

• Don't use stairwells when you're alone, and don't get into or stay in elevators with suspicious-looking people in them. It's better to wait a few extra minutes than to take any unnecessary risks.

• Use common sense when moving through and within *any* area. Avoid dimly lit or deserted areas, and keep your guard up when you're in any crowded area that's a usual target spot for robbing travelers: street markets, festivals, tourist attractions, subways, train stations, airports, and any other area where you're likely to encounter a wide range of people in close, bumping proximity to you. Don't travel alone or separately at night, no matter how close you think the hotel might be from where you are, or even if you think it's safe because you always walk alone at night back home.

• Know a little something about pickpockets. In certain parts of the world, pickpocketing is an art and an entire way of life for some street urchins and criminals. Pickpockets rarely pull magic tricks by slipping your watch off your wrist without you knowing; they often work in pairs or teams, with one person distracting you while the other grabs your wallet. The ploys are amazingly simple but effective:

A stranger might bump you, trip over your bag and yell at you, spill something on herself or on you, point out something that's wrong with your clothing or your bag, or even send her adorable child over to play peekaboo with you. Any distraction will do, as it just takes a second for the distracter's partner to get a hand into your purse or pocket. Groups of street kids can cause a big distraction either by starting a fight and grabbing a few wallets while the crowd is focused on them or scrambling around to avoid the chaos. In some regions, kids offer to shine your shoes, or they go so far as to shove a big item right into your chest so that you're conscious only of the item and not what's being done with your back pocket. The tricks are plentiful, and they work if you aren't aware that *any* distraction or bump can be a pickpocket making an attempt to victimize you:

• Stay away from potentially dangerous situations, like angry crowds, demonstrations, or even gatherings for a political figure's or celebrity's visit. Sometimes it's best to just walk away and not observe the spectacle up close.

• Speak softly. Don't argue. Again, blend in by keeping your voices low.

• Learn a few basic phrases in the native language so you can ask for assistance without coming off as too obvious a tourist. Another great trick is to learn an assertive phrase in that language to disarm anyone who seems to mean trouble. Mind you, I said assertive, not offensive, since you don't want to be the one to incite an incident.

• Don't allow the natives to befriend you. Sure, nine times out of ten, you might have met a kind person who wants to help you out on your travels, but that sweet-looking gentleman who approaches you on the street and offers to take you on a personal tour of the city for a low amount of money could also be a scam artist. Local safety officials advise all travelers to stay with official tour guides and not accept great deals that come to them in the form of a kindly stranger.

• Even if you're lost, try to look as if you know where you are going. Don't wander around dazed, trying to read your map in public, as that's just a drop of blood in the shark tank water to would-be thieves or swindlers. If you need to look at your map, find a bench or a café where you can sit down and look very polished about your next destination plans. A better move is to keep the map tucked away and ask shopkeepers and police officers for directions, not just anyone on the street.

• In case of the worst and you are threatened for your money or your valuables, the State Department advises that you just give them up without a fight or a chase or any other retribution. In some countries, "He took my wife's purse" is not a valid defense for throwing a punch. *You* could wind up in jail—and on the evening news back home.

• Don't do anything stupid. Remember that the laws overseas may be far more strict than our own, so taking a risk by breaking any law, even a minor one, can land you in a world of trouble.

• When out at the clubs, don't accept drinks from strangers, do watch your drinks being prepared, and never leave your drink unattended. Criminals and outright maniacs can slip drugs into your drinks, so be protective of yours. If you do set your drink down to visit the restroom or enjoy a dance, it's better to order a new drink than to continue drinking one that's been left unguarded.

Honeymoon Reflections

Since we were planning our honeymoon in a few major cities where we knew we'd stand out as Americans and where we'd probably wind up in crowded street markets and museums, with a lot of exposure to the locals, we actually both signed up for a self-defense course at a local community education center. Not so much so that we could kick some butt if someone attacked us, but so that we would know the basics and have the right thoughts to keep calm if we were ever in that kind of situation. Thankfully, we didn't need to act on our lessons during our amazing trip, but we were happy to have received them for our overall safety then and from now on.

—Stephanie and Ed

Safety Tips with the Local Cuisine

It can be tough for anyone's system to process foods and spices they're not used to, but some regions' cuisines can be downright dangerous. You probably know enough not to drink the water in various regions of the world, preferring instead to stick with bottled water and avoid ice cubes. You probably would avoid any raw foods anywhere, not just on vacation, and if you have any food allergies, you know what to ask.

On vacations, travelers get into trouble when they eat without their brains involved. That is, they just accept that all foods offered to them are safe, and they don't question any preparation process or basic levels of sanitary practices. I know plenty of travel writers who venture all over the world, and they will not eat anything that comes from a food vending cart in a marketplace. Even if you're a city dweller, and you love a good hot dog right out of the vending cart in front of your office building, you need to be aware that the rules for food safety all over the world sometimes do not match our own food safety standards. So keep your mind on food safety and order your meals only from reputable, established, and clean eateries in any location:

- Again, don't accept food or drinks from strangers, and if something doesn't smell or look right, don't eat or drink it. It's far better to waste the money than to endure a bout of food poisoning, botulism, or any other brutal illness that can ruin your entire trip.

- Drink only bottled water, hot beverages made from water that's been boiled (not just heated), canned beverages, beer, and wine.

- Drink out of the can or bottle rather than use a glass that might have been cleaned with impure water. Wipe off the top and edge of the can or bottle where you will drink from it.

- Don't add ice to anything, even to hot coffee in order to cool it down.

- Believe it or not, brush your teeth with bottled water.

- Choose your foods carefully, depending on where you visit. In some areas, you might want to stay away from salads and salad dressings, unpasteurized milk products, shellfish, and some meats.

- Avoid street vendor foods *especially* in undeveloped or Third World countries and some islands.

- Wash your hands often during your travels and especially before you eat.

- Since traveler's diarrhea is such a common problem to anyone whose system is exposed to unfamiliar foods and microbes, do yourself a favor and pack plenty of antacids, nausea medication, bottled water, and fruit juices.

- If you do get extremely ill, go to a doctor right away. Some contaminations and illnesses can be life-threatening or complicated by delayed treatment.

Health Safety

To check on outbreaks, airborne illnesses and diseases that any traveler might encounter, and further information on any vaccinations you might need, go to www.cdc.gov/travel/index.htm.

Another great site related to health for travelers is that of the International Society of Travel Medicine (www.istm.org), where you'll find referrals to doctors near you who can counsel you on health risks for your location and even immunize you against such nasty illnesses as hepatitis, malaria, dengue fever, and other potentially deadly diseases. Of course, you should also help out your safety factor by getting a complete checkup six months before your honeymoon, when you'll update your regular immunizations like tetanus.

Health Safety on Cruise Ships

You might have heard some reports about airborne illnesses on cruise ships. In the past, there have been some outbreaks of various viral illnesses on boats, and the Centers for Disease Control can answer any of your questions and provide their reports on the best cruise lines based on their safety records. Check out the CDC's link to cruise ship health reports at www.cdc.gov /travel/index.htm.

Tips on Who to Call for Help

• In case of any major problems where you need assistance, call your local embassy or consulate. The Department of State's Web site in the Resources will link you to the Consular Information Sheet for the region you'll be visiting. These pages often contain complete contact information, addresses, phone numbers, and hours of the consulate you might need to contact, so make *three* copies of this sheet: one for your loved ones at home, one for you, and one for your partner.

• In case of any illness or for definitive answers to rumors of outbreak on the road, call the Centers for Disease Control's Traveler's Health Hotline at 877-FYI-TRIP, or check the latest news through www.cdc.gov/travel/index.htm.

Smart Travel Practices

Y ou've just read about how to travel safely, especially if you're going overseas, and now it's time to check out how you can travel more *smartly*. Sure, I know you've planned and been on countless vacations or business trips. You know how and when to make your reservations. You know enough to get to the airport early and bring the specified size and number of carry-on bags. You know what to expect with time changes and jet lag. What you probably *don't* know is that travel for honeymooners can be far different than for anyone else. In this chapter, you'll learn how to get extra perks and the royal treatment—for free!—*just* because you're on your honeymoon. You'll also be reminded of some smart travel practices that will help you avoid the most common travel and resort-stay headaches and nightmares that can annoy you or even ruin your trip. We're planning you a perfect honeymoon here, so read on and ready yourself for the trip of a lifetime.

Right from the Start

Of course, the best way to travel smart is to take the right steps from the start of your planning process, giving yourselves plenty of time to take advantage of the brightest offers out there. Here are a few tips to get you off on the right foot:

• The sooner you start looking for and booking your honeymoon plans, the better chance you have of finding a great trip and a great deal. Just like when planning your wedding, advance action gets you the greatest rewards. This is true for your airline or cruise reservations, your hotel accommodations, and even your car rentals throughout your stay.

• If you're not a member of a frequent flier club or an airline's VIP club, think about joining if you regularly rack up enough air miles each year to qualify. Perks include being ushered to the front of the line at airports, being whisked through security, being allowed access to clubs and VIP waiting areas, and getting regular seating upgrades to first-class. All of which can make your honeymoon trip *so* much more enjoyable.

• Again, consider using the services of a real, live travel agent. When a transportation or rental glitch occurs, you can actually call a *person* to help you out with alternate plans while you're on the road.

• When making reservations, give the travel agent your home *and* cell phone numbers. If the airline, the resort, or the travel agent need to reach you at the last second, they have a better chance of doing so. Thinking ahead and dealing with this tiny detail could prevent the

Simplify It

Many airlines now offer automatic text-messaging services, in which they'll send a message to your cell phone, pager, or personal digital assistant (PDA) to alert you about flight changes or cancellations or relocations of terminals or gates. What better way to stay on time and in the right place than this? Ask your travel agent or airline representative if this service is available.

awful situation of having a message left back on your office voice mail about your flight being canceled at the last minute.

• If travel time stresses you out, plan to fly in the evening hours. Usually, lines at the airport are longer in the morning when business travelers hop their flights. This isn't a failsafe rule, however. Bad weather and increased travel during holiday times can mean long lines at any time of day.

• Want to avoid enormous airports where you actually have to take a *train* to get from one concourse to the other? Ask your travel agent about flying into a nearby alternate airport that's smaller and less in demand.

• Need to make a connecting flight during your travels or as part of a money-saving deal? Again, look into those smaller, alternate airports that might make it easier for you to get from Terminal A to Terminal D in time to catch that second flight.

• Don't book yourself solid during your vacation time. You may *think* right now that a fast-paced honeymoon—touring five different countries in 10 days or getting to jet-ski, parasail, scuba dive, *and* swim with dolphins during your week on the island—sounds like a dream come true. But most honeymooners tell me they were *exhausted* from the wedding activities when they first reached their resort, and the last thing they wanted was another long list of things they *had* to do. Some of these couples canceled their prebooked activities—and didn't get a refund. So spread out the items on your wish list, leave your options open, and plan a more laid-back itinerary. You can always sign up for events, lessons, and tours while your days are unfolding during the trip.

• Plan an amount for your spending money allowance. And then double it. You're going to be shocked at the price of a single martini on that cruise ship, and you're going to flip when you see that some hotels actually *charge* you for plates and silverware to use with your room service order. On a recent trip, for instance, I was charged $7.50 for an extra plate and silverware. Allow yourself a nice chunk of change to be able to take that sunset champagne cruise or shop at that gallery in Paris. It's important to keep a handle on your spending during this vacation, but you don't want to miss opportunities of a lifetime because you didn't plan ahead for spending money. Be generous with yourself so you can splurge once in a while. But plan ahead so you stay within good spending boundaries.

• You read about this in the previous chapter, but I can't stress enough that you should check out your destination *thoroughly* for any governmental warnings about its safety and predicted weather warnings.

Right Before You Leave

Some of the smartest steps are last-minute tasks, those things on your to-do list that occur right at the busiest time in your life as you prepare for both the wedding and your honeymoon. Don't let the hectic countdown pace and your jammed schedule right before the Big Day leave you in a pinch with regard to your trip preparations. Take careful measure to remember the following tips:

• Don't pack too much! Traveling light is the only way to go so you're not burdening yourself with extra, heavy bags, garment bags, and way too much stuff to lug around. Just bring the basics, plan your wardrobe well ahead of time, and leave room in those suitcases for all the great finds and souvenirs you discover during your trip.

• Write out your itinerary, not just for safety's sake, as mentioned in the previous chapter, but for your sanity's sake as well. Especially if you're planning to hit several destinations, it's so much better to start your trip off with an organized printout of your hotel name, address, and phone number, dates you'll be traveling, flight numbers, and your cell phone number. Even if your family back home doesn't need to glance twice at your itinerary, you might find it a time-saver and a big help during your trip.

• Prepare your home life for your absence. In chapter 12, you read about keeping your home and belongings safe while you're away, by turning on the lights, leaving a car in your driveway, and so forth. But before you go, you also need to keep a level of preventive maintenance:

1. Make sure someone can come in to water your plants or take care of the fish tank, mow the lawn, clean and maintain the pool, even make sure the thermostat's at a comfortable level so that all of your candles don't melt (a little something from my own personal experience).

2. A kind helper can also take messages from your home voice mail so that your voice mailbox doesn't get too clogged up to take messages later in the week.

3. On your own, you can set up your office computer to deliver an automatic reply (with your out-of-office status and information on when you will return) to anyone who sends you an e-mail. (This is a smart move, as your clients will know you're not avoiding them or being irresponsible.) I don't advise the same message for your home computer, since such a notice can tip off potential thieves. It's the same as leaving a "Hi, we're on vacation for two weeks" message on your voice mail. That would be like putting out a welcome mat for robbers.

4. Unplug your computer, portable phones, appliances, and any other plug-in items in your home. Even if you have surge protectors, a good lightning storm can fry your equipment.

5. Leave a key to your home with a family member or trusted neighbor, even if you don't need them to stop in and water your ficus. It's just a good move for others to have access to your place, in case you need to call in a request that requires access to your place.

6. Don't forget Fido and Fifi! So many travelers are concerned about boarding their beloved pets at veterinarians or at pet boarding

Simplify It

You already know about checking wedding industry associations for recommendations of well-rated and highly trained experts in their field, but did you know that you can search online for a professional pet sitter? If you can't find a reliable friend to watch your pets, check out Pet Sitters International (www.petsit.com), through which you might be able to find a nearby expert with years of experience, references, training, insurance, and a high degree of reliability. Some of these experts will actually come to your home to spend time with your pet before you leave on your trip, acclimating your pet to their presence. Price packages vary, but you can hire them for a simple feed-and-walk routine, or playtime can be included. In any case, research your expert extremely well, including her safety guarantees and legal responsibilities for the pet's well-being, and leave your pet to a professional only if you cannot find a trusted friend to care for your animals.

centers, fearful of the boarding-house illnesses that can strike pets. Rather than lock your pup in a cage for two weeks, and if no one you know will watch her, find a reliable pet sitter. Your veterinarian can likely recommend a well-rated sitter with plenty of experience.

7. If you absolutely can't miss an episode of a favorite drama or comedy, now's the time to invest in (or learn how to use) TiVo or ReplayTV, the most popular gadgets on the market for scheduling the taping of television programs.

• Plan to get to the airport two hours ahead of time for domestic flights and three hours ahead of time for international flights—at the very least. The airlines aren't kidding about this, especially with greater security measures in place. Allow yourself way more time than you think you'll need to catch shuttles or connecting flights to eliminate the heart-pounding stress of worrying about missing your departure.

• So what do you do with the extra time you're waiting? Don't want to hop from food court counter to food court counter? Don't want to browse the duty-free shops for two hours, or longer, if your flight is delayed? Make arrangements ahead of time to join your airline's exclusive membership clubs for access to their private airport lounges. Behind these doors that are closed to the

Join the Club!

Research the current annual rates and per-use fees through the Web sites listed in the Resources:

- American Airlines: Admiral's Club
- Continental Airlines: President's Club
- Delta Airlines: Crown Room Club
- Northwest Airlines: WorldClub
- United Airlines: Red Carpet Club
- US Airways: US Airways Club

public, you may find reclining chairs, leather couches, cable television, fine food and drink service, Internet access, and even showers and dressing rooms. It's the VIP room of the airport, and that's where you can relax for a few hours until your flight is ready to leave.

• Call a few days before your flight to see if you can get a seat upgrade. This service is often reserved for frequent fliers, so it may be a long shot if you're not of that status. But you never know. Ask again when you check in at the airport—*this* is the time to mention that you're honeymooners. Again, airlines want to keep their special guests happy, and honeymooners are often first on the list for extra perks. Imagine how much better that flight to Australia will be in first class.

• Prepare for the time difference. Know how many hours ahead or behind your present time zone your destination is so you can gradually adjust a week or so before you leave. That might mean going to bed a few hours earlier or later than you're used to, just so you won't be so thrown when you're living in another time zone.

• Call in to confirm your flights and hotel reservations, just to be on the safe side.

Don't Lag!

Other ways to prepare for or avoid jet lag:

• For extreme time differences, set a schedule for going to bed one hour earlier and earlier each day. Or later and later, if the case requires. Over a few days, your body will have adjusted more comfortably to the time change.

• Jet lag worsens when you're dehydrated. So drink plenty of water before, during, and after your flight.

• Your body will need its energy to adjust to the new time zone, so go easy on it. Stick to simpler, lighter foods and not the heavy, spicy, or adventurous local cuisine for the first few days so your system can keep up with you. Don't drink too much alcohol during your flight or even on the first day or two when you arrive.

• Relax! Deep breathing and exercise are good for you in any time zone, so use these natural well-being practices to keep yourself in line for the fun to come.

• Make sure your luggage conforms to the airline's new size restrictions. And remember that you can only bring one carry-on and personal bag (like a handbag) on board with you.

• Triple-check that you have everything on your packing list ready to go so travel day will be hassle-free.

• A few days before, check the weather for your location (www.weather.com) to see if you need to pack additional cooler weather clothing and jackets or bring along a fold-up umbrella.

• Before leaving home, check to see if your flight is going to depart on time or if it's been delayed. You can call the airline directly and talk to a live attendant or an automated system, check the airline's Web site, or log on to www.trip.com. Some people prefer to talk to a live attendant, just to be sure they're getting the most accurate and to-the-minute information. The choice is yours.

En Route

Once you hit the road, still in a state of bliss over the success of your wedding day (and perhaps the wedding night itself!), and as you make your way to your honeymoon destination, you still need to keep some smart travel practices in mind. For many couples, it's the "en route" time that stresses them out the most, but only when they haven't practiced good forethought.

Getting to the Airport

• Whether you're getting a ride to the airport or driving yourself, allow plenty of extra time to get there. Traffic at airports has surged, leading to big backups and extra waits, and many airports have closed their nearby parking lots that are within walking distance to the terminals. This means you'll have to park your car in the long-term lots that are a bus ride away from the airport. Many honeymooners choose to have a limousine or town car take them to and from the airport just so they don't have to deal with the parking hassles and expenses. Especially for your ride home, it's worth the expense.

• Keep your tickets, passport, and ID handy. You're going to need to show them at each step along the check-in process, from signing in to the security gate, even perhaps right before you board the plane.

• Keep an eye on your bags when going to and waiting at the airport. The airlines aren't kidding about making sure that every bag belongs to a passenger. Entire airport terminals have been evacuated because someone left a carry-on bag unattended by the gates. And for nonsafety reasons, just keep your bags near you so you don't forget your garment bag when it's time to board the plane. Such forgotten and left-behind items are a nuisance and a bad start to your vacation.

• If you're checking your luggage with an airport, cruise, or train baggage handler, be sure the handler is wearing an identifiable uniform! This one is a heartbreaker, but it's common among thieves to trick travelers into thinking they're baggage handlers, when they're really just going to take the bags and run. Always get a baggage-claim ticket, and keep it within reach so you can retrieve your belongings once you reach your destination. With security at an all-time high, losing your claim ticket means you're just not going to get your hands on your luggage at all. And that again is a rough way to start your supposedly relaxing getaway.

• Priority check-in of baggage is just one of the perks of frequent flier or airline VIP membership. So if you're a member, skip the long lines and be treated like a star.

• While killing time before your departure, find the best place to hang out in the airport. It might be one of those VIP lounges I mentioned earlier, but it also could be a great bar that's showing a playoff game to a cheering, fun-loving crowd. Airports have gotten into the hospitality business for their waiting passengers, and they've gone to great lengths to make sure your stay is more enjoyable. At some, you might find wonderful art collections to browse or superbookstores with cafés for some leisurely reading and a mocha latte. My favorites: the massage center in the United Terminal at Denver Airport and the wine-tasting centers in San Francisco and Dallas-Fort Worth. You might be surprised at what each airport has to offer, so take a walk around and see what's out there to make your stay go by more quickly and enjoyably. Like it or not, travel time is part of your honeymoon.

Upon Arrival

If only we all got a guarantee that absolute perfection begins the moment we step off the plane at our destinations. But there are still quite a few little details left to cover in order to get the best start to a romantic getaway. Here, you'll find a few smart tips to make your arrival even better:

• "Where the &*#@ is our luggage?!" Lost suitcases are a true thorn in the traveler's side, and when you're on your honeymoon, it can set your dream trip off on the wrong foot. If the airline has sent your luggage to Peru, and you're waiting in Paris, then you'll need to take immediate action for the swift return of your luggage to you. At the airport, fill out a claim form immediately, providing all of your contact information and the address where the luggage must be delivered as soon as possible. This is a good reason to carry a cell phone on you so you can lounge by the pool while you wait for your bags to arrive. And it's also a good reason to pack one of your bathing suits in your carry-on bags so you have the essentials until the rest of your stuff shows up.

Honeymoon Reflections

We were scheduled to depart by train from Paris to Switzerland, and when our taxi driver asked us which train station we needed to go to, we had to dig through our bags to find our tickets for that information. He said it's a good thing he asked because most cab drivers just automatically take people to the other train station, since it's more popular. We would have gone to the wrong one and missed our train entirely!

—Suzie and Ben

• Before you call a cab to get to your hotel, see if the resort has a free shuttle bus that will deliver you for free right to those sliding doors.

• Think twice about hopping on a general resort shuttle bus. If you have no idea where your resort is on the island, or in the country, you could be in for a long ride while that shuttle bus stops at *every* resort on the way to yours. A cab ride could be quicker. Talk to the bus driver and ask for an estimated travel time to your hotel.

Travels During Your Honeymoon

Now don't laugh when I say this to you, but know the name of the airport, train station, or cruise pier you're scheduled to depart from.

The exact name, not just the city. Many major cities have several train stations, for instance, so be sure you're aware of the exact one where you're supposed to be.

When in Rome . . .

The smartest of travelers, particularly overseas visitors, know that the best way to enjoy a vacation in a different land is to play by the rules of the region. Not only is it a smart step to guarantee your safety and well-being, but it's also a deeper way to enjoy the culture, the scenery, and the people you'll meet along the way. Keep these things in mind:

• Respect local laws, in the towns and on the road. If you'll rent a car and drive yourselves, learn ahead of time about local driving rules, road signs, and which side of the road to drive on! Do a little research on local laws, through valuable tip sheets you can get from your travel agent. You might be surprised at what's considered against the law in some countries, and even in some states!

• Respect local customs. I love this story: A couple reported back to me after their honeymoon that they seemed to offend the locals in the Far East when they were trying to gesture an "okay" sign after they'd finally communicated a request or understood directions given by a very patient townsperson. Upon their return, they asked an Asian business associate about the situation, and he informed them that they had been flipping off, or the equivalent of giving the finger to, someone who had spent a great deal of time helping them find their way. Imagine pointing a couple of visitors to the nearest subway system, pointing out street names and landmarks, making sure they knew where they were going, and giving them warnings—and then they just smile and give you the finger before heading off on their way? How odd would that be? Learn the local customs before you head off to another country or island. You can find all the information you need from your travel agent, or head to a bookstore or library for a helpful travel guide for the region you'll visit. So many different tour books and book series exist for just about every country or island out there that it might be difficult to choose between them!

• Respect the land you walk on. Even if you're not a born-and-bred environmentalist, you should respect the parks, beaches, cliffs, rivers, and other natural elements of your destination. This means not chipping a chunk off of the Great Barrier Reef, prying a piece of bark off a sequoia tree, or littering in any national park. In some countries and well-preserved tropical rainforests or game preserves, "protection of the land" rules are taken very seriously. You actually could be arrested or fined for dishonoring the land and its treasures. At any location, know the rules, stay on designated paths, preserve your memories with photographs rather than taking something from its home, and by all means avoid purchasing any souvenir or item made from an endangered species. In some areas of the world, the ivory trade is wiping elephants from the earth—all so that tourists can buy their ivory necklaces, statuettes, and coffee tables. Customs may nab you on your possession of endangered items, as well, so remind yourself at the U.S. Customs Web site (www.customs.gov/travel/travel.htm) of which items are okay to buy. You might not even be aware that tortoiseshell items are on the do-not-buy list, as are various types of furs and even feathers.

Simplify It

For a quick and detailed primer on local customs in more than 170 countries, check out the Culture-Grams from Brigham Young University (www.culturegrams.com).

Smart Self-Care

You might have booked your vacation at a true paradise on earth, lined up an array of once-in-a-lifetime outings during your trip, and

Where the Earth-Loving Honeymooners Go

You might have heard of eco-friendly stocks and bonds, companies that use environmentally sound resources in their productions, but did you know you can also book your honeymoon entirely with environmentally friendly airlines, hotels, tour operators, and cruise lines? The American Society of Travel Agents has a link at its site, www.astanet.com/travel/ecotravel.asp, that will show you which travel industry icons practice excellent environmental procedures such as recycling, water quality, and even noise reduction.

even bought the most fabulous honeymoon wardrobe. But if you're exhausted and dragging your heels the whole time, sick or cranky from the sheer stress of the weeks prior to the wedding, or just running yourself ragged with a way-too-enthusiastic itinerary, you're not going to reap the best benefits of your honeymoon. Take a look at the following tips so you remain in the best shape possible to fully relax and enjoy each other's company:

- Be flexible! Now is not the time to be strict and rigid about your itinerary, mapping out each and every little thing you'll do and at what time each day of your trip. This isn't work, you know. It may be a completely new feeling for you, depending on if you're a Type-A personality or not, but your honeymoon is a time to relax and go with the flow rather than stress yourself out because you can't get through that entire street market in an hour so you can be back at the hotel by 1 P.M. for your scuba lessons and still have time to make the sunset cruise. Lighten up a little, and you'll enjoy your trip so much more.

- Expect the unexpected. This is an offshoot of the whole flexibility thing, but sometimes a delay or a detour in your plans can lead you down a different tropical path right to a waterfall with a rainbow arching over it. Most of the couples I spoke to said that the best parts of their honeymoon were those chance occurrences and surprise events like this:

This was a few years ago, but while we were driving the long ride to the sacred pools of Hana in Hawaii, we hit a big traffic jam. A really big one. Apparently, some road construction on the windy, hairpin-turn road up ahead caused the local police to shut down the entire passage, so we and about 20 other cars were lined up, going nowhere, with no room to turn around. It was hot that day—not a day you want to roast in the car. So we decided to pull out our cooler and dig into the lunch we had planned to enjoy at the sacred pools. We spread out a blanket on the hood of our car, hopped up, and had ourselves a picnic overlooking an amazing view of the valley. Soon, other people in the traffic jam did the same thing, and we basically started a sort of block party! It was a great time, made for great pictures, and we're still e-mail friends with some of the people we met that afternoon!

—DEB AND CHARLES

• Stay in a honeymoon state of mind. For most of us, it's hard to turn off our usual rush-rush, worry-worry mind-set. And it may take a day or two for you to mentally slow down and enjoy your getaway from the rest of the world. But once you've relaxed into that hammock with a frozen drink in your hand, the part of your life with the to-do list and the work worries will start to slip away. When real-world concerns come up, act as a team and remind each other that the business of your lives can be handled when you get back.

• Take no unnecessary risks. If the resort has posted signs about shark or Portuguese man-of-war sightings in the area, go to the pool. Same goes for not drinking the water in certain parts of the world, which some might say is even more treacherous than swimming with sharks.

• Yes, it's true . . . some street drugs are legal in the Netherlands and in other international spots. Some tourists do choose to partake where the practice is legal, but I can only advise you to refrain for the obvious reasons, of course, but *also* for your health and well-being during the rest of your trip. I heard from a recent bride whose groom did choose to try a particular drug during their stay in Amsterdam. He got terribly ill and had a seizure, forcing their early return trip home. I don't need to tell you to use your common sense and avoid what's obviously not a smart idea—you know better.

How to Get Treated Like Gold

Just mention that you're on your honeymoon, and watch the world throw roses at your feet. Well, maybe not roses, but room upgrades, free meals, champagne sent to your room, fruit platters, serenades by violinists and singers, dinner cruises—the list goes on and on. Resorts like to treat their honeymooners like gold, so you're in line for lots of extra niceties that can make your stay extra special. And beyond your honeymooner status bonuses, you can also garner a few extra perks by your decisions during your stay. Read on . . .

• When you're off on your travels, mention that you're on your honeymoon to local restaurant owners who might give you a free drink or dessert. I've heard so many stories from couples who let it be known that they had just tied the knot, and they received offers for free private cruises and other romantic elements that can make a honeymoon unforgettable.

• For those times when you're *not* treated like gold, or when the resort doesn't live up at all to its promises, reputation, or five-star ratings, it's time to lodge a formal complaint. This isn't the time for "resort rage," however, since a brusque manner and threats made to the hotel manager are definitely not going to get you on their favorite guest list. I've heard about too many couples yelling at or belittling managers and concierges, really giving them a horrible time and making *themselves* look and sound horrible as well. It's the diplomatic complaint that will get you far . . . very far.

Our room wasn't up to our standards: peeling paint on the walls and ceiling, a bed that was too saggy in the middle to sleep on, and a few other things. We went downstairs and let the manager know, very nicely, that we were on our honeymoon, and our room was a big problem for us. Could he possibly find us another room within the resort? Simple. Very nice. Very respectful of him. And he found us another room, all right. A great private cabin right on the beach with a stocked complimentary minibar and a fabulous bed surrounded by mosquito netting. And he threw in a complimentary bottle of champagne and a fruit platter as well. All for letting him know we were on our honeymoon and for being nice about our complaint.

—LISA AND VINCE

Remember, as honeymooners, *you* are in the power position here in most cases. The managers of big resorts and getaway locations make a great deal of money from the wedding travel industry—honeymoons and destination weddings alike. They want you to be happy so you'll tell all of your soon-to-be-married friends, siblings, work colleagues, college roommates, and cousins about your terrific experience at *their* resort or on *their* cruise. Advertising costs a fortune, and the best advertising for these destinations is a very positive word-of-mouth recommendation from happy brides and grooms like you. When you have a complaint, and voice it with respect and *requests,* not demands, you're very likely to be upgraded, showered with freebies, and treated like royalty.

For those times when problems at the hotel cost you time and money, prepare your complaint well. Keep receipts of anything you had to spend money on to endure the troubling situation. For instance, if you broke a tooth on a piece of shell mixed in with a crab cake at the hotel buffet, save that bill from your trip to the local dentist. The resort will need to pick up the tab on that one.

Dealing with Others

Unless you've booked a private island and quite happily will spend your honeymoon entirely in solitude with one another, you're going to experience the joys and benefits of interacting with your fellow vacationers. For many couples, this is another highlight of the trip, as social types just love having others to share the fun. When you're spending time with—or even near—others, they can add to your experience in many ways, just as your presence affects their adventures. So be sure to keep the following tips in mind:

• Make friends with other honeymooners! If you're the friendly types, you'll have a blast experiencing that bike ride down a volcano's outer edge or that walk through the Louvre with another couple. Plus, they'll be right there to take pictures of both of you in front of a great sunrise. I've often heard about newly married couples remaining friends with other couples they met during their honeymoon, staying close through e-mails and phone calls.

• Respect your fellow vacationers by keeping the public displays of affection to a minimum. I'm all for affection, but there is something to be said about knowing how to act in public, especially if you're at a family resort.

> We were staying at a great beach resort in Bermuda: swim-up bar, lots of families by the pool, a steel drum band. Just around the bend from the pool was the Jacuzzi, so my husband and I decided to go over for a soak. When we got there, it was obvious we were interrupting something very intimate going on below water level between a honeymooning couple already in the Jacuzzi. My husband and I had already climbed in by the time we realized what had been going on. The other couple couldn't make eye contact with us, and it was just this horrible awkward silence. We got up and left.
>
> —NANCY AND JIMMY

• Ask before taking pictures of people! In one Asian country, a tourist was arrested for snapping an innocent picture of a small child bathing in a river. The photographer loved the shot for the reflection of the child in the water, but the authorities saw it a different way. The tourist was arrested for taking illicit pictures of a minor. Imagine writing *that* postcard home to the family! True, it's a wonderful way to capture the essence of a town or an exotic destination, and *Time* photographers win Pulitzer Prizes for snapping great shots of natives, but this kind of practice can actually frame you (get it?) for unnecessary trouble. Ask permission before taking pictures of anyone, including adorable kids playing on the beach; wonderfully wrinkled Old World natives resting in a fig garden; or members of the military, police, or government. In this last case, your camera could get confiscated.

Keep in Touch!

You may be looking forward to getting away from everything and everyone in your real-life world, detaching from work, family, friends, *everything.* Most couples choose to leave the laptop, the pager, and the cell phone at home so no one can interrupt their bliss with news or questions from the real world.

Most couples simply provide their hotel or resort's main phone number for use in dire situations, and others (especially those with kids back home) will out of sheer conscience call in once in a while to see how everything is going on the home front. However, if your honeymoon will have you on the move, hopping from island to island or even from country to country, the obvious keep-in-touch connection for personal contact (and personal safety during your travels) is a cell phone.

Check to see if your cell phone carrier provides service inclusive of the regions where you will be traveling. Many couples forget about this little detail, not checking to see if their phones will even work in Mexico,

Simplify It

If your carrier doesn't have an international plan and you'd rather not take the time to call cell phone shops around town, another option is to rent an international cell phone. Among the many cell phone companies that offer such a rental (check the list in the Resources), Nextel (800-754-6905) will send you the phone within 24 hours of your trip for a rate of $9.95 each day, plus usage fees and call tolls.

Bali, or Bermuda. Most cell phone carriers do offer international plans, so again, use the list in the Resources to track down a company that offers a wide range of national and international plans.

Couples who do bring their cell phones on their honeymoon say it's a great way to call for a taxi, confirm airline flights while on the road, call ahead to the next city to make hotel reservations, and generally add a lot of efficiency to their trip. Most felt safer having a cell phone on them, in case of any accidents on the road, civil strife in a

Get the Phone

New PDAs come out every day, so look for the best models available right now. What you're looking for if you're going overseas is a global cell phone with tri-band GSM capabilities, which means that the phone in question will work anywhere in the world. Do your research now through the following top telecommunications companies to find the right model at the right price for you:

Casio: www.casio.com
Hewlett-Packard: www.hp.com
Microsoft: www.pocketpc.com
Nextel: www.nextel.com
Nokia: www.nokia.com
Palm: www.palm.com
Samsung: www.samsung.com
Sanyo: www.sanyo.com
Sharp: www.sharp-usa.com
Sprint PCS: www.sprintpcs.com
Verizon: www.verizon.com
Voicestream: www.voicestream.com

foreign country, or the quick reporting of stolen passports and credit cards. Rather than having to seek out a public phone to use—and quickly learn how to use the tricky phone system in another land— they could dial for help immediately.

The new class of cell phones with built-in wireless Internet access al- lows you easy access to airline Web sites to check your flight status, weather Web sites for a look at the five-day forecast, driving directions from point A to point B, and any other online service you could possibly need. It's like having your home computer or laptop right there with you, only you can slip that little phone right into your pocket or bag.

Speaking of pocket PCs, you might also think about bringing along a personal digital assistant (PDA), which gives you full access to the Internet, your address book, a directions finder, or any number of online features—only with a bigger, easier-to-read screen. (You might be using a PDA now to plan your wedding in an organized fash- ion, so if you have one on hand, consider bringing it along on your trip.) In researching the benefits of PDAs to you, the honeymoon traveler, I spoke with a representative from Sprint PCS who showed me the many ways his own PDA might save the day during a vacation and what to look for when buying one for this purpose. First of all, you must make sure your PDA is wireless enabled so it is not simply an organizational tool but will interface with the Internet. On it, you can access Travelocity.com and Expedia.com, which offer special ver- sions of their services to come up specifically on PDAs. Just point and click your way to tracking your flight schedules and making dinner reservations. You couldn't be more organized and better set for smoother travels during your getaway.

Heading Home

Give yourself time to unwind. The smartest couples plan their re- turn-home date for at least two or three days before they have to get

Honeymoon Reflections

I'm so glad we decided to return home four days before our work-week started again. It gave us time to relax, adjust, and—most important—really enjoy being husband and wife in our own home for a while, eating breakfast in bed, checking out our wedding gifts, honeymooning at our own place for a few nights. And then we could get back into the swing of things with our work schedules, our sports leagues, going to the gym, and everything else.

—Thalia and Jeremy

back to work, especially if they'll be overseas and adjusting back to local time zones. Regardless of your destination and your risk of jet lag, leaving a day or two before leaping back into the real world is just a smart move. It will not only give you time to unpack, do laundry, and schedule your week, but you'll also have a day or two to catch up with family members, share stories about your trip, and look at all those candid photographs your friends took at your wedding.

PART IV

How to Get More from Your Honeymoon Budget

Saving Money Right from the Start

In the beginning of the book, you read about planning the right honeymoon for your budget and the time you have to travel, who pays for the honeymoon, and how to register for your honeymoon in its entirety or for special moments like a dinner cruise or a scuba dive. You know the basics of what you can afford, what kind of trip you have in mind, and whether you want a relaxing island getaway or a jam-packed tourist trek across Europe, Asia, Africa, Australia, or the United States. You started sketching out your basic budget and assigning priorities to your most-wanted vacation elements, so you've done the foundational work already.

Now it's time to take your basic budget and play with it, stretch it out, shuffle it, see what you can do with it. It's time to see where you can get even more for the money you have available to spend—perhaps, like some couples, you'll get twice the honeymoon for your original budget!—and save yourself thousands of dollars just by choosing the right honeymoon package. Let's get started.

Stretching Your Honeymoon Fund

I'll keep this short and simple because chances are you've planned vacations before and you know enough to shop around for the best-priced flights and resort packages. However, when the honeymoon factor comes in, you'll certainly have to take a few new notes, even if you are an experienced trip planner.

According to the Travel Institute of America, honeymooners spend *three times* the money on their trip compared to the budget allowance of regular everyday vacationers. These statistics prove that many couples give themselves permission to spend a fortune on their trip of a lifetime, whether subsidized by parents, a honeymoon registry, or smart savings for a few years before the wedding. Regardless of your budget, whether it's enormous or limited, you can still use the many smart ways to make the most of your money and stretch that honeymoon fund out even further.

Cash in Your Miles

Let's start with the biggest potential money saver first. Your existing frequent flier miles or credit card reward miles and bonuses can save the financial day if you choose to cash them in for free airfare, hotel stays, upgrades, and car rentals during your honeymoon, making your trip, in essence, *free* or highly discounted. If you travel a lot for work, you may have thousands upon thousands of frequent flier miles racked up just waiting to be a part of your honeymoon plans. If your everyday credit card usage has been netting you points, perks, and potential freebies, now is the time to look into cashing out on those deals as well.

Many couples plan ahead to use their frequent flier miles as a payment plan for their honeymoon, saving up their points during their extended engagement periods and even far before then. Some switch to credit cards that earn them points with every purchase so their every charge for the wedding, their summer wardrobe, gifts for others, and lunches and dinners out are earning them credits toward their honeymoon. It's a wise move, if you have plenty of time, and if you can find a great credit card that delivers big points for every purchase.

The one thing you need to know about cashing in your frequent flier or credit card bonus points is that some restrictions do apply. Read the fine print on your information pamphlets or brochures, or call the credit card 800-number to ask for specific details on cashing in your points. Some companies require many months of advance notice for your points to be activated for use in upgrades and freebies, and many establish blackout dates during which frequent flier miles or bonus points cannot be used. You need to research this information well ahead of time so you know about any restrictions or timing delays that can turn this great opportunity into a missed opportunity.

Simplify It

A fabulous source for researching frequent flier and air mile partnership programs is www.frequentflier.com, which links you directly to all of the airlines' point programs and hotel partnership programs, plus dining and credit cards that deliver points for travel. This site is must-stop shopping, answering all of your frequent flier program questions. In addition, the Resources provides you with a complete list of Web sites for the various airlines, credit cards, hotels, and bank cards that can help you earn free flights, rooms, upgrades, and more.

Finding the Best-Priced Flights

Is Priceline.com the way to go when you want to get a steep discount on your plane fare? Some people swear by that online flight reservations site—and other people swear *at* it. Sure, these time-saving Web sites can net you a great price, but some of them do ask you to give up a lot of control over which airline you fly, when you fly, and even which city you'll fly into. If you regularly book your trips through Priceline.com and the like, check out the service thoroughly to see if you'll want to hinge your travels on decisions a site makes *for* you. Many

Honeymoon Reflections

We each travel a lot, and we've often run into situations where the airline has overbooked a plane. Passengers are then asked to voluntarily give up their seat on one flight in exchange for either an upgrade on a flight later in the day or vouchers for a free additional domestic flight at a later date. We took the airline up on this offer several times, and we were able to trade in those vouchers for future flights as our honeymoon travel freebie.

—Jessica and Henry

honeymooners keep this type of site in mind as a research step, and they may come back to it if their search through various airline Web sites doesn't turn up a better deal. The choice is yours. If you're a flexible traveler, this may be a good money-saving option for you.

If you'd like to steer clear of online flight reservation finders, then it's time to check with the airlines. You'll find an extensive list of airlines' phone numbers and Web sites in the Resources. Do some hunting around to compare and contrast quoted rates for your time of travel. Of course, a travel agent can take over this research work for you—for many couples, saving time is the true benefit of going to a quality travel agent.

During your search, check out the following options to see if you can turn up even better prices along the way:

- Flying on a Saturday, as opposed to a Sunday
- Flying on a weekday
- Flying at different times of the day: early morning, afternoon, evening, late night
- Flying into and out of a hub airport versus a smaller, alternate airport
- Using frequent flier miles for free air travel or seat upgrades
- Using airline club discounts for free air travel or seat upgrades

Don't forget that some honeymoon resort travel packages *include* airfare, so keep that in mind as you look for great airline deals. You might not have to pay for it in addition at all, even without voluntarily giving up your seat on a flight right now or cashing in all of your frequent flier miles. Just remember that you'll have to itemize such an air travel—

included deal to see if you're really getting the best bargain all around. (We'll talk more about all-inclusive packages shortly, so read on.)

Finding the Best Hotel Rates

No doubt about it, you'll have to shop around to find the resort or hotel package that offers you everything you want and need, comes with a sterling reputation and great ratings in the travel industry, and is offered at a fabulous price. Your travel agent can help you out by narrowing the field and pointing out the best deals for your time of travel, but you can help your own mission by knowing where to look for the best-priced rooms and amenities.

Penny-Wise

Consumer Reports Travel Letter (a must-read for the latest travel news) says that you can capture the greatest bargains if you book your airline tickets during the months of January through March and October through December.

Although you're free to conduct your search through the Internet, you might be surprised to find out that you can often discover the best deals by calling the hotels directly. And by directly, I mean going a step *beyond* talking to a receptionist at the hotel's 800-number reservations center. Very often these clearinghouse operators are *not* in the loop about the newest deals and bargains at, say, the Westin in Providence, Rhode Island.

Your best source, then, is to talk to the reservations specialist at the hotel itself. So ask to be connected to that hotel's own desk. Is this more time-consuming? Yes. Is it a bit of an expense to dial that 401 area code to reach the hotel? Yes. But the effort and expense can net you a much better discount when you're dealing directly with the resort. Plus you'll be able to talk to a live representative at the hotel to ask many other questions, such as which rooms have the best view (that 800-number operator wouldn't know), if the convention center is in walking distance (nope, no information at the 800-number), and if it's easy to get a taxi in that city, which would keep you from having to rent a car. Perks abound everywhere for the investment of your time.

Now let's talk about your Internet research that can lead you right to a timesaving lineup of deals and packages that meet your requests. I've listed in the Resources some of the top hotel reservation networks, so find your list of must-visit Web sites there. Many of these sites offer excellent tools for efficiency, asking you to list your requirements very specifically so the program can deliver only the options that fit your profile. And here is where shopping for your honeymoon resort is going to differ from any other time you've ever made travel arrangements over the Internet. Many sites offer special categories of room and resort options that include packages for honeymooners. You didn't even think about clicking on that icon when you were planning your business trip to Rome last year, but it's a wise move now. Go to the honeymoon sections of these sites, or click on the honeymoon categories of their regular click-and-choose section. See what they have to offer by way of freebies and discounts for honeymoon travelers. Some sites put their best deals in the honeymoon section, knowing that at least 2 million American brides and grooms are shopping specifically for honeymoon deals at any point in the year. It's just good marketing for them to put those deals where you, the bride and groom, will find them quite easily.

This is not to say that a honeymoon package is always better than a regular travel package at any resort. Indeed, it may be quite the opposite. Of course, resorts want to attract the marrying kind to their establishments, but as with anything else you'll come across during your wedding planning, some professionals will choose to offer true discounts, and others will jack up the prices of anything with the words *bridal, wedding,* or in your case, *honeymoon* attached. It's just a condition of the entire wedding industry—slap on a wedding label, and you can charge 15% more for the exact same item or package. Wedding industry experts are quite savvy about the huge bridal consumer market out there, and they are aware that some brides and grooms are able to throw caution to the wind and spend an obscene amount of money on their weddings and honeymoon trips. These carte blanche couples aren't out there looking for the best deal like you are. They hold a blank check, they're not constrained by budget, and they're ready and willing to spend twice what their honeymoon is worth without batting a high-society eye.

The entire wedding and honeymoon industry also knows that many couples just want to get their plans *over with*. They're stressed and harried. Everyone's on their back about the wedding plans, and they're insanely busy at work. Booking the honeymoon seems like an easy thing to accomplish—just check the honeymoon packages at some major resorts, pick the best-sounding one, and book it.

These two examples are of course a look at extreme ends of the spectrum. You probably would never rush through your honeymoon plans just to get it done, and you probably have to look at your budget more carefully than the anything-goes couple. I include them here to give you an idea of why you might not find the best deals attached to a "honeymoon special" label. Resort coordinators know that some people will pay anything for their honeymoon, some people's parents will splurge for their kids' honeymoon, and some people just don't take the time to research well. So they feel they can increase the costs of some of their honeymoon packages and get away with it.

Although that's the exception more than the rule, I've heard enough regret stories from recently married couples to warn you about bad deals listed as honeymoon packages.

So what does this mean to your planning? It means that you shouldn't limit yourself just to honeymoon packages and plans. Very often you can construct an equally fabulous honeymoon by booking a standard room or suite in a resort as *regular guests,* not specifically as honeymooners. Yes, I know I told you to tell everyone at the hotel, on the island, and in the country that you're on your honeymoon. Great deals can be had with that classification once you're there with those shiny new rings on your fingers. But for the sake of planning with a budget in mind, sometimes it's best to step outside the classification of honeymooner, particularly when you're building your honeymoon

Playing the Numbers Game

Always compare a honeymoon package to a regular vacation package with no H-word attached. I did so with several major resort chains and found that when you boiled it down to just the stay in the hotel, amenities, package elements like breakfasts or all meals included, and taxes and tips, I found a better-priced deal 45% of the time when I wasn't looking at the honeymoon package in a resort. Not the majority, but still enough to get you to think twice and comparison shop between both classes of stays.

piece by piece at the very beginning. Just check out regular versus honeymoon deals, and see what the numbers say for you. Is it twice the work? Yes, unfortunately so. But just as with your wedding, devoting extra time to research before booking can save you a fortune.

All-Inclusive versus A La Carte Honeymoons

Right at the start of your resort researching, you'll discover a world full of all-inclusive travel packages, honeymoon-specific or not. Everything comes at one price: transportation from the airport, a honeymoon suite or oceanfront room for X number of nights, all meals, all activities, a champagne and sunset cruise, taxes, tips, and mints on your pillow. Sounds like a fabulous deal, and in many cases it is. Just listen to this story from a couple who wished they *had* booked an all-inclusive honeymoon package:

> We knew that our resort offered all kinds of restaurants and lounges, scuba diving, jet-skiing, horseback riding, tennis—everything we wanted for our vacation. We knew these things would be pricey, but we had no idea until we got to the resort just how high the prices would be. One drink at the swim-up bar was $12. Just for one drink. Our first meal dropped our jaws at $200, and we didn't even order appetiz-

ers and dessert. It would cost us $150 to go horseback riding for an hour at sunset. If we'd thought ahead of time to ask for an itemized price list of everything we wanted to do at our resort, we would have taken their all-inclusive plan. And if we had done that, we would have spent only a few hundred dollars during the course of our trip on everything from food to activities, instead of paying thousands and having to skip a few of the day trips we wanted to take. We really wish we'd looked into that ahead of time, and my husband even got snippy with me because I hadn't thought of checking the individual price ranges. It was a nightmare and almost ruined our stay.

—Vanessa and Tim

Vanessa and Tim's example shows the importance of evaluating the all-inclusive plan offered at any resort or on any cruise. Very often, the all-inclusive arrangement can take away the hassle of worrying about money during your trip. Except for tips, you can order anything on the menu, sign up for any included activities, and not have to sweat dollar bills every time you want a drink or to enjoy a great sport or activity. All-inclusive plans *can* mean a huge savings to you *if* you plan to live it up during your trip. Take a look at the following sample breakdowns showing how two couples used an all-inclusive plan:

Mandy and Jeffrey's Week in Jamaica

Mandy and Jeffrey paid a $3,000 all-inclusive fee for their stay at a popular resort, and they put their fun-loving selves right into the heart of the action. Here is their list of what they enjoyed during their week:

- A week of lodging in an oceanfront bungalow (cash value: $1,500)
- All meals and drinks at the resort's five different eateries, room service, and drinks at the oceanside bar during the day (cash value: $1,200)
- Horseback riding (cash value: $100)

- Scuba diving lessons and two dives (cash value: $200)
- Nightclubbing at the resort's disco, bars, and late-night beach bashes (cash value: $500)
- Tennis (cash value: $40)
- A private dinner cruise with a champagne toast at sunset (cash value: $100)
- A tour cruise on a glass-bottom boat (cash value: $30)
- Massages for two (cash value: $120)
- Taxes and tips (cash value: they didn't keep track, but it was high, owing to the resort's auto-charge of 18% tip on all food service and drink tabs)

TINA AND ROB'S WEEK IN JAMAICA

Tina and Rob stayed at the same resort in Jamaica, for the same $3,000 all-inclusive fee. This couple is way more laid-back than Mandy and Jeffrey. They're not big drinkers or partiers, so their idea of a great honeymoon was a leisurely week with nothing written in pen on their calendar. Both were stressed out from the wedding plans and from trying to get all their office work done before this time of taking their wedding and honeymoon weeks off, and they truly needed some downtime at the beginning of their trip. Here's their list of what they did within that $3,000 all-inclusive plan:

- A week of lodging in an oceanfront bungalow (cash value: $1,500)
- All meals and drinks at the resort's five different eateries, room service, and drinks at the oceanside bar during the day (cash value: $600, since they didn't order too many mixed or frozen alcohol drinks)
- Scuba diving lessons and two dives (cash value: $200)
- Nightclubbing at the resort's disco, bars, and late-night beach bashes (cash value: $100, since they only did the nightlife thing on two nights of their stay)

- A private dinner cruise with a champagne toast at sunset (cash value: $100)
- Taxes and tips (cash value: high, with that 18% tip on all food service and drink tabs)

Tina and Rob clearly didn't get as much from their all-inclusive payment as did Mandy and Jeffrey, but they still loved their getaway, even if they didn't set out to squeeze activity and festivity out of every minute of their trip. For them, the vacation was exactly what they needed. I used these couples as a way to get you to analyze your own trip style. Do you want the laid-back vacation like Tina and Rob needed and enjoyed, with long unscheduled hours of relaxation and bliss with each other and some activity thrown in when they felt like it? Or is your dream honeymoon vision more like Mandy and Jeffrey's, packed with activity, sport, perhaps touring, and full freedom to eat, drink, and do whatever you want, whenever you want? Before you sign up for an all-inclusive plan, you'll need to see if you'll make the most of it . . . or if it's not a smart money move.

Here's a detailed rundown of what you might find offered in a high-quality all-inclusive honeymoon or vacation package, all choices and luxuries provided as part of your one payment and reservation:

- Round-trip airport transfers to and from the hotel
- Air-conditioned deluxe room or suite
- All meals and snacks from a variety of restaurants, clubs, bars, and room service
- 24-hour room service
- Wine or drinks with meals
- Unlimited premium brand cocktails
- Champagne dinner or oceanfront champagne sunset toast
- Satellite TV in your room
- CD player in your room
- Luxury robes in your room
- Hair dryer in your room

It's Not Just the Money…

All-inclusive plans look like a great deal, and many really are. But just keep in mind that you might not want to spend all of your time at the resort. Even if the resort has a wide range of restaurants, clubs, bars, nightclubs, and activity centers, you might want to venture off into town or into the port city for lunch or dinner several times during your stay. Factor in that expense, and see if you really will make the most of an all-inclusive plan at your resort.

- Jacuzzi in your room
- Water sports: scuba diving, jet-skiing, windsurfing, sailing, boogie boards, snorkeling, etc.
- Land sports: golf, horseback riding, volleyball, tennis, mountain biking, etc.
- Fitness center
- Full-service spa and beauty salon
- Beach towels and floats for pool or ocean
- Poolside Jacuzzis
- Au naturel or topless beach nearby
- Cruises: dinner, sunrise, touring, glass-bottom, etc.
- Daily and nightly planned activities
- Daily and nightly planned activities for children
- Dance clubs
- Piano bar
- Taxes
- Tips included, so no tipping necessary

So many options can make your head spin. But at resorts that offer such an incredibly long list of possibilities within an all-inclusive plan (such as Sandals and SuperClubs, which provided me with the preceding list), you might find that you can make the most of such a deal and actually get two to three times the honeymoon for what you're going to pay. Do the math, figure out your needs and wants, and then hold these deals to comparison scrutiny at any destination you have in mind.

All-Inclusive Resorts versus All-Inclusive Packages

You need to know the difference between an all-inclusive resort and an all-inclusive package. At an all-inclusive resort, everything's included in your plan because that's the way they do it at the resort as a whole. Everyone is on the all-inclusive plan and not carrying around their wallets to cover every drink, meal, and activity. As an example, or as a starting point for your research, here are some all-inclusive resorts to check out.

> ## Just the Facts
>
> A recent *Consumer Reports* survey says that couples save an average of 25% on their vacation when they book at an all-inclusive resort versus one in which they must pay for every meal and attraction.

Mexico (includes Cancún and Cozumel)
- Sol Melia resorts
- El Presidente resorts

Caribbean
- Sandals in the Bahamas, St. Lucia, Jamaica, and Antigua
- SuperClubs in Jamaica and Nassau
- Swept Away in Negril, Jamaica
- Beaches in the Turks and Caicos Islands and in Negril, Jamaica

Resorts that offer all-inclusive *packages* offer you the option of signing up for a full run of their luxuries and attractions, as well as the options of making regular reservations like a regular guest. Such resorts' honeymoon packages might include a minilist of perks, such as a champagne dinner, a certificate to their on-site spa, vouchers for a water sport, and massages for two.

Watch Out!

Keep an eye out for resorts that claim to be all-inclusive but actually are not quite so. I collected information on a wide range of all-inclusive resorts and found that many labeled themselves with that attractive title but actually held some items off the all-inclusive list. For instance, one resort said that all drinks were included in the plan, but on closer inspection, I found that only some types of liquors and drinks were included. If you didn't know any better and ordered drinks made with premium-brand liquors rather than house-brand, those drinks would go on your bill. Some resorts also said that scuba diving was included in the plan, but a teeny tiny asterisk next to the listing of scuba diving on their lineup said that additional expenses applied. My warning to you here: Read the fine print and find out *exactly* what is and isn't included in your plan. Don't be one of those honeymoon couples who get a big bill at the end of their stay and finds out only then that they'd been "breaking the rules" the whole time.

So many resorts offer these honeymoon packages that it would be hard to find a resort in a popular honeymoon destination that *doesn't* have some sort of package plan for your consideration. While you're looking through the various packages, whether it's at an all-inclusive resort, a standard honeymoon package, or a mix-and-match arrangement you create yourself, know that you have even *further* power over creating the honeymoon of your dreams. Some resorts that draw big honeymoon or romantic getaway crowds specify that they are adult-only destinations, where no children will be playing by the pool or building sandcastles on the beach. Some are designed as wild party resorts, and others guarantee your complete privacy with a secluded beach or cove outside your room, or even a private swimming pool *in* your room. I love the resorts in Cozumel and Cancún that have these private pools right on your room's terrace, overlooking the ocean, and offering unlimited skinny dipping potential at all hours of the night (or day, if you're so inclined). Since your honeymoon is a once-in-a-lifetime trip, you should know that many all-inclusive or hot honeymoon resorts out there have dreamed up such romantic arrangements as this for your ultimate enjoyment. And it's up to you to find the package and the enticements you have in mind.

Off-Island All-Inclusives

It's not just the island resorts that offer these all-inclusive packages. Most of the cruise lines also offer honeymoon deals, filling them with spa treatments, port call specialties like meals or a drink at a native hot spot, water sports, and flowers or champagne brought to your room. If you're among the cruising honeymooners, check each cruise line for its all-inclusive, no-worries packages—remembering to check out the regular, nonhoneymoon packages as well.

> ## Honeymoon Reflections
>
> Being at an all-inclusive resort made our honeymoon so much more special. Not because of the money we saved—which was nice, don't get me wrong—but because we never would have taken the time to sign up for windsailing if we'd had to pay for it ourselves. Since it was included, we did it. And although we were both terrible at it, we had a blast, and it made for great pictures and great memories afterward.
>
> —Theresa and Seth

On land, you're still within reach of great all-inclusives. Most of the major hotel chains offer these attractive packages, and even smaller, independent resorts also have their own versions of this arrangement. Safaris, now growing in popularity among adventure-minded honeymooners, also offer great all-inclusive deals, as do other types of trips, such as winery and culinary tours, spa vacations, and even family trips to Disneyworld. In short, there's no category that doesn't offer some sort of all-inclusive plan for your ultimate enjoyment and savings, so check out what's out there to explore.

Additional Money-Saving Tips Right from the Start

• Plan to honeymoon at a place near home. If you can drive or take the train to your destination, you'll save a fortune on airline travel and on transportation to and from the airport.

• Stay domestic. Of course, a trip to Italy or to Australia is the trip of a lifetime, but perhaps you'd rather wait until later in your lifetime for a trip of this magnitude. Especially if you're paying for your entire wedding yourselves, you can unburden your budget by planning to stay in the United States or go to a nearby island destination. Our major cities are attracting more and more honeymooners right now, with New York City leading the list of hot spots. Recent Big Apple honeymooners say that the city is kinder than ever and that its culture, shopping, and romantic restaurants make it a sure thing. Other big cities to enjoy include Chicago, Boston, Aspen, Los Angeles, San Diego, Austin, and of course, Orlando. Even better: no passports.

• Let your travel agent find the cheapest airfare for you. Sure, you can research until your fingers turn blue from punching computer keys, but a true in-the-know professional can track down the best rates as part of her job.

• Know that air travel ticket prices fluctuate constantly. Booking way in advance, then, isn't always going to get you the best rate as a rule. That's just one of the many travel misconceptions out there. I wouldn't advise waiting before you book because availability is the bigger issue, especially if you're traveling at a popular tourism time or to a popular tourism destination (or both!), but I wanted you to realize that a ticket purchased way in advance isn't always going to pay off in the end. It's all in your research, not necessarily in your timing.

• Avoid last-minute bookings. Now *these* are the deals that will probably cost you more.

• Compare flight prices at Web sites like Trip.net, Orbitz.com, Travelocity.com, and Expedia.com. *Then* go to your travel agent and see what he or she can do for you in comparison.

• Know that these online travel sites are *not* going to be there to help you in the event that your flight gets canceled. A real, live travel agent can help with that and will be your safety backup in case of problems on the road. Even better, she can find you an inexpensive alternate flight right away and even make some calls for you to get you reservations at another hotel.

• Read the fine print on cruise packages that include making arrangements for your flights. This wording means that the cruise line will find you the flight, but payment is up to you. Now do you really want some cruise line taking on the job of finding you the best flight for the best price?

• Look for fly/drive packages, which include the costs of airfare, transport or car rental, and your hotel.

• Know what's *not* included in package deals. Port charges during your cruise? Insurance for the rental car? Valet parking at the hotel? It's these little extra expenses that can surprise you during your trip and cost you way more than you planned on spending.

• Use your spine. When the hotel quotes a room price to you, ask if there are any special packages or discounts. Ask if a different class of rooms is available, if you're willing to stay in a room without an ocean view. Speak up and ask, politely, for a better deal, and you might just get it.

• See if your professional association offers travel discounts as part of their benefits plan. Expert associations exist in just about every business and industry, and they offer their members some excellent perks. If you're already a member of an association, research the benefits. They may have added some new ones since the last time you looked. If you're not a member of any association, do a bit of checking to see if it might be advantageous for you to join right now, not just for the travel deals and rental car discounts but for future networking and educational opportunities as well. Just bear in mind that it can cost a few hundred dollars to join an association, so be sure you're going to make the most from that investment during the year.

On-Site Expenses

Dinners, snacks by the pool, drinks, buying that cute little T-shirt in the gift shop—you can spend *lots* of money during your honeymoon without even realizing it. While couples who stay at all-inclusive resorts don't have to keep track of what they're spending on daiquiris at the swim-up bar or on that enormous breakfast buffet, the average couple does face a mountain of extra expenses during their stay.

If you're not on the carte blanche plan where "budgeting" is a word with no meaning to you, and if you're not planning to bring a suitcase full of cash with you on your trip, you can easily look for ways to slash your on-site spending without cutting any of the enjoyment from your trip.

This is, after all, the most important vacation of your life. You want to live it up. Now is not the time for cutting corners and living frugally, you might say. And you don't have to. This chapter is all about spending your money wisely and finding great values during your trip. You'll learn to avoid unnecessary expense and stay in control of your spending money *most* of the time so you can truly splurge on any grand gestures and romantic treats you desire the rest of the time.

Food and Drinks

• Eat lightly half of the time. Of course, you'll want to enjoy your destination's great cuisine, but you don't have to order appetizers, entrées, and desserts at every meal. Split an appetizer, skip dessert once in a while, and save a fortune while also preventing honeymoon weight gain and lethargy during your trip.

Just the Facts

The Association of Bridal Consultants recently ran a survey and found that honeymooners spend more money in and around their hotel than at any other spot at their destination. Since this is such an important trip, the survey goes on to say that couples will spend top dollar during their stay.

• Find out the price list for alcoholic mixed and frozen drinks. Some of those bright red, icy concoctions can cost you from $10 to $15 each, so look at an actual menu for specialty drinks and choose the most affordable tropical beverages.

• See if you can't tell the difference between top-shelf and house brand liquors. Ordering the second-best rum can save you a few bucks, and you're unlikely to be able to tell the difference, especially after the first two or three drinks!

• Stay away from tourist trap restaurants, where the prices are high and the food isn't spectacular. Research ahead of time to find well-rated restaurants near your resort or hotel (check the Web site lists of hotels, resorts, and city information searches in the Resources to get you started), or ask the concierge for recommendations. Many concierge desks offer their guests a look at a collection of menus from local eateries for price comparisons and cuisine selection, so take a look at that book and explore your dining options in the area. Locals might also point

> ## . . . And the View Is Free!
>
> Eat out on your terrace. If room service is too expensive, you can either bring in some food or call for a delivery to your hotel room. Create a romantic setting on that great terrace you paid to enjoy, and have a private candlelight dinner overlooking the sunset or the ocean. Lunch on the terrace is also a great idea, with some honeymooners highly recommending freshly baked bread, wonderful cheeses, fruit, and wine as an afternoon pick-me-up and a welcome break from peak sun time.

you toward the great seafood place they always go to, with no threat of inflated prices, long waiting lines, and rushed service.

• Stay away from that minibar! Snacks and sodas, spring water, and minibottles of Stoli run a high price in those convenient little refrigerators, so keep your distance. You should also know that the newest models of minibars are sensor-activated, so if you remove that Snickers bar from its place for more than 10 seconds, the minibar itself rings it up as sold. Check your minibar for this feature so you'll know not to move items to make room for soda or water bottles and snacks of your own.

• Stop in at a local grocery store, or even at the gift shop downstairs, to buy a few bottles of spring water, sodas, and juice, plus some snacks. These items, as well as bottles of wine bought in a nearby town, are going to be far less expensive, and they can be kept cold in your ice bucket or portable cooler.

• Stop in at a local liquor store or duty-free shop to buy wine and liquor to store in your hotel room. Especially on the islands, you might be able to find a very inexpensive source for your cocktails and romantic sunset toasts, and you'll save a fortune over buying each drink or bottle at the hotel.

• Order in. Many hotels allow the local pizza or sandwich delivery person to deliver directly to your room, so ask the concierge for the best takeout in town. One honeymoon couple shared the story of how they had the Pizza Hut delivery guy meet them in the lobby, and then they took their steaming, hot pepperoni pie out to poolside for a mouthwatering lunch. Other guests in the hotel were practically drooling, they said, and over the course of the next few days, many families and couples were ordering pizzas to enjoy by the pool. It was the best $20 they spent the entire trip, they said, and it also earned them some new pizza-loving friends among the resort's other honeymooners.

• Don't get the breakfast plan if you don't eat breakfast. Some hotels' modified American plans include breakfast, precharging you from $8 to $20 per person within your plan. If you don't normally eat a big breakfast, or if you doubt you'll ever wake up before noon during your trip, this is an expense you might be able to skip.

Sporting Activities

• If the sport is included in your package plan, by all means try to take advantage of the offering. You are, after all, already paying for it.

• Before signing up, be sure you're aware of all the extra expenses involved in any sporting activity. Just because it's offered through your all-inclusive package doesn't mean the entire outing is free. You might learn, a little too late, that you have to pay a nonrefundable tax or security fee for use of the scuba tank or for that surfboard. Check out hidden surcharges well before signing on the dotted line.

• Don't rent equipment if you don't have to. If you own golf clubs or a tennis racquet, bring them along. Renting sporting equipment like this can add up. The same goes for tennis balls, golf balls, golf tees, and so forth. Hotel sports shops will gladly sell these necessities to you at a steep price, so avoid the extra waste of money and pack these items ahead of time.

• Comparison shop among sporting centers. Sure, that dive shop right at your hotel is convenient, but for half the price you might be able to take scuba lessons at the next resort over or at a highly rated scuba center in town. Do a little bit of checking first to see where you can get a better value for your money.

• Don't forget about what it will cost to get to these sporting centers, piers, or even ski slopes during your trip. In some locations, expensive cab fare might convince you to take the scuba lessons in the hotel pool.

Tours and Trips

• If you'll be in Boston, Philadelphia, New York City, Seattle, San Francisco, Chicago, or Hollywood for your great getaway, you can visit from five to seven (depending on the city) of each city's most popular attractions for just one ticket. CityPass (888-330-5008, www.citypass .com) is your discount golden ticket into each city's greatest museums, aquariums, observation decks, and other big draws. At about $30 to $60 per CityPass, that's an incredible bargain when you add up existing entry fees to each of the five attractions on each city's list of possibilities.

• See if your hotel concierge has free or discounted tickets to nearby tours, wineries, shows, and other events. Very often your hotel will set a large selection of brochures by the entrance, but the real deals are with the concierge or guest services desk.

• See if free tickets to local tours and attractions are part of your all-inclusive plan. Couples frequently forget what's included in their package deal, and they naively shell out for tickets that are already free to them.

• Nothing to do on a rainy day? On five rainy days in a row? If you've already watched the best in-room movies (not a bad deal for two people to watch a first-run movie for $9.99), head out on the town to take in the latest film release in a nearby city. To make it fun, check out www.dinnerandamovie.com, which will suggest the best restaurants and movie theaters near your ZIP code. Go in the afternoon and save more with matinee tickets and lunchtime's more inexpensive menus. It's all in the timing.

Getting from Here to There

• If you're going to rent a car for use during your trip, you can save a bundle by taking some steps ahead of time:

Show your AAA or travel club card to gain a savings of from 10% to 20% off the cost of the rental or to receive free upgrades.

See if booking your rental car online can net you a bargain. (Some car rental agencies are rewarding their electronic renters additional discounts or free upgrades for doing the work themselves.)

Skip the airport car rental counters (which often charge more for their convenience) and get your rental car from a different rental agency in town that you've found through an online search of the most reputable companies.

Call your car insurance and credit card companies to see if your existing policies or cardholder benefits cover you enough to avoid buying extra collision and liability coverage with your rental. (This alone can save you from $10 to $25 each day you have the car.)

Reserve a fuel-efficient car that's no bigger than you need it to be.

Refill the gas tank before returning the car to the rental company's lot. This simple step can save you from $1 to $3 per

Save Money and Snuggle at the Same Time

Just rent one moped and take turns driving it rather than renting two of them. It's economical and it gives you cuddle time during your ride from site to site. Many honeymooners tell me they loved leaning into the turns together, with their passenger's arms wrapped around their waists.

gallon, perhaps more overseas, for what rental companies claim as their refill expenses.

• If you're not already a member, join AAA for its great discounts and free travel help with rental cars and information on your transportation needs.

• Know that it will cost you more to drop off your rental car in a city other than the one where you picked it up. See if the price differential will make it cheaper for you to just travel by train from city A to city B.

• Renting an RV for your adventure ride through the mountain states? Learn all you need to know about the best value deals and how to work that giant vehicle at Cruise America (800-327-7799, www.cruise america.com) and the Recreation Vehicle Rental Association (www .rvra.org).

• See if your hotel offers free shuttle service to bring guests into town for shopping or to special events in the area.

• Ask the concierge if the hotel has any coupons or freebies for bike rentals or boat launches that you can use. Sometimes, departing conference attendees leave behind a treasure trove of unused discount coupons and two-for-ones, so see if that nice concierge will hand out a few leftovers to make your honeymoon even more special.

• When renting bicycles or mopeds to get around the city or island, do some comparison shopping to see if you can get a better rate at a rental shop down the road rather than through your resort. At some destinations, it's just a few minutes' walk to the nearest moped rental shop and a savings of $10 to $30 for each rental.

• If you'll be taking the train from city A to city B, or country A to country B, invest in Eurailpasses (www.eurail.com) for a great transportation deal through Europe.

Communication

• Use your cell phone rather than the phone in your room. Many resorts charge exorbitant amounts for your long-distance and even local calls made through their system, so avoid these charges by using your own minutes.

• Keep a list of important phone numbers on you, such as phone numbers of your hotel's main switchboard, your concierge, a good local taxi company, and the horseback riding stable for later in your trip. Having to call Information for these numbers because of disorganization adds up to extra expenses.

• Need to check your e-mail? Don't rent a laptop from your hotel for a daily fee. Learn how to use a handheld PDA or your cell phone's Internet access and check your e-mail without paying a price.

• Bringing your laptop along? Sometimes this isn't a sign that you simply can't detach from your worklife but rather a great tool for doing research on your destination, staying in touch with kids at home, or checking up on the weather forecasts at your next destination. A great site with complete details on traveling with your fliptop friend is Laptop Travel (www.laptoptravel.com), which can provide you with important details on traveling internationally with your laptop.

• Postcards may be inexpensive, as are the stamps for the postcards, but you might prefer to send all your loved ones a great e-mail with a fabulous digital photo of the two of you when you get home. Many couples are skipping the postcards in favor of detailed e-mails because there's more space to write out their messages and it saves them a lot of time and trouble.

• Want to communicate with the locals? You could invest in a handheld computer gadget that translates words and phrases, or you could get a simple traveler's phrase book at a bookstore or at the library. Sometimes, being able to communicate well with the locals can actually save you time and money when you're able to get your request across clearly.

I Gotta Have That Tiki Doll!

• If you want that souvenir, get it! Sometimes it's the fun little trinkets and T-shirts that bring home the greatest reminders of your wonderful honeymoon. Just don't hit the gift shop when you first arrive at the resort, even if you have time to kill before checking in. Leave a little time for comparison shopping at other resorts, at shopping centers, at outside markets, and from beachside vendors. Especially if you have several family members to buy for, waiting to see the true offerings around you might net you some better catches.

• Check out the smaller, more inexpensive souvenirs. A refrigerator magnet is likely to stay a part of your home decor for far longer than that wide-rimmed sombrero, and a quirky shot glass will remain in your cupboard for years.

• Look for free souvenirs, like a perfect abalone shell from the beach, that conform to customs rules. One couple brought home fabulous, pearlized shells from their Hawaiian honeymoon and with a weekend's worth of work turned them all into shell necklaces for their nieces and sisters. The cost: $2 for a spool of necklace string.

Just the Facts

According to the Association of Bridal Consultants, 74% of honeymooners regularly use travelers' checks during their big trip, and 86% use credit cards as their main payment method. Try to stay within a spending budget as best you can, and plan to pay off those balances when you return home.

• Shopping can also mean looking for a ladies' shaver when you forgot to pack one. At the hotel gift shop, that one Lady Bic might cost the same as four or five back home. Pack well, paying special attention to morning-of-travel toiletries you'll be packing at the last minute so you don't have to buy any necessities in the gift shop or on the local economy.

• Pack way more film than you'll need. Hotel gift shops charge a fortune for those little rolls of camera film, as well as batteries to run your camera. Get both in bulk or on sale before your trip, and save leftovers to use in the future.

Get Your Hands on Your Cash

• If you'd rather not use your credit card for all of your purchases but you need some extra cash, find out where the nearest ATM machine is by calling Cirrus at 800-307-7309 or Plus at 800-843-7587.

• Using travelers' checks or plastic is much safer than carrying around a roll of cash, so think ahead about your credit card limits and budget for impulse spending during your trip.

When *Not* to Pinch Pennies or Pesos

• Your honeymoon should be filled with extravagances, grand gestures, and as many activities and special events as you care to enjoy.

Spare no expense on these important elements of your trip, but find a balance in your everyday spending. Like on any other trip, there are plenty of ways to get more trip for less money, and your honeymoon is no exemption from all the cost-cutting opportunities.

Many of the honeymooners I counseled before their trips said they were glad they took my advice about splurging on only half their meals and eating lightly at others. They were able to enjoy some true indulgences: fabulous five-course meals, champagne toasts, and crème brûlée at midnight. They took sunset dinner cruises, reserved secluded beaches for a fantasy afternoon, took helicopter rides across the canopied treetops of rainforests. But they didn't blow their spending money because they balanced out their purchases throughout their trip, like eating a pizza at poolside and drinking hydrating ice water with a bright curl of lemon between every other piña colada.

There's something to be said about smart spending habits, but there's also something to be said about giving yourself permission to treat yourself on your honeymoon. So don't rip yourself off and regret your decisions for years down the road. Don't pinch pennies while you're on your trip. That's as large a problem as going way overboard with your spending and maxing out your cards before it's time to check out of the hotel (which has happened to several couples I've heard from). Just look for reasonable deals along the way, and enjoy the freedom you've given yourself to splurge on the special elements that mean the most to you.

Tipping

If you're a great tipper right at the start of your honeymoon, you'll be treated like gold by the service professionals (waiters, bartenders, doormen), who will meet your every need with a smile during your stay. This is no place to scrimp, and it is not a time to insult the bartender with a measly mound of change at the swim-up bar. So many couples tell me that they received fabulous service from their waiters and concierge when they tipped an impressive amount from the first day of their stay, and as such they were granted special favors and no-wait service that made their vacation a joy.

Following is a general guide to the going rates for tips, but I encourage you to tip above and beyond these figures when the service is especially good. Before you cash out a $100 bill into singles for tips during your vacation, find out ahead of time if you'll be staying at an all-inclusive that does not allow tipping. Some resorts encourage you to leave your wallet in the hotel safe because the tips are already included in your package. Know this ahead of time so you're not double-tipping.

The Honeymoon Tip Sheet

Airport skycap: $1 per bag, $2+ for extra-heavy bags.

Bartender: 15% to 20% of bar tab; $1 to $2 per individual drink ordered, slightly more if you've ordered a complicated drink to make, not just a beer or wine.

Concierge: When the concierge helps you find dinner reservations or show tickets, a general tip of $5 to $10 is an appropriate thank-you. If you expect to use the concierge's services several times during your stay, tip him well the first time ($20+) and get ready for the royal treatment throughout your honeymoon.

Doorman: $1 to $2 for getting you a taxi; $3 to $5 if he helps with your bags.

Helpful native: For giving you great directions or saving the day when you're helplessly lost and without access to a phone, a helpful native should receive a small monetary or item gift.

Hotel bellhop: $2 to $3 per bag. Be extra generous if you have many bags or heavy luggage, or if he brings your suitcases to your room.

Housekeeping staff: $3 to $5 per night for the maid, slightly more if you're enjoying an extended stay; $5 tip when housekeeping brings you extra towels or pillows you've requested. (Note: You should leave a tip for the maid every night, not just an amount at the end of your stay. This way, the maid who cleans your room to spotless perfection on Monday through Thursday of your stay gets her just rewards, while the "weekend maid" is paid only for her Friday and Saturday work, not for her work as well as for that wonderful weekday maid's time and labor.)

Musical artists: $5 to $10 for a street artist's or restaurant musician's serenade.

Parking attendant: $1 to $3 each time they retrieve your car.

Taxi driver: 15% of your fare, more if he helps you with your bags.

Tour guide: $5 to $10 optional tip for already-paid-for tours, if the guide was exceptionally helpful, knowledgeable, or entertaining.

Train station porter: $1 per bag, $2+ for extra heavy bags.

Waiters: 15% to 20% of your bill is standard. (Note: Many hotels and restaurants automatically add on a generous 18% to 21% tip for waitstaff, so read your room service bill and restaurant bills well to avoid tipping an *additional* 15% on top of that.)

> ## Simplify It
>
> A great travel guidebook for your location will enlighten you about tipping customs in the country you're visiting, letting you know if tipping is even done at all in that country or on that island. In some lands, tipping is socially unacceptable, but the taxi driver will accept a small gift.

Tipping Overseas

If your honeymoon is taking you to a foreign land or island where international currency is used, you'll need a solid working knowledge of that currency in order to tip well. A good currency converter calculator can make your job of handing out lira quite easy, as can a simple written-down equation that will help you figure out how many lira are appropriate as a tip for your taxi driver. International travelers tell me that tipping was a tough job, since they were so afraid of over-tipping or, much worse, undertipping a kind waiter or bellhop when they had no clue about the local currency exchange rate. Avoid any insult to the locals, then, by educating yourself to international money rates and tipping customs where you will be traveling.

In some regions, an automatic 10% service charge might be added to all of your bills, tabs, and checks. This doesn't mean that the establishment has set a 10% tip for you and you're free from any further gratuity. If the service was great, your waiter kind and attentive, or your bartender patient about making a drink he or she has never heard of before, add on an extra amount of money to bring that 10% closer to a generous 15% or higher. If, however, the waiter snubbed you all night and the bartender gave you a death look when you asked for a glass of ice, then leave the tip at that automatic 10%. Tipping is all about rewarding good service, after all.

Smart Packing to Save Money

So what's going in *your* luggage? Pack too much and you're likely to slip a disc hefting those suitcases around. Pack too little and you could wind up shelling out big bucks at the hotel gift shop, where a single-dose packet of Advil runs for no less than $5. Or, even worse, you could be stuck trying on highly unflattering replacement bathing suits in that gift shop because you left all your stylish and sexy one-pieces at home. Smart packing can make your honeymoon so much more enjoyable and so much less expensive. This chapter shows you how to further organize your packing list so you don't forget anything important and so you choose the right number, size, and quality of luggage and carry-on bags. Also, learn from the experts which fun travel gadgets you need.

Get Ready to Pack Your Bags

Before you start making your list and checking it twice, you'll need to start with the very basics. Do you have good luggage? "Even if they've traveled often throughout their lives, there's one thing that honey-mooners seem to invest in more and more," says Laurie Borman, who is an editorial director at the travel-based company Rand McNally (www.randmcnally.com). "This is when couples invest in really good, solid-quality luggage they'll use for many years to come."

I highly recommend luggage as a featured registry item, since that's a fabulous group gift option from your bridal party. Splitting the costs, it's an affordable choice for them, and you'll get great use from it in the future.

There are so many reasons to look into getting great new luggage and carry-on bags for this trip and forever after. And I'm not just talking about having matching his and hers sets (although you could if you wanted to!). Today, the airline industry has levied some serious restrictions on luggage and carry-on numbers and sizes. Most airlines allow you to bring only one carry-on and one separate purse or personal item apiece, and these must conform to set measurements. At the time of this writing, for example, United Airlines posts that the allowable measurement for carry-ons is 9 inches by 14 inches by 22 inches, and purses must measure under 25 inches all the way around. These aren't the days anymore where these rules were stretchy and bendable; at many airline security screening checkpoints, you'll find premeasured plastic screens set up at the X-ray machines. If your bag doesn't fit through the screen area, you'll have to go back and officially check your carry-ons that are too large. It's precisely these size and weight measures that could send you packing (get it?) to the luggage store to buy a new set of regulation bags.

Another reason to get great new luggage is the improved designs out there. I spoke at great length with Laurie Borman from Rand

Simplify It

You can check each individual airline's Web site for its most current size and weight restrictions for both luggage and carry-ons. And keep these rules as golden for your own trip's ease and convenience. Check again a few days before you depart to be sure the same regulations are in force.

McNally, and she suggested the following guidelines for smart luggage shopping:

• Be willing to spend some extra money for a really high-quality set of luggage from a reputable company. Better-made bags are sturdier, are safer, and come with great compartments for efficient packing. One model she suggests, as found among the many top-notch choices at www.randmcnally.com, is the Eagle Creek expandable bag.

• Be sure to choose a model with a sturdy, expandable zipper. Today's best luggage models allow for a good amount of give at the zippers, providing even more room for your return-trip goodies and extra strength in the bag's ability to hold all of your things securely. In contrast, hard-sided suitcases with clasp locks instead of well-made zipper lines aren't quite as giving or forgiving when it's time to close and lock them.

• Look for luggage that has a good set of wheels, for obvious reasons.

• Look for luggage that features a pull-out handle that twists. The new designs allow handles to work with your movements as you walk, preventing your bag from tipping over all the time behind you or being harder to maneuver through airports and crowds.

Simplify It

To find companies that feature great luggage pieces, carry-ons, and backpacks, look in the Resources for a lengthy list of great travel gear Web sites.

• Look for luggage with aluminum and titanium frames (which make them much lighter in weight and easier on your neck, back, and shoulders), plus tough nylon pack cloth.

If you'll also be shopping for new and improved carry-on bags, look for those bags that will fit size and weight standards for travel (obviously) but also offer you all the nooks and crannies and special features you'll need for more efficient packing. In some cases, these well-designed bags allow you to get more stuff into a smaller-sized tote, making those size restrictions not matter so much anymore. Most travelers recommend styles of carry-ons that offer great slots and compartments for laptops, cell phones, water bottles, and pens, as well as zippered inside pockets for safekeeping of itineraries, birth certificates, cell phones, or passports.

Choose a model with a wide shoulder strap as well, since that can make carrying a heavier bag a little easier. For example, latch on the Human Curve Strap. Sounds like a sex toy, but it's really a wonderful new carry-on or bag strap that's wide, extra-cushioned, non-slip, and very sturdy (www.nationalgeographic.com).

Additional bags you might need include garment bags for your suits and dresses, backpacks for your adventurous outings or moped rides across the island, or beach totes to hold your sunscreen and trashy summer beach reading. What about those fanny packs that fasten around your waist? While some people do use these during their travels, devious criminals and little street urchins have targeted these types of bags for thievery. If the waist bag has no lock on the zipper, that's an easy unzip-and-grab while you're being distracted or bumped by an expert pickpocket's partner in crime. Some robbers even cut the bottom of the waist bag so your items will just slip right out into their greedy little hands. They're so good and so quick at it, especially if you're wearing the pouch to the back, you won't even notice. A far better option, according to travel experts I spoke to, is a new, slim

Professionally Speaking

When you're out shopping for carry-ons and travel bags, look for a hanging toiletry bag. This great, foldout organizer has compartments for all your makeup and get-ready gear, and it has a slip-out hanger that allows you to suspend it from a hook or from a shower bar. Since many hotels have limited counter space in the bathroom (some in foreign countries have no counter space above pedestal sinks), you can keep organized by hanging your toiletry kit for easy access in one easy step. No unpacking of all those little bottles, jars, wands, and accessories needed.

—Laurie Borman, editorial director at Rand McNally

pouch worn under the jacket or under the shirt. Check the pictures and descriptions at www.containerstore.com and www.randmcnally .com for a better look at these great little items.

You're not done with bags yet! Be sure to pack an empty duffel bag in your luggage for use on your return trip. If you're planning to do a lot of shopping during your travels, whether for clothing or for souvenirs for your loved ones back home, this bag is at the ready, waiting to be filled with all your loot and checked with the rest of your luggage for the flight home.

Tags for Your Bags

Be sure you have attached high-quality identification tags on *all* your luggage and carry-on bags. For your own protection, choose ID tags that obscure your personal information (like your address) from any potential thieves who might use that information to target you for crime. The new lines of ID tags do come with safety in mind, and you may even find them in fluorescent colors or patterns for easier or immediate identification on that slow-moving luggage carousel. Another tip for quickly spotting your luggage is to fasten a brightly colored, thick elastic luggage band around your bag. Not only does this announce your luggage's approach from far away, but it can also help prevent another traveler from accidentally picking up your standard black travel suitcase that resembles his or her own.

Remember, too, that having an identification tag on the outside of your luggage is not enough to ensure that your bag reaches you. For optimum protection, pack *inside each suitcase* an index card on which you've written your name, your hotel name, and the hotel phone number and/or your cell phone number. Include your itinerary so the airline can find you even a few days into your trip. Baggage handlers tell me that rough handling can sometimes knock poorly attached ID tags right off suitcase handles, so if you skip this step, that tag-free bag is sent right to luggage purgatory, leaving you empty-handed at baggage claims and for the first days of your trip.

And since we're talking about luggage safety, check out the new class of luggage locks at www.worldtraveler.com, www.sharperimage .com, and www.randmcnally.com. At these sites you'll find standard key-in-lock models, number combination locks that eliminate the need for those tiny little keys, and other newfangled latches that will keep your gear more secure.

General Packing Rules

• Pack lightly! Bringing way too many outfits is a space waster and a backbreaker. So this means being organized and bringing only what you'll really need.

• Think of the climate when you're packing. Be prepared for cooler nights or seasonable rainstorms even at the warmest destinations, and pack the right jackets or sweaters for the weather you'll be facing.

• Choose color coordinates that allow you to build several great outfits from just a few basics plus accessories. Also, keeping your clothing in one or two color families means you can get by with bringing fewer pairs of shoes! But be sure to add some color to those outfits—dressing purely in black or white isn't the great effect in photos that a beautiful rose-colored dress would be.

• Bring washable items, like knits that fold and pose no wrinkling threats. Bring along a pair of jeans, even though they take up extra room. Especially if you'll be riding horses on the ocean's edge at sunset, you'll be very happy you brought the thigh-protecting jeans.

• When packing, put smaller items, socks, and even snag-threatening hairbrushes inside shoes.

• Add a few empty resealable plastic bags to your suitcase, in case any of your bathing suits are still wet when it's time to pack for home.

• Find out what you won't need to bring. Call the hotel's front desk and ask if they supply hair dryers in their rooms, robes, irons, and other basics that you will then not have to lug along with you.

• If you're cruising or taking an adventure or active tour as your honeymoon, the cruise line or company might provide you with a list of recommended packing items (such as for a mandatory dress-up night with formal attire or even a list of important camping gear for those adventure treks). Ask the tour director if such a list is available to you.

• Don't overload your luggage! Overpacking is a big, big mistake, and not just because of how much your gear weighs. If your suitcase's zipper bursts during your travels—or especially when airline handlers are tossing your bag around on the tarmac—you may lose valuable items or find your suitcase gliding along the luggage carousel as an open box of overflowing and strewn objects.

• Share toiletries where you can. There's no need to bring two bottles of shampoo, two cans of shaving cream, and so forth.

• A must-have is the most recent touring guidebook available for the state, island, country, or region you're visiting. Travel agents tell me that even year-old travel books get out of date. Restaurants close or change

Professionally Speaking

In the last few days before the wedding, there are a lot of last-minute details, arriving in-laws and guests, and so on. But don't forget to spend time planning what you'll wear on your honeymoon and packing what you'll need. If packing becomes an afterthought, you'll set yourselves up for (1) overpacking, thinking you'll need everything in your wardrobe; (2) forgetful packing, not bringing the essentials and then incurring extra expenses when you have to buy them on your trip; and (3) unnecessary stress, making packing an unpleasant task when the details get out of hand. Remember, your honeymoon is the time to start making memories of your new life together. A little preparation now will ensure that you spend your time enjoying your honeymoon!

–Elaine Luce, travel expert and spokesperson
The Container Store
www.containerstore.com

menus, local attractions have now become the site of a new WalMart, and even highway exits and road names change in just a short amount of time. "In the last two years alone, many exit numbers have changed in Florida, Georgia, Pennsylvania, and other states," says Laurie Borman from Rand McNally.

• If you'll be bringing along your golf clubs, skis, snowboard, tennis racket, or other big items, call the airline to ask if special travel containers are provided to hold and protect this gear. Many airlines offer the use of these tubes and carriers for free.

• Finally, bring your complete packing list with you on your trip so when it's time to pack back up and head for home, you're less likely to forget any items in your hotel room or on your balcony.

Carry It with You: What Goes in Your Carry-On

Luggage can sometimes wander off into the friendly skies on its own little misadventure, leaving you at your destination's airport with a shocked look on your face and only what's in your carry-on bag. Smart travelers prepare for the worst and pack a few extra must-haves in their smaller, take-along bag just in case they'll have to wait a few hours (or days) for their lost luggage to be delivered to their hotel. Here's what to put in your carry-on so you won't miss a moment of fun if your luggage is lost:

❏ One of your bathing suits

❏ A sarong or light cover-up

❏ A pair of flip-flops or beach shoes

❏ One change of clothing, in case of longer waits (be sure the outfit you pack goes with whatever footwear you have on that day)

❏ A spare set of underwear

Stressbuster

When I'm flying, I like to bring a little roll-on tube of lavender-scented oil. Lavender is very relaxing, especially if you're a nervous flier and vodka isn't your calm-down answer. Also, the roll-on applicator is more considerate of your fellow travelers than a spritzer.

- ❏ Your toothbrush and a small tube of toothpaste
- ❏ Breath mints
- ❏ Hand wipes
- ❏ Moisturizer lotion
- ❏ Makeup items (eyeliner, powder, and lip gloss for touch-ups)
- ❏ Pain relievers
- ❏ Tissues
- ❏ A comb or travel brush
- ❏ A travel pillow
- ❏ Travel eye-shades
- ❏ Your birth control items (Who would want to be left without these?!)
- ❏ Extra feminine protection products, just in case
- ❏ Medical supplies, such as asthma inhalers and insulin kits
- ❏ Cameras, including video cameras
- ❏ PDAs
- ❏ Laptops
- ❏ CD players
- ❏ Handheld video games
- ❏ Other breakables or valuable items

What Stays with You

Certain things need to stay on your person, in your purse, or in a secure safety travel pouch worn under your jacket or at your waist. These are the must-haves that stay with you at all times:

- ❏ Your wallet
- ❏ Your passport
- ❏ Travel visas
- ❏ Travel itinerary
- ❏ Marriage license
- ❏ Birth certificates
- ❏ Credit cards
- ❏ Travelers' checks
- ❏ Health insurance cards
- ❏ Driver's license
- ❏ Auto insurance card
- ❏ Traveler's club card (like AAA or Disney rewards cards)
- ❏ Cash and foreign currency
- ❏ Prescriptions
- ❏ Key phone numbers and contact information
- ❏ Your cell phone
- ❏ Your car and house keys
- ❏ Other valuables that would devastate you if they were lost
- ❏ Any special travel coupons you plan to use during your trip

Wrinkle-Free Packing Tips

• If you're bringing dresses or button-down shirts, have them professionally cleaned, pressed, and slipped into plastic dry cleaner bags. Then just lay those plastic-covered outfits into your suitcase for a better chance of avoiding wrinkles.

Better Off in Your Luggage?

The jury's out on whether or not it's better to pack your liquid toiletries (shampoo, conditioner, lotion, perfume, nail polish remover, etc.) in your carry-on bag or stow them in your luggage. Logic says that it would be better to pack all of your liquid toiletries in your carry-on bag, but that may not be the best place for these items. Lots of airlines do not allow you to bring liquids on board for safety's sake, plus the air pressure in high-flying planes can wreak havoc on some types of containers. So seal up your travel bottles of liquid beauty products well, using leakproof bottles from Nalgene (a favorite brand among flight attendants). For further protection, put these in a *double-ply plastic bag* sealed at the top, and stow the bag in your suitcase in a zippered or meshed compartment separate from your clothes. Now that you can only bring one carry-on per person onto planes, you might have to send your toiletries in your suitcase. The choice of your space usage is up to you.

• Another frequent-traveler wrinkle-busting secret: Lay a thin sheet of tissue paper between each item of clothing, and pack all items snugly in an appropriately sized bag. When your items shift during transit, the tissue paper keeps fabric from bringing other outfits into wrinkle positions with them.

• Seriously consider investing in travel organizing kits, such as the Pack-It organizer products at www.containerstore.com. This line has fabulous folder systems for packing shirts, skirts, blazers, and pants; packing cubes for organizing socks, underwear, and accessories; sacs that will hold your shoes; and the vacuum-sealable Pack-Mates that give you 75% more space in your luggage by removing excess air from each bag or container.

• Practice rolling T-shirts and other clothing into tight circular bundles to keep them in shape and less wrinkle-prone.

Simplify It

Can't tell which travel organizer items you need, how many to get, or how to pack unusual objects in your bags? Get some advice from a packing professional—for free!— by contacting The Container Store's Customer Solutions Department at 800-786-7315 or through www .containerstore.com.

• Pack a travel-sized clothing steamer to get out any noticeable creases or wrinkles in fabrics or jackets.

• Pack shoes at what will be the bottom of your bag when you lift the bag upright onto its wheels. Having that weight at the bottom of the luggage means your clothing won't get "stomped" throughout your travels.

• As soon as you get into your hotel room, unpack completely, hanging up your dresses and other wrinkle-prone items, filling dresser drawers with your additional clothing (refolding T-shirts and shorts well if you have to), and setting out all other items where needed. Valuables like cameras and jewelry go right in the hotel room safe, for good measure.

In Your Luggage

You've just read a lineup of smart packing tips to make your bags lighter and more organized and to keep your items wrinkle-free, leakproof, and in one piece. Now it's time for you to get specific about what you'll bring along with you. In Appendix 7 at the back of this book, you'll find detailed packing checklists with special categories of must-haves for any type of honeymoon you have in mind. I hope you'll use these checklists to plan out your own packing lists specific to your honeymoon, then tear them out and bring them with you as a handy reminder to *repack* everything you brought with you at the end of your trip. Do the same with the carry-on packing list on page 254 as an extra reminder of the important items that should travel with you on the way home.

It's the Little Things That Make Travel Easier

Sometimes it's the little extra gadgets you pack, and the online services you find, that can make a trip more enjoyable. These are a few of my favorite things for traveling:

- Folding travel minisize umbrella.

- Alarm clock that keeps track of which time zone you're in by setting itself to the right time and keeping track of daylight saving time switches. One to check out is the ExactSet Travel Alarm Clock, www.oregonscientific.com, less than $60 at the time of this writing.

- White-noise player. This great little gadget will help you sleep, as its sounds of light rain falling or gently lapping ocean waves will ease you into a deep slumber or a relaxed state of mind. Frequent travelers tote this godsend along on their trips, saying that it blocks out noisy traffic outside, sounds within the hotel itself, and brain buzz from your stimulating daily adventures. Two to check out: The Sharper Image's Travel Soother, which is compact and runs on four AA batteries, and The Sharper Image's Sound Soother, which is a bit larger but also provides a radio, a CD player, a thermometer, a barometer, and other handy tools (www.sharperimage.com). If these gadgets are too pricey for you, stick with the sound of the room's air conditioner for your white noise.

- Noise-reduction headphones. This one is new to me, but it sounds like an amazing thing. You pop on Bose QuietComfort headphones, and the microphones within the earpieces come very close to eliminating most outside noise. If you don't want the soundwave suppressor, then use the headphones to plug into the airplane's armrest sound system.

- Spillproof travel toiletry bottles. Check out the line of Nalgene travel bottles at www.containerstore.com. These top-of-the-line bottles hold up well to airline travel altitude pressure and are a favorite choice of airline attendants. Tip from the attendants: Label each bottle to avoid mixing up your hand lotions with your hair conditioner.

• Well-padded makeup bags. Especially if your bags will be packed tightly, these can protect your eyeliners from snapping and your compact mirror from shattering. Who wants to start a honeymoon off with seven years of back luck?

• Currency organizers. If you'd like to keep your American currency separate from your francs, or if you'll be visiting several different countries with several different types of coins or bills, then invest in a great currency organizer (available at www.containerstore.com), which features several pockets and color-coded zippers to keep everything easy to find. Later on, you can use this organizer for your business travel needs.

• E-ticket organizer. Also from The Container Store, this handy organizer will store your e-tickets, rental car confirmations and coupons, passports, and other tickets or IDs you'll need easy access to.

• Travel candles (for those romantic shared bubble baths). With their safe, metal containers and secure lids, these travel candles are easy to carry along and easy for peace of mind. Check out the many scents and sizes from Aveda (www.aveda.com), The Body Shop (www.the-body-shop.com), and Illuminations (www.illuminations.com).

• Aromatherapy spritz bottles for your hotel room.

• Air freshener minispray for your bathroom.

• A roll (or two or three) of good toilet paper in your suitcase if you're traveling to a rustic or underdeveloped area.

• TeleAdapt (www.teleadaptusa.com), a PDA- or laptop-saving Web site that will explain the varying voltages around the world so you'll know where it's safe to plug in your cell phone, PDA charger, or laptop. This site also provides you with free, 24-hour e-mail assistance to help you figure out the how-tos for where you are, along with instructions for getting your handheld PDA to function despite those foreign dial tones. (If you're traveling without handheld Internet-connect gadgets, you can still access the Internet. Just go to www.net cafeguide.com for a list of more than 3,000 Internet cafés where you can log on in some 150 different countries!)

• Download reading material and travel information on your handheld PDA at www.memoware.com, or go with RCA's REB1100 eBook, which allows you to read (on its screen) the novel of your choice from the many its powerful memory can provide.

• Portable DVD players. Especially if you have kids traveling with you, it's handy to pop in a movie at a moment's notice.

• Cars that tell you where to go! If you rent an Infiniti i30, QX4, or Q45, you can use its built-in computer to find your way through city streets and countrysides, and you can even see the view of the road you're on from overhead. The car acts as your tour guide, scrolling down lists of notable sites you're now driving past.

• Want to listen to the radio while in the car? Finding a good radio station overseas can be tough without some help, so log on to www.tvradioworld.com or www.mikesradioworld.com, which are the best locators of overseas stations playing your favorite rock, classical, oldies, or jazz music.

• Panoramic and underwater one-time-use cameras. I love these little cameras for the interesting shots they allow you to take. What better way to catch your scuba adventure on film or that breathtaking view from the top of a volcano than with a wide-angle panoramic camera?

• Pocket city language guides. If you're not the techno-type, *Fodor's to Go* magnet guidebooks (www.fodors.com or www.amazon.com) will give you all the phrases and wording you need to know to get around town and find your way back with all of your shopping complete.

• The Swiss Army knife. You won't be able to take it on board with you in a carry-on, so ask your airline where it's best to stow such an essential travel tool.

- A locking jewelry case from www.nationalgeographic.com.

- Special surprise gifts that you give to your new spouse through-out the trip (see chapter 17).

Ready to shop for your great travel gear? Check the Resources to find out where the best buys and best luxury items can be found. If you're disappointed that I haven't talked much about cameras and video camera equipment here, then I have good news for you! All of chapter 18 is devoted to your picture-taking pleasures.

PART V

How to Make Your Honeymoon Sizzle!

Romantic Gestures

Candlelight dinners . . . champagne toasts . . . rose petals on the bed . . . waking up in each other's arms at 11 in the morning and not getting out of bed until 2 in the afternoon. A fabulous honeymoon is filled with these kinds of romantic moments, since this is you starting off your married life in idyllic surroundings with nothing on your to-do list but to love one another and enjoy each other's company. For many, this is *the* most purely romantic time of their lives, and it may be so for you. If you're lucky, neither of you need my ideas on how to make your honeymoon romantic. You already shower each other with affection and reminders that you're each adored. Your fiancé already creates fantastic dates for you, and you return the favor with love notes in his briefcase. If you're like the rest of us, daily life and work stresses crowd out some opportunities for romance, and the ideas that follow might just work well in your honeymoon plans. So read this chapter together, get those ideas flowing, and remind yourself that your honeymooner status welcomes complete spoiling of one another during your time away. This is, after all, the very beginning of your married life. Start it off with pure romance.

Using the Location's Most Romantic Elements

Like most couples, part of your decision about where you should go on your honeymoon hinged on the location's potential for romance, great scenery, balmy breezes, breathtaking sunsets, or handheld strolls through bistro-lined city streets. Some of the most popular destinations in the world encompass all the stereotypical romantic environments, so you've undoubtedly placed yourself where everything around you sets the mood for your most romantic fantasies. Here are some ways to use your site's most attractive romantic qualities to make a regular day into one of your most romantic experiences on the trip:

• See if your resort will plan for a single formal dinner table set up at sunset on the beach, where you'll be served by your own private waiter. As the sun sets, shimmering over the purple and blue waters on the horizon, lift your champagne flutes and toast your future together.

• Take a private dinner cruise on a well-appointed yacht, and make that tropical coastline a part of your scenery as well as that sunset.

• Kiss and cuddle under the cascades of a natural waterfall.

• Swim in a private underground cavern lake, which you've reserved for your own personal use.

• Stop at a scenic overlook during your adventurous bike tours, and look out at the vast mountainous landscape before you.

• Take advantage of clear skies in the desert or on mountaintops to see the magical nighttime display of constellations and shooting stars as you never have before.

• Be on the lookout for rainbows after a brief summer rain shower. These are especially common above or near waterfalls (where some of my honeymooning couples report seeing double or triple rainbows at once) or over the ocean in a wide-ranging arc of color.

• Take your romance under water. While scuba diving or snorkeling, hold hands, twirl one another in a deep sea dance, and let the schools of fish try to figure out what species *you* are.

• Research for little-known romantic spots, such as a private gondola ride or tubing trip through a maze of sea tunnels to emerge in an underground cavern with walls that sparkle with embedded crystals and gemstones. It's like being at the center of a geodome in a soft glow of romantic lighting that very few people will ever see.

• Find out about nature conservatories, which offer up elements of romance when you find yourself delighting your way through a butterfly conservatory or a wild animal park. Honeymooners tell me that it's this kind of day trip that is surprisingly romantic, with nature opening up a whole new arena of romance.

• Add some heartstrings to your dinners out. Spontaneously slow dance by your table, at a piano bar, or on a wharf overlooking a lineup of impossibly gorgeous private yachts.

• Go skinny-dipping or night swimming in that crystal azure water that looks even more inviting than it did in the brochure (but pay attention to any safety postings regarding shark or Portuguese

Honeymoon Reflections

We did a little checking to see which of the local hotels in New Orleans had well-known resident ghosts who roamed the halls and staterooms looking for a lost love. We adore the supernatural, so it was so romantic to us to actually tour these supposedly haunted places and even stay in a stateroom where one particular apparition was known to leave the scent of roses in the room for honeymooners. Unless the ghost forgot to put the toilet seat down in the morning, we weren't visited, but it still made for an exciting, romantically charged experience.

—Janie and Paul

man-of-war sightings—for this one, you're taking all the risks on yourselves).

• Find out the romantic history of your location. In Bermuda, for instance, you'll see many tall circular stone moon gates that are often set up to overlook the ocean. Legend, in its many variations, says that it's great luck for newlyweds to kiss under a moon gate for eternal luck and happiness. In big cities, find out from the tourism board where the most romantic eateries and the most historically romantic spots are, like where they filmed a romantic part of a movie.

• Take the concierge up on recommended romantic tours, whether they're steamer trips past historical estate homes on the river, the spots where literary greats penned their eternal sonnets to the great loves of their lives, five-course gourmet meals at the top romantic eateries in town, or even a horse-drawn carriage ride for a touristy but still memorable trip across town.

• Ride horses on the beach at sunset. Even if it's at a beginner's pace and not a wind-in-your-hair gallop like in a perfume commercial, it's still really romantic.

• Rent one moped instead of two, and hang on tight for a close-contact ride.

• Follow your senses. What could be more romantic than walking down a cobblestone path lined with fragrant gardenias, delicate lilies of the valley, and birds-of-paradise. The air is scented and charged with a pure level of aroma that you will never forget, and even just a walk across the hotel grounds to the dinner buffet becomes a few steps through heaven.

• Stuck in your room on a rainy day? Take the example of that well-known camera commercial and go out and splash in the puddles, taking the waterproof camera with you.

• Reserve a secluded beach area and reenact that scene from *From Here to Eternity* as you roll around on the beach with a light surf crashing around you and rolling up to wash over your legs and bodies. Or reserve that private beach—even if you have to row out to it—for a private picnic, a romantic swim, or a playful romp on the beach with no one else the wiser.

• Biking through vineyards in Napa or Provence? Take a break from pedaling and stop off to breathe in the lush and fertile air. Ask a field manager if you can wander through the vineyards and sample a few grapes or figs right from the trees. One couple tells me that this spontaneous walk through immaculate vineyards transported them to what their grandparents must have lived like on their own vineyards in wine country in the Old World. The couple picnicked on the grounds, in the shade of an old fig tree, relaxing and absorbing the scenery and scents around them, before biking off into the rest of their adventures.

• If your resort has spa amenities, sign right up. The environment at a great spa, or at a resort with spa offerings, is meticulously planned to relax your every nerve ending, fill your senses, and set your bodily and spiritual tone for the rest of your trip. If one of you is not the mudbath and seaweed wrap type, then bestow upon your new spouse an afternoon of pampering, or look into a muscle-melting massage or hot rock therapy that suits your spa-going style. (Like the spa treatments idea but not planning to visit a spa resort? Check out chapter 10, "Spa Honeymoons," for ideas to borrow for your own honeymoon trip.)

• Get a massage outdoors. Some resorts bring you right out to a waterfall or a flower-strewn gazebo, a beachside oasis or a tented rainforest retreat for your massage out in the elements. At Negril in Jamaica, you can schedule your couples' massages to take place on the beach right at sunset.

• Take a romantic gondola ride through the canals of Venice, Amsterdam, or even American cities like Providence, Rhode Island, that offer the same ultracuddly option.

• Take a romantic plunge. Hold hands and jump from a divers' point right into the ocean. Make sure someone gets a picture of that!

Creating a Romantic Atmosphere

No doubt you'll be spending some time in your hotel room or cruise ship cabin, and as well decorated and cozy as the room may be, there are definite steps you can take to make your home-for-now environment even more romantic:

• Book a room that's all about romance. Choose a suite that opens up to a beautiful view of the ocean and features a private pool out on the terrace, a Jacuzzi on the deck, a canopied bed, great decor, and even your own garden terrace with fragrant island flowers and tropical birds that come right to your ledge.

• Bring in cut flowers from your trips through the street markets, and ask housekeeping to deliver several vases from their ballroom supplies. Set those floral centerpieces around your room, next to the bed, and even in the bathroom for a luxurious atmosphere at a low cost.

• Set scented travel candles around the room, and light them for even greater ambience in the evenings.

• If possible, switch the hotel's bright white-light lamp lightbulbs with ones in a soft pink or gently hued tone. This simple lighting trick sets the mood for love, and most couples say they like how their bodies look in such flattering lighting.

• At least on the first night of your honeymoon, sprinkle rose petals on the bed.

• Ask the hotel if you can have your bed set with satin sheets, if you like that sensation, or in colder climates, ask for a fluffy goose-down comforter and lots of pillows.

• Have champagne or wine chilling on ice.

• Keep a bowl of fine chocolates in the room—a little nibble of Godiva is a sensual pleasure.

• Take a bubble bath together.

• Stock your tubside with plenty of luxurious bath products that you've brought from home: scented oils, scented soaps, a soft loofah sponge, body butters, and so forth. (See the shopping list at the end of the chapter.)

• Make music a part of your romantic room environment. Set up a portable CD player to serenade you with classic jazz or instrumentals, or play "your song" for your first dance during your honeymoon.

• Have breakfast in bed together.

Dressing the Part

Ideally, your honeymoon is a time when you've never looked better. You're glowing from the joy of your wedding, you may be tan from your first day on the beach (or from those hours at your outdoor wedding), and your trousseau is waiting to be shown off during your travels. For the ultimate in romance, be sure your garment bag is waiting to reveal several gorgeous dresses in flowing fabrics with a romantic neck scarf or a wrap. Show some skin with a plunging back or a bare midriff, but go with what your personal style makes you most comfortable in. When you step out onto the terrace, your handsome groom can only remark how beautiful you look, and you'll enjoy watching his jaw hit the floor. New husbands I spoke to said they love seeing their wives all dressed up in something they feel very confident in. It doesn't have to be too revealing or too clingy—many husbands said they wouldn't want their wives to dress out of character just to try to act a part—just something they look and feel fabulous in.

For romance in a more private time, you can't beat the look of fine lingerie. Perhaps you received boxes and boxes of peignoirs, camisole and panty sets, silk robes, bustiers, and sexed-up garters and thigh-high stockings as gifts at your bridal shower. Well, now's the time to use them, as well as any other lacy, silky, sexy lingerie you have on hand. For a full line of honeymoon lingerie, go right to the source at VictoriasSecret.com. Men, you too can dress the part in the boxers, briefs, or boxer briefs your new wife finds you most captivating in, and don't forget to pack a smart evening-out suit or crisp pants and shirt set that will knock her stockings off as well.

- Watch the sun rise or set from your terrace.

- Wake up together, but don't jump out of bed ready to start your day. Lounge around under the covers for a few hours, cuddle, talk, trace a connect-the-dots over each other's freckles:

"We spent every single morning in bed together like this," says Tracy, fresh upon her return from her honeymoon trip in Europe. "In our real-world lives, we never get to do that. It's always smacking the alarm clock and jumping out of bed to get to work or to the gym. So we took advantage of our complete freedom from any schedules to just lie around and spoon each other, hold hands, pick at breakfast; we even did a crossword puzzle together one morning. That's one of my most surprising favorite memories—doing a crossword puzzle together on our honeymoon! Now, whenever I see one in the newspaper, I'm going to remember that."

Romantic Gestures

Julia, a bride from Tennessee, broke into a deep blush when she told me about her new husband's surprising romantic gestures during their honeymoon in Hawaii. "It was about 4 o'clock in the afternoon, and we'd spent the whole day on the beach. My husband, Dan, said that he was going back up to the room to take a shower before dinner and that I should come up there in a half hour so that I could take my own shower before we went out to dinner that evening." Here's where Julia's blush turned a deeper shade of crimson and her smile made her eyes twinkle. "When I got up to the room, he had filled it with candles and roses, rose petals on the floor and on the bed, a fruit and shrimp platter also sat waiting on the bed with a bottle of champagne chilling nearby, and when I went into the bathroom, he had drawn up a bubble bath with candles all around, just for me. He told me to step in and relax in the tub and when I was ready to come out to join him for fruit and champagne on our terrace as a beginning to our night." Dan wins Honeymooning Husband of the Year for that kind of forethought and pampering of his new wife. It's a story that Julia tells everyone, and one she'll keep with her forever.

It really is the simple, thoughtful, romantic gesture that warms the heart and makes the trip special. You don't need to spend a fortune or make a hundred phone calls to pull off an elaborate scheme. All you need is the knowledge of what your sweetheart will enjoy, what will make her *or him* feel special and adored, and to pace yourself well. Remember, romantic gestures are best offered in small doses when the honored one isn't expecting something. So there's no need to exhaust yourself and cross the line into sappy by doing too many over-the-top romantic gestures during the honeymoon. Here are some ideas:

• Plan for a surprise romantic dinner at a place he'll love. If he's not the dress-up-for-dinner type, then a loving gesture might be to take him someplace that's more his style. Leave the suit and dress at home, and go to a great ribs and pulled pork joint. Shoot pool and drink beer on one of your evenings so that the trip really is a reflection of what you always enjoyed doing together.

• Incorporate something you know your partner loves. If she's a big butterfly fanatic, then plan ahead to take her to a butterfly garden. If he likes a good beer, then surprise him with a tour of an authentic German brewery—it's just an afternoon, of course!

• Use your sense of humor. Especially now, your ability to make each other laugh does a lot to seal your affection for one another. Creating inside jokes from things that happened during your honeymoon is something that will last a lifetime, and couples tell me that their ability to laugh at a plan that goes awry or an awkward canoe trip, a truly bad bottle of wine, or a bad hair day—anything that could ruin a less lighthearted couple's trip—just makes the love grow all the more.

• Give gifts throughout your trip. It might be a beautiful silk robe for her or a nice cologne for him, or it can be as simple as a shell necklace that will remind her of your trip. One groom told me that his new wife had eyed a beautiful antique bracelet at a street fair, but the

Ahhhhhhhhhh!

Get a couple's massage, or massage one another. Many resorts will send a pair of masseurs right to your room so you can get kneaded and unknotted in tandem. Massages are more than just a little bit of sandalwood oil rubbed between the masseur's hands. You have your choice now of the following:

• Hot rock massage: Warmed-up rocks or volcano stones are set right on your back for a heated, soothing sensation.

• Lomilomi: A relaxing and healing massage, lomilomi uses broad, long strokes and a soothing rocking motion.

• Lurlur: A little more involved, this one starts with a jasmine-scented oil massage, followed by a gentle sandalwood exfoliation of your skin, then a cooling slathering of yogurt, followed by a floral bath to wash it all off.

• Shiatsu: This is the standard massage you've probably had before, with lots of pressure at just the right points.

• Swedish: A bit more relaxing, Swedish massage works your muscles, getting out all of that postwedding tension from your neck, back, shoulders, and arms.

Would you rather give each other the massages? Take an inexpensive couples' massage course at a community education center or yoga school near you, pop in a how-to video, or read a book found through Barnes and Noble (www.bn.com) or Amazon (www.amazon.com) or at your local bookstore.

vendor stalled her bargaining and she walked away disappointed. Later in the day, the groom excused himself for a moment from their nearby lunch in a restaurant, went back and bought the bracelet at the seller's price (the groom noted that "it was worth every penny"), and then gave it to her later that evening as a surprise. She was so touched, she broke into tears.

• Give compliments. Genuine ones. Tell him he looks great when he comes back from the pool to get his towel. Tell her she looks beautiful when she wakes up in the morning. Don't stop yourself from speaking what's in your heart, because when life speeds back up again at home, it'll be very easy to forget to compliment your partner. One of the best things anyone can hear on a honeymoon is, "That's why I'm so glad I married you. You're always so kind/fun/romantic /sweet/adventurous/spontaneous." Everyone is warmed by a genuine compliment and affirmation from those they love.

• Touch one another. Even if you've been together for years and years, way past the days when you were attached at the hip or the hand or the lips, remind yourself and your partner of the power of your touch. Hold hands, slip your arm through his as you're walking in true gentleman-lady fashion, touch her from time to time when you're having a conversation, find a reason to make any skin-to-skin contact at all. Sometimes it's just a brush of your hand across the shoulder, face, arm, or bare leg that is incredibly romantic and connecting.

• And finally, *talk* to each other. What's more romantic than reminiscing about the wedding or dreaming out loud about the future as you swing together in an oceanside hammock? Talking is romance all in itself, so use this time together to share your thoughts and dreams.

Honeymoon Reflections

We made it a game during our honeymoon that we each had to give a compliment to the other that neither of us had ever been given by anyone else before. They had to be genuine, too. So there we were, saying things like, "You have the cutest earlobes I've ever seen!" Even though it started out as a game, the compliment thing made our honeymoon extra special—and we're carrying on with it now even a year after our wedding.

—Evie and Peter

The Can't-Fail Romantic Touch for Men

Guys, if you don't have this one down as part of your romantic repertoire, learn it now. There is nothing sexier than when a man gently places his hand against the small of his partner's back, whether he's escorting her into a room, guiding her to take steps ahead of him up a flight of stairs, or just standing next to her. Especially if our backs are bare or we're wearing a thin-fabric dress. Your gentle, leading touch on the small of our backs (that's the curve right above our bottoms)—someplace we're very rarely touched at all by anyone—is one of the most romantic gestures ever.

Your Romance Shopping List

❏ Scented massage oils

❏ Travel candles

❏ Flowers (once you get to your destination)

❏ Fine chocolates

❏ Romantic sentiment greeting cards (prebought and filled out)

❏ Notepad and pen (for spur-of-the-moment love notes)

❏ Lingerie, silk robe, silk boxers to look the part

❏ A great scent: perfume or cologne

❏ Scented linen mist spray

❏ Softly hued lightbulb for the bedroom

❏ Bubble baths, scented bath oils, and scented soaps

❏ Loofah sponge

❏ Mood music and CD player

Just keep some of these romantic ideas in mind, use the ones you often shower upon one another in your regular, everyday lives—

hopefully you do that, especially during the stressful wedding-planning time, to remind you why you're marrying each other in the first place—and make your honeymoon the most romantic and love-filled time of your lives. Because you know what a good dose of romance can lead to.

18

Capturing the Moment

No doubt the memories of your honeymoon—from the most romantic grand gestures to the scenic vistas, and even to the blood-boiling hassles of finding the right baggage carousel in a supersized airport—are going to stay in your mind forever. But there's nothing better than capturing those great moments on film for eternity. A picture, after all, is worth a thousand words, even more so if a thousand words could never do justice to the beauty of that sunrise over the ocean, the scents of that bakery in the Italian villa you stumbled across during your journey, and the sixth sense feeling of swimming with dolphins in Florida or sighting a mother whale with her newborn calf off the coast of Alaska. Some moments you just want to capture forever, make eternal, and in some small way hold on to so the feeling you experience never fades away.

In years to come, you'll flip through your pictures or view your video and smile at the radiance of your fresh, young marriage. In further years to come, you'll share those pictures with your kids and grandkids. So it only makes sense to invest some time, thought, and, of course, money in your choices of cameras and how you'll use them.

Cameras

The beauty of any shot begins with what you're aiming at, but the quality of the picture depends on the camera you have in your hand. Today's new models of cameras feature top-of-the-line technology with little to no thinking involved. Digital cameras let you work magic with your pictures, giving you the best shots possible, allowing you to wipe away those eyes-closed mistakes, and automatically eliminating those raccoon-in-the-headlights red-eye glares that make you look more possessed than passionate. You'll find both regular point-and-shoot cameras out there, which take great pix, and upper echelon digital cameras. Whatever your technology skills and needs, look for the best-rated cameras as written up in *Consumer Reports* and in industry magazines that talk about the newest, hottest cameras out there.

For nondigital point-and-clicks, look for a new-model camera that has automatic focus and zoom, red-eye elimination features and even an option to capture wide-angle or panoramic views. Today's choices are small, lightweight, and easy to tote, and they work on regular batteries (see the section on batteries coming up later in the chapter).

If you're shopping for a new digital camera or looking to upgrade your old one, here are a few features to ask that slick salesman about:

- As many megapixels as possible (Megapixels are like your computer's resolution numbers—the higher the megapixel amount, the more crisp your photos will be)
- The ability to take a portion of any picture and enlarge it, crop it, magnify it, or work it in several other ways

Simplify It

Your wedding photographer uses only the best cameras and equipment (well, that's true if you hired a great professional!), so ask him or her for some recommendations on the best cameras to consider for purchase. Photography pros receive the latest information on the newest and best equipment possible, so think of this as going right to the source for a fabulous recommendation.

Capture the Action

A snapshot camera that takes video . . . and a video camera that takes snapshots? What is going on here?

It's true. Many digital cameras have a feature that lets them record short bursts of video footage, and many digital camcorders will allow you to capture still images right off your rolling footage and print them as snapshots. Consider these as bonus safety options and *not* a release from having to choose between one or the other. It's better to have one of each on your trip, since technology on still-digital cameras that take short video have a little bit of improving to do yet in the near future.

- 2x to 3x optical zoom features (Know this lingo! Optical zoom is better than digital zoom.)
- Autoexposure adjustment
- Autolight exposure adjustment
- Autoflash
- A very powerful multimedia card (The more pictures you plan to store, the more memory you'll be reserving in your system)
- Delivery of footage to mini-DVDs, which you will then label and store in a safe place to avoid taping over important, earlier honeymoon footage
- The ability to switch from automatic to manual controls (if you prefer)
- A small and lightweight size for easier toting and use
- Weatherproof (Important!)

One of your top priorities might be that your camera is *small*. It's not just the digital cameras that are coming out in palm sizes; 35mm cameras are also shrinking in size but growing in power as well. These tiny treasures claim a modest space in your carry-on and even slip into pocketbooks and beach bags with little heft to them.

Video Cameras

Capture all the action in real time with a great digital camcorder. Now that big-time movie directors are using digital cameras to shoot their films (like *Star Wars: Attack of the Clones*), why shouldn't you take advantage of the same sterling technology to get the best footage of your own adventures? The brightest models on the market might run you upwards of $1,500, but you'll find that the crisp image and idiot-proof usage make that a drop in the bucket compared to the ultimate value of the action and priceless moments you capture on film.

What are you looking for in a great camera? Ask a qualified professional for the full list because technology is improving and new models are released every day. Some of the top features I can recommend right now are:

- 1+ megapixels for capturing all the details (A $2,000 camera model gives you 1.92 megapixels, among the top quality imaging out there right now.)
- 20x optical zoom (to be able to capture that faraway gathering of dolphins)
- 2.5-inch LCD screen, which allows you to easily see what you're filming without having to squint into a little eyepiece
- Long battery life
- Still image capabilities

The list goes on and on, but it's the digital camcorder's ability to capture still photos that makes this lightweight handheld a must. With just a few of the right commands and a multimedia card, you can download stills from your moving images onto your Web site, send them in e-mails (even *during* your trip, if you'd like), and develop them into standard photographs. This option increases your ability to catch that once-in-a-lifetime moment and keep it in a safe and lasting place.

Already own a digital camcorder? Fabulous. Ready to upgrade your older video camera for a newer model? Read up in *Consumer Reports* to find the most highly rated options out there, and spend some time seeking out the best purchase for your honeymoon and future needs.

Try not to swallow your tongue when you see some of these prices, though. They do reach up into the stratosphere for some of the best models, and you might not think it's worth it to invest in Spielberg-worthy camera equipment. Some of the digital-shy couples I spoke to said they preferred medium-tech cameras because they didn't need their honeymoon footage to be worthy of an Emmy or an Oscar. They just wanted reliable footage from an easy-to-use camera. In that case, research standard VHS cameras, which also come in smaller styles and lighter weights now. In the happy medium zone, look at the Hi-8 cameras like Sony's Handycam. Hi-8 cameras give you great footage (you might not be able to tell the difference between its results and a digital camera's output), equally impressive zoom and auto controls, and high battery power. Even better, a Hi-8 camera might run you $400 to $500, while cameras will all of those editing options are more in the neighborhood of $1,000 to $1,500 right now. If you're not obsessed with editing, cropping, and turning your honeymoon footage into a slick documentary, this might be the option for you.

Specialty Cameras

You've seen them in camera shops, bulk food warehouses, and even your beauty supply store. Those brightly colored one-time-use, throwaway cameras with kitschy quotes printed out on the bottom of each picture make spontaneous shutterbugging fun at times. On my own honeymoon, we loved our bright yellow underwater disposable camera for those deep-sea dive kisses and playful underwater surprise shots (don't ask!). I highly, highly recommend that you grab at least one underwater disposable camera so you don't miss your scuba diving, snorkeling, and swimming with sealife moments, nor those submerged kisses and great shots of you swimming away from the camera while holding hands. These are pictures that capture you in a beautiful underwater world that you might actually never visit again.

Another specialty camera not to miss is the panoramic disposable camera. Sure, some high-tech digital and 35mm cameras will give you the option of wide-angle shots and Imax-theater worthy scopes of a rainforest all around you. But there's a big advantage to investing a small amount of money in a few disposable panoramic cameras: if you drop them during your wild ride down the side of a volcano, you haven't lost a $2,000 camera. Honeymooners love the stress-free options of the throwaway camera, and some choose these as their primary mode of picture taking. Today's models take some great quality shots, and they do come with flashes, elementary zoom options, and other features that make these smart choices if you'll be on an active honeymoon or a hot-weather trip or even if you'd rather not have to worry about that obscenely expensive camera during your entire trip.

Get ready to be impressed when you start shopping for your throwaway cameras. Sure, many of them come in those bright yellow wrappings, in those clear plastic protective covers for underwater shots, and in other designs that just scream "Tourist!" But you'll also find attractive designs that look more like real cameras, with the gray color, the pop-up flash, and all.

Simplify It

A few top companies to check out:

Canon: 800-652-2666,
    www.canondv.com
Olympus: 800-622-6372,
    www.olympus.com
Pentax: 800-877-0155,
    www.pentaxusa.com
Sony: 800-222-7669,
    www.sony.com

For a great collection of travel-worthy cameras, with explanations and updated reviews and recommendations, look at *Travel and Leisure* magazine's Web site shopping section on cameras and camcorders: www.tlstore.com.

You could buy these throwaways from wedding Web sites, with jacked-up prices attached to their titles as "bridal cameras." Or you could save a few bucks by buying them in value packs at stores like WalMart, Target, and Kmart; at beauty supply stores; and at warehouse clubs like Costco (www.costco.com), Sam's Club (www.samsclub.com), and BJ's Wholesale (www.bjswholesale.com).

Batteries and Chargers

Don't miss that sunrise! Be sure your cameras are well fueled by batteries and effective and long-lasting chargers. Your individual cameras will probably come with chargers and instructions for their optimum use, so read up well on the process, the length of time it takes to charge your camera, and how to read the battery levels on an LCD screen.

As for batteries for all of your cameras, you don't need to spend a fortune for high-tech batteries with supernatural shelf lives. Those brand name alkaline batteries you find in the store will do the trick just fine, thank you very much. Just get plenty of them. You should be aware that digital camcorders and some flashes are huge power drains on batteries, so you'll need to be sure you stock up in bulk on the best brands out there. *Consumer Reports* recently suggested that Duracell's Ultra M3 batteries are the best bet for the camcorder-happy.

If you'd rather invest in high-powered chargers, know that a specialized charger that goes with your new camera can reach up there in price. I saw a nice one recently for $150 at Sony, and I considered that price tag worth it, since the charger extended the camera's recording time from 2 hours to 10-plus. Such an efficient gadget will keep you from having to worry so often about whether the camera's charged up and ready. And if it saves you time and worry, it's worth it.

Smart honeymoon travelers told me that they kept their chargers, unused film and batteries, and *well-labeled spent film* securely tucked

Stressbuster

Worried about your cameras getting ruined during your travels, even if they're throwaways, for the value of the pictures they hold? Well, there's a product that can give you some peace of mind. Otter Boxes are sturdy plastic containers with compression latches and watertight silicon seals that keep your safely tucked away cameras protected from damage by water, wind, sand, mud, dirt—basically anything you're likely to encounter during especially active honeymoon trips. You can get the smaller boxes for your point-and-click camera and larger boxes with foam padding for larger cameras and more cumbersome equipment. Go to Otter Boxes at www.otterbox.com, or call 888-695-8820, for their safety containers in the $20–$40 range.

away in a sealable plastic bag in one of their carry-ons. When they left their room for a night on the town or a day at the beach, they stowed their cameras, film, batteries, and chargers in their hotel room safe for extra security.

Getting the Best Shots

The first rule of honeymoon photography: You can never take too many pictures.

The second rule of honeymoon photography: You can take really bad, boring pictures if you don't think ahead about what kind of range of shots to get, about using different lighting, and about including some candid shots in your repertoire. I've seen way too many collections of honeymoon shots where it's just the bride standing in front of a sign for the Crystal Caverns underground tour in Bermuda or it's a series of shots of the Eiffel Tower. Ho-hum. If it's a shot you can get from a postcard, don't waste your film. Here are some ideas to get better-quality photos of all your unforgettable honeymoon moments:

• Mix it up. Get some shots of you as individuals, and get more shots of you as a couple. Ask a friendly fellow resort-goer to snap a picture of the two of you slow dancing on the beach or toasting one another with a bright blue frothy frozen drink at a swim-up bar. Ask your tour guide to get pictures of you on the horses you've been riding on the beach. Don't be shy, because it's the pictures of the two of you together that show the true story of your shared experience.

• Use lots of color. Whether it's the flowers in a Dutch field of tulips or the amazing hues in a rainforest, be sure your high-tech camera with the great color resolution has something to work with. The same goes for the outfits you'll wear during your trip. This is another thing I see in bland honeymoon photo albums. Couples who try to color-coordinate their clothing for easier packing stick with basic black, white, or neutrals and pastels to make 20 outfits out of eight pieces of clothing. Then they look washed out in their pictures. Try a bright blue bathing suit with a blue and black sarong, a passionate red evening dress with a red neck scarf—something that's going to make you stand out in that amazing scenery.

• Go with candid shots. Surprise one another with pictures of your facial expressions when you first look upon a hilltop view you've

Honeymoon Reflections

We loaded up on a few of the different types of disposable cameras out there. Since we were traveling with our kids on a blended family trip, we gave each of them one throwaway camera to use as they wished. It actually was a great thing, since we were able to see some of the shots from their Maui Loves Kids day camp: the sandcastles they built, their first rides on a boogie board, their tan little faces smiling during their hula lessons. While we spent our days taking our own underwater shots during our private time, we were so happy that our kids could share with us what they had done with their six hours of camp time on the trip. Although we're not going to show them our underwater pictures!

—Tammi and Brent

climbed hours to reach, or get a shot of your groom walking out of the ocean surf like a god of Greek mythology. Sometimes it's the unplanned, surprise shots that are the most fun and revealing.

• Use the light. Experiment ahead of time with your camera to see if you can take silhouette or backlit shots. Shoot pictures without a flash as one of you looks out the window of your hotel room, which glow-lights the face but then fades the rest of the shot gradually into a slight level of darkness.

• Get a camera that allows action shots. Some models are better for catching you whipping by on bicycles past the Mayan temples.

• Use your panoramic camera for those great vistas and the view from your hotel balcony.

• Do something! Don't just stand next to each other and smile at the camera in every European city. Add a little flavor to your shots, like sipping that glass of French wine at a sidewalk bistro, admiring the artwork at a street market, dancing the limbo at that cheesy tourist nightclub the cabby recommended.

• Add some romance to your shots. Write your names and "Just Married" in the pink sand at the ocean's edge, arrange some seashells or starfish around it, and snap the picture. Hold the rose your husband gave you at dinner. Get a modest shot of the two of you in a bubble bath, using your camera's timer.

• Use your imagination and snap away. Make an effort to get great pictures.

• Pick up postcards for the general shots of landmarks and cityscapes. They're great to use not only as picture savers but also for you to write down your favorite memories from that city on the back rather than mailing them to friends.

• Think *really* hard about whether or not to take sensual or sexual pictures or video of each other. Plenty of couples love to capture these types of honeymoon memories on film, and for many couples it's an enjoyable part of their sex life. Those great, sexy photos of you wrapped up in a silk sheet with your hair splayed out on the pillow might become one of your favorite photos of yourself in the future. A tasteful picture of your husband sitting shirtless in front of you (also shirtless but with all vitals obscured from view) might be a great way to remember your daring day at that topless beach. But when it comes to full frontal pictures and explicit videotape, search your soul for the answer to that one. It would be stressful and potentially humiliating if you lost that videotape during your travels. And imagine the horror of living through Jeannine's story:

> We'd just gotten back from our honeymoon, and all of our family and friends had come over for dinner and drinks. We told them all about our honeymoon, the great tours we went on, the countries we visited, how we reached Milan just in time for the fashion shows and saw a lot of my favorite celebrities. Wanting to share that footage, I grabbed the tape labeled "Milan" out of our carry-on bag and popped it into the VCR player. Well, we'd done something else while we were in Milan as well, and I couldn't run fast enough to find the remote while my entire family and bridal party watched more than a few seconds of my husband and me making love and talking dirty, really acting out a sexual fantasy for the camera. It was a horrifying, horrifying experience, especially to see my parents turn that shade of white. My advice: If you're going to tape your sexual exploits, footage of you on a nude beach, even just sensual nudes of each other, put it on its own tape, label it with fluorescent stickers, and store it in a safe. And don't plan to run for any political office in the future.

> —JEANNINE

Storing and Sharing Your Pictures

Naked footage nightmares aside, what's better than showing everyone how great you looked on the beach in Borneo or that magical shot of

Penny-Wise

Want to share some of your honeymoon pictures with family and friends after your return? Don't bother paying to get extra copies made of that perfect picture of the two of you, and don't waste money mailing your portrait to people. Instead, go online to photos.yahoo.com and download your best pictures from your cameras or through your scanner right into their system, add your titles and captions to each shot, and fully design your virtual photo album. What would you pay for this kind of time- and money-saving option, not to mention the thrill of sharing your best honeymoon memories with the people who may have even paid for the trip or registered for some of your most special activities or meals? $50? $100? $199.99? Put your wallet away. At the time of this writing, this service is free. (If this sounds like the ideal plan, check to see the site's current fees and procedures.)

you at the butterfly conservatory, that surreal picture of you on safari, or even the adorable shot of your exhausted new husband sleeping on a hammock with a coconut-shell drink still clutched in his hand? When those pictures come in, you'll definitely want to store them in great photo albums, frame them, and even get copies made for your loved ones. One couple I spoke to used a cute honeymoon photo of themselves as the picture for their Christmas cards—they had thought ahead to pack Santa hats to wear with their bikini and swim trunks at their October island getaway. Ingenious!

Tuck all of those great shots away in a top-quality photo album, or store them in specially marked photo boxes that you can get for just a few dollars at a craft store. Frame your photos to decorate your living room walls, or go with the new talking picture frames and photo albums from The Sharper Image (www.sharperimage.com). I *love* The Sharper Image for just these kinds of fun memory keepers. The Sharper Image's Talking Pictures Photo Album ($29.95 at the time of this writing) looks like a regular album for pictures 4 inches by 6 inches, but each page is equipped with a digital voice chip that allows you to record a 10-second statement on what each individual picture is showing, adding the excitement in your voice as you explain just what it was like to bike through that vineyard or swim past that stingray.

However you display them, whether or not you give them a soundtrack, be sure to keep all of your pictures and videos safe. Store the negatives in your family safe or bank safety deposit bank. A firefighter friend of mine tells me that family and wedding photos are the one thing people want to grab from their burning homes, and some risk their lives to do so! These pictures are priceless treasures of your once-in-a-lifetime trip, so ensure their safety with the right storage.

Speaking of safety, pop the tab on any VHS videotapes you use so you cannot mistakenly tape an episode of *Sex and the City* over that fabulous champagne-at-sunset cruise, label all of your tapes and DVDs well, and invest in plastic videotape storage cases. Skip the engraved bridal videotape boxes and go with something simpler that you can label yourselves with an easily printed label off your own home PC. The savings here: $5 to $30.

Preserving Your Memories Without a Camera

Keep a honeymoon journal in which you write down the best moments of your trip, any funny catchphrases you encounter, or names of notable strangers you meet along the way. It's these kinds of memory catchers that live on forever and will bring a smile to your face in the future, on your anniversaries, when you relive the best times of the greatest trip of your life. Some couples share a journal, with her notes in her handwriting and his notes in his. Sarah and Tom of Portland, Oregon, took turns writing and adding romantic messages to each other within the pages of their journal. When Sarah was taking a shower or blow-drying her hair, Tom would write a few lines about their day in the journal. "I love you more today than yesterday," in his handwriting, fluttered Sarah's stomach. "You looked so beautiful sleeping on the train today" earned him a great big kiss. When Tom was in the shower or shaving, Sarah wrote about the events of their day and then filled in her messages to Tom with plenty of "I love yous" and a "This is only the beginning of our adventures together." What they had at the end of their trip, just by filling downtime with a few sentences at a time, was a journal of their trip and heartfelt expressions and messages of love to one another.

Now *that's* capturing the moment.

Appendix 1

Souvenirs List

Name	Item to Get	Shirt Size	Check Off for Bought

Name	Item to Get	Shirt Size	Check Off for Bought

Appendix 2

Postcards List

Name	Address	E-mail (for e-postcards)

Name	Address	E-mail (for e-postcards)

Appendix 3

Itinerary

Tear out to leave with family or friends.

Date of arrival:

Airline (or cruise line):

Flight number(s) (or cruise name):

Limo or transport company name and number:

Name of hotel:

Hotel address:

Hotel phone:

Our cell phone #1:

Our cell phone #2:

Our pager number:

Our e-mail:

Additional stops during our trip, and dates we're planning to be there:

Date of departure:

Airline:

Flight number(s):

Limo or transport company name and number:

Appendix 4

Instructions for House and Pet Sitters

Tear out for sitters' use.

Lawn and garden should be watered on these
days (depending on rain):

Pets' care and feeding schedules:

Name and number of veterinarian:

Deliveries expected at home on the following dates:

Service workers (lawn crew, pool cleaner, maids, etc.)
expected on the following dates:

Emergency numbers:

How to reach us in case of emergency:

How to reach home alarm service company:

Home alarm code:

Additional instructions:

Appendix 5

Contact List

Travel agent name:

Address:

Phone number:

E-mail:

Cell phone:

Fax:

Airline name:

Phone number:

Web site:

Hotel/cruise name:

Phone number:

E-mail:

Fax:

Hotel reservations clerk:

Additional contacts:

Name:

Phone number/e-mail/fax:

Name:

Phone number/e-mail/fax:

Name:

Phone number/e-mail/fax:

Name:

Phone number/e-mail/fax:

Appendix 6

Notes and Reminders

Appendix 7

Packing Lists

GENERAL PACKING LIST

Necessities

- ❏ Airline and travel tickets
- ❏ Identification
- ❏ Car rental vouchers
- ❏ Credit cards and travelers' checks
- ❏ Passports and visas
- ❏ Important contact phone numbers and Web site addresses for hotel, travel agent, consulate or embassy, at-home house sitters, etc.
- ❏ Prescriptions for medications, eyeglasses, contact lenses
- ❏ Medic alert bracelet
- ❏ Birth control items

Clothing and Accessories

For clothing items, determine the numbers of articles you'll need for the length of your stay.

- ❏ Bathing suits
- ❏ Cover-ups
- ❏ Jeans or pants
- ❏ Formal dresses

- ❏ Formal suits
- ❏ Sundresses
- ❏ Alluring evening dresses
- ❏ Casual men's attire
- ❏ Jackets
- ❏ Wraps or shawls for those chilly evenings
- ❏ Windbreakers for breezy days
- ❏ T-shirts or tank tops
- ❏ Shorts
- ❏ Socks
- ❏ Stockings
- ❏ Underwear
- ❏ Bras (including sports, racerback, strapless bras)
- ❏ Lingerie
- ❏ Robes
- ❏ Casual pajamas
- ❏ Shoes
- ❏ Sneakers
- ❏ Sandals
- ❏ Flip-flops
- ❏ Slippers
- ❏ Accessories for each outfit
- ❏ Purse or evening bag

Other clothing items or accessories:

- ❏
- ❏
- ❏
- ❏
- ❏
- ❏
- ❏
- ❏
- ❏

Nonclothing Items

- ❏ Tote bag for beach, pool, or travels
- ❏ Cameras
- ❏ Film
- ❏ Battery chargers for cell phone, laptop, cameras, etc.
- ❏ Extra batteries
- ❏ Electrical adapters as needed in foreign countries and on islands
- ❏ Reading material for flights, travels, and beachside
- ❏ Travel reading light, if necessary
- ❏ Address book for sending postcards
- ❏ Postage stamps
- ❏ Pens
- ❏ Mini battery-operated radio or portable CD player
- ❏ Childproof lighter
- ❏ Lint brush
- ❏ Spray bottle of laundry scent freshener, such as Febreze or Bounce spray, to take that smoky smell out of the blazer you wore at that crowded bar last night
- ❏ Scented laundry dryer sheets (Having one in each suitcase keeps your clothing smelling fresh during multiple stops on your trip. One cigar-scented evening wrap can make your entire wardrobe smell foul after a few hours next to it in a closed suitcase.)

For the Germ Freak

Worried about how clean your hotel sheets really are? Did you recently see an investigative report about the transmission of hanta virus from beddings to human? Whatever your level of germophobia, ease your mind with Silk Liner, a bring-along sheet liner that will keep the bed-bugs from biting. Find Silk Liner at home decor stores or at Summit Hut (www.summithut.com). If you're traveling through some underdeveloped areas on your adventure trip, this little purchase is one you might favor strongly.

SPECIAL ITEMS FOR SPECIAL PLACES

The Island Getaway

- ❏ Waterproof sunscreen
- ❏ Sunscreen for lips
- ❏ Sun hat or visor
- ❏ Sunglasses
- ❏ Beach towels
- ❏ Inflatable beach pillow
- ❏ Insect repellant
- ❏ Aloe vera for those sunburns
- ❏ Talcum powder (to sprinkle gently in your bed when your sunburned legs are hurting–keeps the sheets from giving any traction on your skin)
- ❏ Waterproof swim boxes (cigarette-pack-sized sealable boxes that hold your room key, money, and ID safely on you while you're in the water and away from your lounge chairs)
- ❏ Rain jackets and miniumbrella for rain bursts
- ❏ Lightweight jacket or wrap for evening breezes
- ❏ Sneakers or sturdy shoes for activities
- ❏ Beach shoes
- ❏ One nice dress-up outfit for a formal night out
- ❏ Lots of film and batteries for your cameras
- ❏ Portable radio for the beach
- ❏ Special identification cards and vaccination documents

Cold-Weather Trips

- ❏ Sunscreen and lip sunblock
- ❏ Warming packs for inside boots
- ❏ Parkas
- ❏ Gloves
- ❏ Hats
- ❏ Scarves
- ❏ Ski goggles

❏ Thermal underwear
❏ Thermal socks

Active Trips

❏ Sports bras and protective clothing
❏ Good sporting shoes
❏ Workout outfits
❏ Thicker sporting socks (of them!)
❏ Protective hand- and headgear
❏ UVA and UVB sunglasses
❏ Travel ice pack
❏ Bandages (just in case)
❏ Motion sickness medication
❏ Eye lubrication, such as Visine
❏ Water bottles
❏ Sporting equipment
❏ Cell phone
❏ Compass
❏ Camera and film
❏ Backpack

Adventure Vacations

See all items under "Active Trips."

❏ Waterproof shoes, hiking boots, jackets, cameras, and travel pouch or wallet
❏ Convertible pants that zip off into cargo shorts
❏ Convertible jackets that zip off into vests
❏ Many pairs of socks
❏ Thermal underwear
❏ Microfleece poncho
❏ Ibuprofen or painkillers
❏ First-aid kit, including Swiss Army knife, bandages, callous protectors, Ace bandage or flexible knee wraps for that troublesome knee pain, and other fix-its
❏ Cameras and film

- ❑ Binoculars
- ❑ Two-way radios
- ❑ Shoes that can get ruined
- ❑ Waterproof sunscreen
- ❑ Insect repellant
- ❑ Childproof lighter or waterproof matches
- ❑ Vaccination documents
- ❑ Sleeping bag
- ❑ Hand-protecting gloves, like weight-lifting gloves
- ❑ Water purification kit (if you're really going off the beaten path!)
- ❑ Mosquito netting (packs in a tight bundle, and you'll be so happy you brought it along to hang over your bed in some parts of the world)

Big City Touring

- ❑ Tour guidebooks
- ❑ Guide to subways or public transportation
- ❑ Pepper spray or safety whistle
- ❑ Two-way radios or cell phone
- ❑ Subway or public transportation tokens
- ❑ Safety travel pouch worn under a jacket or shirt
- ❑ Blister pads
- ❑ Bandages
- ❑ Good footwear for lots of walking
- ❑ Binoculars
- ❑ Umbrellas or rain gear

Family Vacations

- ❑ Kids' games and activities (Check out the electronic handheld version of Scrabble, with several levels of play, a dictionary, and a timer, from www .hasbro.com, and Trivia Trek, a fun handheld geography quiz game from www.nationalgeographic.com.)
- ❑ GameBoy or other handheld toys
- ❑ Kids' medications
- ❑ Motion sickness medication or sea-bands for kids' wrists

- ❏ Kids' prescriptions and important medical contact information
- ❏ Kids' clothing
- ❏ Kids' shoes
- ❏ Beach shoes
- ❏ Kids' accessories
- ❏ Two-way radios or beepers on the kids at all times
- ❏ Educational tour guidebooks
- ❏ Addresses for the kids to send postcards of their own (to grandparents, friends, etc.)
- ❏ Kids' journals and pens
- ❏ Disposable cameras for each child (If they get lost or damaged, it's not a big loss; plus it's fun to see what kids choose to take pictures of!)
- ❏ Portable CD player with headphones for each child who can't live without his or her music for very long
- ❏ Snacks and beverages for the kids during the trip (Tip: Keep any chocolate snacks in a cooler if you're driving by car; hot temperatures cause melting and mess in the backseat.)
- ❏ Water (Parents suggest you hydrate your kids with something other than sodas—caffeine-hyped kids can cause travel headaches.)
- ❏ First-aid kit
- ❏ Sunglasses
- ❏ Baby supplies: diapers, diaper rash ointment, baby wipes, formula, waterproof bedsheets, changing pad, diaper bag, car seat, stroller, pacifiers, bottles, drink cups, bibs, supply of baby food, baby spoons, baby medications, baby relaxation music, baby monitor
- ❏ Strollers for toddlers
- ❏ Nightlight for the hotel room
- ❏ Lots of resealable bags for kids' toy pieces, wet bathing suits, sandy beach shoes, etc.
- ❏ Wet wipes for sticky hands and faces
- ❏ Antibacterial hand sanitizers

Simplify It

A great idea if you're taking the kids along is to allow them to plan their own packing lists of clothing, shoes, accessories, gadgets, and toys. Let them draw up a list, and then you step in to make sure all the essentials are included. Kids can then fold and pack their own luggage with your supervision.

One Toy Per Hour

If you're traveling by car or taking a long flight with the kids, you can help pass the time more peacefully by handing out small wrapped presents for each of the kids to open every hour on the hour. They don't have to be expensive gifts; just little travel games will be fine. And parents offer this advice: Be sure that kids have more to do than just read books or do crossword puzzles in the car. Some children can get motion sickness while reading in a moving vehicle.

Cruises

- ❑ Motion sickness medications
- ❑ Indigestion medications (for all of that great food!)
- ❑ Cameras and film
- ❑ Weather-appropriate clothing and jackets (see clothing list)
- ❑ Sporting gear and clothing
- ❑ At least one formal dress-up outfit and full accessories, shoes, stockings, and jewelry for many cruises' mandatory dress codes
- ❑ Hairbands or scarf to keep hair in place while on deck

Spa Getaways

- ❑ Workout outfits
- ❑ Comfy loungewear
- ❑ Bathing suits
- ❑ Sarongs
- ❑ Clothing and footwear appropriate for the activities you'll enjoy: hiking, horseback riding, golf, yoga classes
- ❑ Flip-flops for walking and postpedicure times
- ❑ Aromatherapy products and candles for use in your room
- ❑ Sunscreen and lip sunscreen
- ❑ Skin-calming lotions, in case that facial irritates your skin

- ❏ Several dress-up outfits or slinky dresses (Some spas have formal dining environments.)
- ❏ Lush beach towel
- ❏ Hairbands for sweeping hair into a ponytail
- ❏ Cameras and film
- ❏ Relaxing music
- ❏ Light reading
- ❏ Healthy snacks for your room
- ❏ Prepurchased luxury beauty products and treatments (because some spas will charge you a fortune in their gift shop!)

Going Overseas

- ❏ Electrical adapters
- ❏ Currency converters
- ❏ Language translators
- ❏ Cell phone coded to function in that region
- ❏ Important embassy or consulate contact information
- ❏ Complete travel itinerary
- ❏ Some amount of foreign currency
- ❏ Current tour guidebook
- ❏ Maps of public transportation routes
- ❏ Pepper spray and alert whistles for your own safety
- ❏ Upset stomach or diarrhea medication

ODDS AND ENDS

Toiletries

- ❏ Shampoo
- ❏ Conditioner
- ❏ Soap
- ❏ Shaving cream
- ❏ Shavers or razors
- ❏ Toothbrushes
- ❏ Toothpaste

- ❏ Mouthwash
- ❏ Dental floss
- ❏ Deodorant
- ❏ Perfumes, aftershave, or cologne
- ❏ Makeup
- ❏ Makeup remover
- ❏ Moisturizers
- ❏ Aloe vera
- ❏ Sunblock
- ❏ Lip sunblock
- ❏ Nail polish
- ❏ Nail polish remover
- ❏ Cotton balls
- ❏ Cotton swabs
- ❏ Tweezers
- ❏ Miniscissors
- ❏ Emory board
- ❏ Nail clippers
- ❏ Comb
- ❏ Hairbrush
- ❏ Curling iron
- ❏ Hair spray
- ❏ Hair gels and styling lotions
- ❏ Bandages
- ❏ Pain relievers
- ❏ Antinausea medication
- ❏ Antihistamines
- ❏ Antibacterial sprays, wipes, or hand gels
- ❏ Laxatives
- ❏ Calamine or skin irritation lotion
- ❏ Foot powder
- ❏ Birth control items
- ❏ Lubricant, such as KY Jelly or Astroglide

❏ Maxipads, tampons, additional feminine care products

❏ Contact lenses, solution, carrying pack

❏ Extra pair of glasses

❏ Eye care items such as Visine

❏ Vitamins

❏ Stain remover wipes

❏ Liquid laundry detergent, like Woolite, for washing your bathing suits or lingerie

❏ Ear plugs

❏ Motion sickness wrist bands

Gotta Get Your Gadgets

❏ Electrical adapter (Great for not blowing up your hair dryer when another country's electric system is different from our own. Buy the full set, with several marked converters that work anywhere in the world. Tip: Many European countries work on 220 volts rather than 110, so look for adapter kits that have the plug-ins you need.)

❏ Currency converters (Great for making sure street vendors aren't ripping you off.)

❏ Language translator handhelds (Great for finding out where the restroom is.)

❏ PDAs (Great for getting driving directions and making travel itinerary changes.)

❏ Cell phones (Great for calling the hotel to change your dinner reservations.)

❏ Two-way radios (Great for checking in with the kids at the resort's play camp without having to walk all the way over there.)

❏ Beepers (Great for letting kids in the arcade know when to meet you back at the Ferris wheel.)

❏ Flashlight (Great for navigating your unfamiliar hotel room at night, looking for the bathroom, while your partner sleeps.)

❏ Alarm clock (Be sure it automatically adapts to time-zone changes!)

❏ Extra batteries for gadgets

❏ Chargers and cables for gadgets

❏ Carrying cases for gadgets

Other gadgets:

❏

❏

❏

❏

❏

❏

❏

Resources

Please note that the following information is for your research use only. The author and the publisher do not personally endorse any company or professional. Please note that at the time of your reading this book, some phone numbers and Web sites may no longer be the same because of changes in area codes or Web addresses. We apologize if such a change has occurred since the writing of this book.

Airlines

Aer Lingus: 800-474-7424, www.aerlingus.ie

AeroMexico: 800-237-6639, www.aeromexico.com

Air Afrique: 800-456-9192, www.airafrique.com

Air Aruba: 800-882-7822, www.interknowledge.com/air-aruba

Air Canada: 888-247-2262, www.aircanada.ca

Air France: 800-237-2747, www.airfrance.com

Air New Zealand: 800-262-1234, www.airnz.com

AirTran Airways: 800-247-8726, www.airtran.com

Alaska Airlines: 800-426-0333, www.alaskaair.com

Alitalia: 800-223-5730, www.alitaliausa.com

Aloha Airlines: 800-367-5250, www.alohaairlines.com

America West: 800-235-9292, www.americawest.com

American Airlines: 800-433-7300, www.aa.com

British Airways: 800-247-9297, www.british-airways.com

Continental Airlines: 800-525-0280, www.flycontinental.com

Delta Airlines: 800-221-1212, www.delta.com

Gulfstream International: 800-457-4835, www.gulfstreamair.com

Hawaiian Airlines: 800-367-5320, www.hawaiianair.com

Iberia of Spain: 800-772-4642, www.iberia.com

Japan Airlines: 800-525-3663, www.japanair.com

JetBlue Airways: 800-538-2583, www.jetblue.com

KLM Royal Dutch Airlines: 800-556-1000, www.klm.com

Korean Air: 800-438-5000, www.koreanair.com

Lufthansa: 800-645-3880, www.lufthansa-usa.com

Mexicana: 800-531-7921, www.mexicana.com

Midwest Express: 800-452-2022, www.midwestexpress.com

National Airlines: 888-757-5387, www.nationalairlines.com

Northwest Airlines: 800-225-2525, www.nwa.com

Olympic Airways: 800-223-1226, www.olympicair.com

Qantas Airways: 800-227-4500, www.qantas.com

Singapore Airlines: 800-742-3333, www.singaporeair.com

SkyWest: 800-453-9417, www.skywest.com

Southwest Airlines: 800-435-9792, www.southwest.com

Spirit Airlines: 800-772-7117, www.spiritair.com

United Airlines: 800-241-6522, www.ual.com

U.S. Airways: 800-428-4322, www.usair.com

Virgin Atlantic Airways: 800-862-8621, www.virgin-atlantic.com

World Airways: 800-274-3601, www.worldair.com

Discount Airfares

Air Fare: www.airfare.com

Best Fares: www.bestfares.com

Cheap Fares: www.cheapfares.com

Cheap Tickets: www.cheaptickets.com

Discount Airfare: www.discount-airfare.com

Airline Frequent Flier Program

For the latest and most complete information on frequent flier programs, plus the tracking of your own air miles and alerts for new plans, go to www.frequentflier.com.

Check the Web sites of these popular American-based airlines for details on their frequent flier programs and affiliated partnerships:

- Air Canada: Aeroplan
- Air Tran: A Plus Rewards
- Alaska Airlines: Mileage Plan
- America West: Flight Fund
- American Airlines: AAdvantage
- Canadian Airlines International: Canadian Plus
- Continental: OnePass
- Delta Air Lines: SkyMiles
- Hawaiian Airlines: HawaiianMiles

- Legend Airlines: Travel Awards
- Midwest Express: Frequent Flyer Program
- National Airlines: National Comps
- Northwest Airlines: World Perks
- Southwest Airlines: Rapid Rewards
- TWA: Aviators
- United Airlines: Mileage Plus
- U.S. Airways: Dividend Miles

Among the many foreign-based airlines with frequent flier programs are the following:

- Aer Lingus: Travel Award Bonus Program
- Air France: Frequence Plus
- Alitalia: Club Mille Miglia
- British Airways: Executive Club

- Iberia: Iberia Plus
- KLM: Flying Dutchman
- Lufthansa: Miles and More
- Olympic Airways: Icarus
- Virgin Atlantic: Flying Club

Expedia.com: www.expedia.com
Hotwire: www.hotwire.com
Low Airfare: www.lowairfare.com
Lowest Fare: www.lowestfare.com

Mr. Cheap: 800-MR-CHEAP

Orbitz.com: www.orbitz.com

Priceline.com: www.priceline.com

Travelocity.com: www.travelocity.com

Trip: www.trip.com

You Price It: www.youpriceit.com

Cruises

Alaska's Glacier Bay Tours and Cruises: 800-451-5952,
www.glacierbaytours.com

American Canadian Caribbean Line: 800-556-7450,
www.accl-smallships.com

American Cruise Lines (East Coast from Florida to Maine):
800-814-6880, www.americancruiselines.com

American Hawaii Cruises: 800-765-7000, www.cruisehawaii.com

American Safari Cruises: 888-862-8881,
www.americansafaricruises.com

Carnival Cruise Lines: 800-327-9501, www.carnival.com

Celebrity Cruises: 800-437-3111, www.celebritycruises.com

Clipper Cruise Lines: 800-325-0010, www.clippercruise.com

Club Med: 800-258-2633, www.clubmed.com

Costa Cruise Line: 800-462-6782, www.costacruises.com

Cruise Lines International Association: www.cruising.org

Cruise West: 800-426-7702, www.cruisewest.com

Crystal Cruises: 800-820-6663, www.crystalcruises.com

Cunard: 800-728-6273, www.cunardline.com

Delta Queen Coastal Voyages: 800-846-8000,
www.coastalvoyages.com

Discount Cruises: www.cruise.com

Discovery Cruises: 800-866-8687, www.discoverycruiseline.com

Disney Cruise Line: 800-951-3532, www.disneycruise.com

First European Cruises: 888-983-8767, www.first-european.com

Holland America Line: 877-724-5425, www.hollandamerica.com

Norwegian Cruise Lines: 800-327-7030, www.ncl.com

Orient Lines: 800-333-7300, www.orientlines.com

Princess Cruises: 800-774-6237, www.princess.com

Radisson Seven Seas Cruises: 800-285-1835, www.rssc.com

Regal Cruises: 800-270-7245, www.regalcruises.com

Renaissance Cruises: 800-525-5350, www.renaissancecruises.com

Royal Caribbean International: 800-327-6700,
    www.royalcaribbean.com

Seaborn Cruise Line: 800-929-9391, www.seaborn.com

Silversea Cruises: 800-774-9996, www.silversea.com

Society Expeditions: 800-548-8669, www.societyexpeditions.com

Star Clippers: 800-442-0551, www.starclippers.com

Swan Hellenic Cruises: 877-219-4239, www.swan-hellenic.co.uk

United States Lines: 877-330-6600, www.unitedstateslines.com

Windjammer Barefoot Cruises: 800-327-2601,
    www.windjammer.com

Windstar Cruises: 877-827-7245, www.windstarcruises.com

World Explorer Cruises: 800-352-2752, www.wecruise.com

Hotels and Resorts

All Hotels: www.all-hotels.com

AmeriSuites: 800-833-1516, www.amerisuites.com

Best Western: 800-528-1234, www.bestwestern.com

Choice Hotels: 800-424-6423, www.hotelchoice.com

Clarion Hotels and Resorts: 800-252-7466, www.clarionhotel.com

Club Med: 800-258-2633, www.clubmed.com

Concorde Hotels International: 800-888-4747,
    www.concorde-hotels.com

Crowne Plaza Hotels and Resorts: 800-227-6963,
    www.sixcontinentshotels.com/crowneplaza

Days Inn: 800-329-7466, www.daysinn.com

Doubletree Hotels: 800-222-8733, www.doubletree.com

Embassy Suites: 800-362-2779, www.embassy-suites.com

Four Seasons: 800-332-3442, www.fourseasons.com

Grand Hyatt Hotels: 800-233-1234,
    www.hyatt.com/explore_hyatt/grand_hyatt

Hershey Entertainment and Resort: 800-437-7439,
    www.800hershey.com

Hilton Hotels: 800-445-8667, www.hilton.com

Holiday Inn: 800-465-4327,
    www.sixcontinentshotels.com/holiday-inn

Howard Johnson: 800-446-4656, www.hojo.com

Hyatt Hotels and Resorts: 800-223-1234, www.hyatt.com

Inter-Continental Hotels and Resorts: 800-327-0200,
    www.interconti.com

La Quinta Inns and Suites: 800-687-6667, www.laquinta.com

Leading Hotels of the World: 800-223-6800, www.lhw.com

Loews Hotels: 800-235-6397, www.loewshotels.com

Marriott Hotels, Resorts and Suites and Marriott International:
    800-228-9290, www.marriott.com

Marriott Vacation Club International: 800-845-5279,
    www.marriott.com/vacationclub.com

Omni Hotels: 800-843-6664, www.omnihotels.com

Orient Express Hotels: 800-237-1236,
    www.orient-expresshotels.com

Outrigger Hotels and Resorts: 800-688-7444, www.outrigger.com

Quality Inn: 800-228-5151, www.qualityinn.com

Radisson Hotels Worldwide: 800-333-3333, www.radisson.com

Ramada Inns: 800-272-3333, www.ramada.com

Renaissance Hotels and Resorts: 800-638-8108, »
    www.renaissancehotels.com

Ritz-Carlton Hotels: 800-241-3333, www.ritzcarlton.com or
    www.fourseasons.com

Sandals Resorts: 888-726-3257, www.sandals.com

Sheraton Hotels and Resorts: 800-325-3535,
    www.starwood.com/sheraton

Sonesta International Hotels: 800-766-3782, www.sonesta.com

Hotel Partnership Programs

For special deals through frequent flier and hotel partnership perk accounts, check out the following programs at the Web sites in the Hotels and Resorts list:

- Best Western: Best Western Gold Crown Club International
- Crowne Plaza Hotels and Resorts: Priority Club (same as Holiday Inn)
- Hilton Hotels: Hilton HHonors
- Holiday Inn: Priority Club
- Hyatt Hotels and Resorts: Hyatt Gold Passport
- Inter-Continental Hotels and Resorts: Six Continents Club
- Marriott Hotels, Resorts, Suites: Marriott Rewards
- Radisson Hotels Worldwide: Gold Rewards
- Ramada Inns: Club Ramada
- Renaissance Hotels and Resorts: Marriott Rewards
- Sheraton Hotels and Resorts ITT: Starwood Preferred Guest
- Westin Hotels and Resorts: Starwood Preferred Guest

W Hotels: 877-443-4585, www.starwood.com/whotels/index.html
Westin Hotels and Resorts: 800-443-4585, www.westin.com
Wyndham Hotels and Resorts: 800-996-3426, www.wyndham.com

Adventure Tour and Expedition Companies

Abercrombie and Kent: 800-323-7308, www.abercrombiekent.com
Adventure Travel Society (an association that rates and provides information on various tour companies and expeditions,and a great place to research the following and additional sources): 719-530-0171, www.adventuretravelbusiness.com

American Society of Travel Agents: 703-739-2782,
www.astanet.com

Backroads: 800-GO-ACTIVE, www.backroads.com

Expeditions: 800-EXPEDITION, www.expeditions.com

General Tours: 800-221-2216, www.generaltours.com

Geographic Expeditions: 800-777-8183, www.geoex.com

Intrav: 800-456-8100, www.intrav.com

Mountain Travel Sobek: 888-MT-SOBEK, www.mtsobek.com

Tauck World Discovery: 800-788-7885, www.tauck.com

Travcoa: 800-992-2003 (US), 800-563-0005 (Canada),
www.travcoa.com

Wilderness Travel: 800-368-2794, www.wildernesstravel.com

Bed-and-Breakfasts

Bed and Breakfast International Guide: www.ibbp.com

Bed and Breakfasts in Canada: www.bandbinfo.com

Internet Guide to Bed and Breakfasts: www.traveldata.com

Victorian Inns: www.victorianinns.com

Car Rental Agencies

Alamo: 800-327-9633, www.goalamo.com

Auto Europe: 800-223-5555, www.autoeurope.com

Avis: 800-331-1212, www.avis.com

Budget: 800-527-0700, www.budgetrentacar.com

Dollar: 800-800-4000, www.dollarcar.com

Enterprise: 800-325-8007, www.pickenterprise.com

Europe By Car: 800-223-1516, www.europebycar.com

Hertz: 800-654-3131, www.hertz.com

National: 800-627-7777, www.nationalcar.com

Thrifty: 800-367-2277, www.thrifty.com

Car Travel Services

AAA: www.aaa.com

Car Club: www.carclub.com

Car Rental Agencies' Partnership and Perk Programs

For tie-ins with frequent flier and hotel partnership programs, check out the following perks at the Web sites in the Car Rental Agencies list:

- Alamo: Travel Partners
- Avis: Travel Partners
- Budget: Travel Partners
- Dollar Rent a Car: Travel Partners
- Hertz: Travel Partners
- National: Emerald Club
- Thrifty Car Rental: Travel Partners

Limousines (for transport to and from airport)

National Limousine Association: 800-NLA-7007, www.limo.org

Train Travel

Acadian Railway Company (northeastern United States and Canada): 866-91-TRAIN, www.thetraincollection.com

American Association of Private Railroad Car Operators: 202-547-5696

Amtrak: 800-872-7245, www.amtrak.com

Eurailpass: www.eurail.com

Orient Express Trains: 800-237-1236, www.orient-express.com

Rovos Rail (in South Africa): www.rovosrail.com

Society of International Railway Travelers: 800-IRT-4881

VIA Rail Canada: 800-681-2561, www.viarail.ca

Credit Card Companies

American Express: 800-528-4800, www.americanexpress.com

Diners Club International: 800-234-6377, www.citibank.com/dinersus

Discover Card: 800-347-2683, www.disoverfinancial.com

MasterCard International: 800-247-4623, www.mastercard.com

Visa International: 800-847-2911, www.visa.com

Tourism Departments

• To find any island, country, or state's tourism department Web site or current contact information, check the Tourism Office Worldwide Directory at www.towd.com.

• To find more detailed information on any state listed below, go to www.travel-library.com or www.travel.org.

State and Location Tourism Departments

Alabama: 800-ALABAMA, ww.touralabama.org

Alaska: 800-862-5275, www.travelalaska.com, www.anchorage.net, www.explorefairbanks.com

American Samoa (U.S. Territory): 684-633-1092, www.amsamoa.com

Arizona: 888-520-3433, www.arizonaguide.com

Arkansas: 800-NATURAL, www.arkansas.com

California: 800-GO-CALIF, gocalif.ca.gov (also directly: 800-5-SONOMA, www.sonomacountry.com; www.bigsurcalifornia.org, www.virtualtahoe.com, www.lacvb.com, www.monterey.com, www.sandiegonorth.com, www.sfvisitor.org)

Colorado: 800-265-6723, www.colorado.com

Connecticut: 800-CT-BOUND, www.tourism.state.ct.us

Delaware: 800-441-8846, www.visitdelaware.net

Disney Honeymoons: 877-566-0969, www.disneyhoneymoons.com

Florida: 877-7-FLA-USA, www.flausa.com, www.floridakeys.org, www.floridakiss.com

Georgia: 800-847-4842, www.georgia.org, www.atlanta.com

Hawaii: 800-353-5846, www.visithawaii.org, www.visitmaui.com

Idaho: 800-635-7820, www.visitid.org

Illinois: 800-2-CONNECT, www.enjoyillinois.com

Indiana: 800-ENJOY-IN, www.enjoyindiana.com

Iowa: 800-345-IOWA, www.state.ia.us

Kansas: 800-2-KANSAS, www.travelks.com

Kentucky: 800-225-TRIP, www.kentuckytourism.com

Lake Tahoe: 800-824-6348, www.go-tahoe.com

Louisiana: 800-334-8626, www.louisianatravel.com

Maine: 800-533-9595, www.mainetourism.com

Maryland: 800-MD-IS-FUN, www.mdisfun.org

Massachusetts: 800-227-MASS, www.mass-vacation.com

Michigan: 888-78-GREAT, www.michigan.org

Minnesota: 800-657-3700, www.exploreminnesota.com

Mississippi: 800-WARMEST, www.visitmississippi.org

Missouri: 800-810-5500, www.missouritourism.org

Montana: 800-VISIT-MT, visitmt.com

Nebraska: 800-228-4307, www.visitnebraska.org

Nevada: 800-NEVADA-8, www.travelnevada.com (for Las Vegas:
    www.vegasfreedom.com)

New Hampshire: 800-FUN-IN-NH, www.visitnh.gov

New Jersey: 800-JERSEY-7, www.state.nj.us/travel,
    www.atlanticcitynj.com

New Mexico: 800-545-2040, www.newmexico.org

New York: 800-CALL-NYS, www.iloveny.com, www.nycvisit.com

North Carolina: 800-VISIT-NC, www.visitnc.com

North Dakota: 800-435-5663, www.ndtourism.com

Ohio: 800-BUCKEYE, www.ohiotourism.com

Oklahoma: 800-652-6552, www.travelok.com

Oregon: 800-547-7842, www.traveloregon.com

Pennsylvania: 800-VISIT-PA, www.experiencepa.com (for the
    Poconos: www.poconos.org)

Rhode Island: 800-556-2484, www.visitrhodeisland.com

South Carolina: 803-734-0235, www.travelsd.com

South Dakota: 800-732-5682, www.travelsd.com

Tennessee: 800-491-TENN, www.tourism.state.tn.us,
  www.memphistravel.com, www.nashvillecvb.com
Texas: 800-888-8TEX, www.traveltex.com
Utah: 800-200-1160, www.utah.com, www.visitsaltlake.com
Vermont: 800-VERMONT, www.travel-vermont.com
Virginia: 800-VISIT-VA, www.virginia.org
Washington: 800-544-1800, www.tourism.wa.gov
Washington, DC: 800-422-8644, www.washington.org
West Virginia: 800-225-5982, www.state.wv.us/tourism
Wisconsin: 800-432-8747, www.travelwisconsin.com
Wyoming: 800-225-5996, www.wyomingtourism.org

Hawaiian Islands

Big Island Visitors' Bureau: 800-648-2441, www.bigisland.org
The Hawaii Visitor and Convention Center: 800-GO-HAWAII,
  www.hawaii.com
Lanai Visitors Bureau: 800-947-4774, www.visitlanai.com
Maui Visitors' Bureau: 800-525-MAUI, www.visitmaui.com
Molokai Visitors Association: 800-800-6367,
  www.molokai-hawaii.com
Oahu Visitors' Bureau: 877-525-OAHU, www.visit-oahu.com

Other Islands

Anguilla: 800-553-4939, www.anguilla-vacation.com
Antigua and Barbuda: 888-268-4227, www.antigua-barbuda.org
Aruba: 800-862-7822, www.arubatourism.com
Bahamas: 800-224-3681, www.bahamas.com
Barbados: 800-221-9831, www.barbados.org
Bermuda: 800-223-6106, www.bermudatourism.com
Bonaire: 800-266-2473, www.bonaire.org
British Virgin Islands: 800-835-8530, www.bviwelcome.com
Caribbean Tourism Commission: www.caribtourism.com
Cayman Islands: 800-346-3313, www.caymanislands.ky or
  www.divecayman.ky

Cozumel: www.islacozumel.com.mx

Curaçao: 800-445-8266, www.curacao-tourism.com

Dominica: 212-949-1711, www.dominica.dm

Dominican Republic: 800-752-1151, www.dominicana.com.do

Fiji: 800-932-3454, www.bulafiji.com

Galapagos Islands: www.galapagoschamberoftourism.com

Grenada: 800-927-9554, www.grenadagrenadines.com or
    www.grenada.org

Honduras: 800-410-9608, www.letsgohonduras.com

Jamaica: 800-233-4582, www.jamaicatravel.com

Marianas (Saipan, Tinian, and Rota in Northern Marianas):
    670-664-3200, visit-marianas.com

Martinique: 800-391-4909, www.martinique.com

Mauritius: www.mauritius.net

Private Islands Online: www.privateislandsonline.com

Puerto Rico: 800-815-7391, www.prtourism.com

Santorini: 212-421-5777, www.gnto.gr

St. Kitts and Nevis: 800-582-6208, www.stkitts-nevis.com

St. Lucia: 800-456-3984, www.st-lucia.com

St. Maarten: 800-786-2278, www.st-maarten.com

St. Vincent and the Grenadines: 800-729-1726, www.svgtourism.com

Tahiti: 800-365-4949, www.gototahiti.com or
    www.tahiti-tourism.com

Tahiti, Kiribati, New Caledonia, Niue, Papua New Guinea,
    Solomon Islands, Tonga, Tuvalu, and Vanuatu: www.tspc.com

Tourism Council of the South Pacific (Includes: American Samoa,
    Cook Islands, Fiji, Turks and Caicos): 800-241-0824,
    www.turksandcaicostourism.com

U.S. Virgin Islands: 800-372-8784, www.usvi.org

Foreign

Australia: 800-369-6863, www.australia.com

Belize: 800-624-0686, www.travelbelize.org, www.belizetourism.org

British Tourism Office: 800-462-2748, www.visitbritain.com

Canada: 877-BONJOUR (Quebec), www.travelcanada.ca,
     www.canadiantourism.com
China: 212-760-9700, www.cnto.org
Costa Rica: 800-343-6332, www.tourism-costarica.com
Dominican Republic: 800-752-1151, www.dominicana.com.do
England: www.travelengland.org.uk,
     www.londontourist board.com
Egypt: 877-773-4978, www.touregypt.net
France: www.francetourism.com,
     www.paris-touristoffice.com
Germany: www.germany-tourism.de
Greece: www.gnto.gr
Hong Kong: 800-282-4582, www.hkta.org,
     www.Discover HongKong.com
Ireland: 800-223-6470, www.shamrock.org
Israel: 800-596-1199, www.goisrael.com
Italy: www.italiantourism.com
Japan: www.jnto.go.jp
Kenya: www.africanvacation.com/kenya
Korea: 800-868-7567, www.knto.or.kr
Mexico: 800-446-3942, www.mexico-travel.com
Monaco: 800-753-9696, www.monaco-tourism.com
New Zealand: 800-388-5494, www.purenz.com
Nice: www.nicetourism.com
Portugal: 800-767-8842, www.portugal.org
Russia: www.russia-travel.com
Scotland: www.visitscotland.com
Singapore: www.singapore-usa.com
South Africa: 800-822-5386, us.southafricantourism.com
Spain: www.okspain.org
Switzerland: www.switzerlandtourism.com,
     www.myswitzerland.com
Vietnam: www.vietnamtourism.com

National Parks

E.S.C.A.P.E.: www.park-escape.com

GORP: www.gorp.com

U.S. Parks System: www.us-parks.com

Camping and RV Trips

American Camping Association: 765-342-8456, www.acacamps.org

Cruise America: 800-327-7799, www.cruiseamerica.com

Kids' Camping Association: www.kidscamps.com

Mike's Radio World: www.mikesradioworld.com

National Park Service: 800-365-2267, www.nps.gov

Recreational Vehicle Association: www.rvra.org

USDA Forest Service: 877-444-6777, www.reserveusa.com

Woodall's Campground Directory: www.woodalls.com

Embassies and Consulates

Find your intended foreign embassy and consulate offices both overseas and in the United States at travel.state.gov/foreignentryreqs.html.

Travel Agencies

AAA: 888-869-5161, www.aaa.com

American Society of Travel Agents: 800-965-ASTA, www.astanet.com

API Travel Consultants: 800-401-4API, royalinsider.com/4API.htm

Institute of Certified Travel Agents: www.icta.com

Travel Information: General

ATM Finder: Cirrus at 800-307-7309 or Plus at 800-843-7587

Bureau of Consular Affairs: travel.state.gov

CultureGrams: www.culturegrams.com

Currency Converter: www.currencyguide.com

Flight Tracker: www.trip.com

Foreign Entry Requirements (passports, IDs, visas, travel restrictions and aid while overseas): travel.state.gov

Overseas Citizens Services: 202-647-5225, travel.state.gov

Passports, Visas, Travel Advisories: travel.state.gov/passports

Pet Sitters International: www.petsit.com

Tourism Office Worldwide Directory: www.towd.com

Travel Facts: www.travelfacts.com

Travel Institute of America: www.tia.org

Traveling with Pets: www.travelpets.com

U.S. Postal Hold Mail Form: new.usps.com/pdf/ps8076.pdf

Travel Research: Newspapers

AsiaWeek: www.asiaweek.com

Chicago Sun Times: www.suntimes.com

Los Angeles Times: www.latimes.com

Newsday: www.newsday.com

Philadelphia Inquirer: inq.philly.com

San Francisco Examiner: www.examiner.com

Time: www.time.com

Washington Post: www.washingtonpost.com

Travel Research: Magazines

Arthur Frommer's Budget Travel: www.frommer.com

Caribbean Travel and Life: www.caribbeantravelmag.com

Conde Nast Traveler: www.cntraveler.com

Cruise Travel: www.travel.org/cruisetravel

Frequent Flyer: www.frequentflyer.oag.com

Hemispheres: www.hemispheresmagazine.com

Islands: www.islands.com

Porthole Magazine (cruises): www.porthole.com

Spa: www.spamagazine.com

Spa Finder: www.spafinder.com

Travel and Leisure: www.travelandleisure.com

Travel Holiday: www.travelholiday.com

Travel Research: Bridal Magazines with Extensive Honeymoon Features and FYIs

Bridal Guide: www.bridalguidemag.com

Bride Again: www.brideagain.com

Conde Nast Bride: www.brides.com

Destination Weddings and Honeymoons:
www.destinationweddings.com

Grace Ormonde Wedding Style:
www.weddingstylemagazine.com

Martha Stewart Weddings: www.marthastewart.com

Modern Bride: www.modernbride.com

Today's Bride: www.todaysbride.com

Wedding Bells: www.weddingbells.com

Travel Research: Online

4 Deals.com: www.4deals.com

About.com: www.about.com

All Hotels: www.allhotels.com

Arthur Frommer's Budget Travel Destinations:
www.frommers.com/destinations

Away.com: www.away.com

BedandBreakfast.com: www.bedandbreakfast.com

Best Fares: www.bestfares.com

Best in the World Travel Directory:
www.thebestintheworld.com

Cheap Tickets: www.cheaptickets.com

Citynet.com: www.citynet.com

Citysearch: www.citysearch.com

Concierge: www.concierge.com

Connected Traveler: www.connectedtraveler.com

Cruise: www.cruise.com

Digital City: www.digitalcity.com

Dine: www.dine.com

Ecotraveler: www.ecotraveler.com

Ettractions (attractions across North America):
www.ettractions.com

EventsWorldWide: www.eventsworldwide.com

Excite Travel: www.excite.com

Expedia.com: www.expedia.com

Fodor's: www.fodors.com

Hidden America (little-known spots in the United States):
www.hiddenamerica.com

History Channel Traveler: www.historytravel.com

Honeymoons: www.honeymoons.com

Hotel Guide Network: www.hotelguide.com

Hotwire: www.hotwire.com

iExplore: www.iexplore.com

Island Honeymoons: www.islandhoneymoons.com

My Travel Guide: www.mytravelguide.com

National Hotel Directory: www.gothotel.com

Orbitz.com: www.orbitz.com

Rand McNally: www.randmcnally.com

Resorts Online: www.resortsonline.com

Snap: www.snap.com

Travel Web: www.travelweb.com

Travelocity.com: www.travelocity.com

Trip.com: www.trip.com

USA Citylink: www.usacitylink.com

Vacation Spot: www.vacationspot.com

Web Flyer: www.webflyer.com

Yahoo! Travel: www.travel.yahoo.com

Maps

AAA: www.aaa.com

Go.com: www.go.com

Lycos Roadmaps: www.maps.lycos.com

MapQuest: www.mapquest.com

Yahoo! Maps: maps.yahoo.com

Foreign Language Translators and Lessons

Accent Language: www.accentlanguage.com

Alta Vista: babelfish.altavista.com

Travel Language: www.travllang.com

Staying Connected

Etrieve: www.etrieve.com

Go to My PC: www.gotomypc.com

Yahoo! by Phone: phone.yahoo.com

Weather

AccuWeather: www.accuweather.com

CNN Weather: www.cnn.com/weather/

Lycos Weather: www.weather.lycos.com

National Hurricane Center: www.nationalhurricanecenter.com

National Weather Service: www.nationalweatherservice.com

Rain or Shine: www.rainorshine.com

Weather Channel: www.weather.com

World Climate: www.worldclimate.com

Yahoo! Weather: weather.yahoo.com

Consumer and Fraud Help

Better Business Bureau: www.bbb.org

Better Business Bureau Online: www.bbbonline.org

Federal Trade Commission: 877-FTC-HELP, www.ftc.gov

Luggage and Gadgets

In Motion Pictures: www.inmotionpictures.com

Handheld Organizers and PDAs

Casio: www.casio.com

Compac: www.compac.com

Hewlett-Packard: www.hp.com

Microsoft: www.microsoft.com

Nextel: www.nextel.com

Nokia: www.nokia.com
Palm: www.palm.com
Samsung: www.samsung.com
Sanyo: www.sanyo.com
Sharp: www.sharp-usa.com
Sprint PCS: www.sprintpcs.com
Verizon: www.verizon.com
Voicestream: www.voicestream.com

Luggage and Travel Gear Gadgets
Coach: 800-223-5689, www.coach.com
Container Store: 888-266-8246, www.containerstore.com
Eagle Creek: 800-874-9925, www.eaglecreek.com
eBags: 800-820-6126, www.ebags.com
Eddie Bauer: 800-625-7935, www.eddiebauer.com
High Sierra Sport: 800-323-9590, www.hssc.com
Lands' End: 800-332-0103, www.landsend.com
LeSportsac: 800-486-2247, www.lesportsac.com
L. L. Bean: 800-441-5713, www.llbean.com
Louis Vuitton: www.vuitton.com
Magellan's: 800-962-4943, www.magellans.com
Mercury Luggage: 800-888-5844, www.mercuryluggage.com
National Geographic: 800-437-5221, www.nationalgeographic.com
Royal Case Company: 903-868-0288, www.royalcase.com
Samsonite: 800-223-7267, www.samsonite.com
Sharper Image: 800-344-5555, www.sharperimage.com
TravelPro USA: 888-741-7471, www.travelpro.com
TravelSmith: 800-950-1600, www.travelsmith.com

Shopping for Honeymoon Treat Items
Body Shop: www.bodyshop.com
Burt's Bees: www.burtsbees.com
Illuminations: www.illuminations.com
Primal Elements: www.primalelements.com

Red Envelope: www.redenvelope.com
Space NK: www.spacenk.com
Xandria Collection: www.xandria.com

Honeymoon Beauty

Avon: www.avon.com
Beauty.com: www.beauty.com
Bobbi Brown Essentials: www.bobbibrown.com
Clinique: www.clinique.com
Elizabeth Arden: www.elizabetharden.com
Estée Lauder: www.esteelauder.com
Eve (carries Lorac, Elizabeth Arden, Calvin Klein, etc):
    www.eve.com
Lancôme: www.lancome.com
L'Oréal: www.loreal.com
Mac: www.maccosmetics.com
Max Factor: www.maxfactor.com
Maybelline: www.maybelline.com
Neutrogena: www.neutrogena.com
Pantene: www.pantene.com
Rembrandt (tooth-whitening products): www.rembrandt.com
Revlon: www.revlon.com
Sephora: www.sephora.com

Warehouse Stores

BJ's Wholesale: 800-257-2582, www.bjswholesale.com
Costco: 800-774-2678, www.costco.com
Price Smart: www.pricesmart.com
Sam's Club: www.samsclub.com

Index

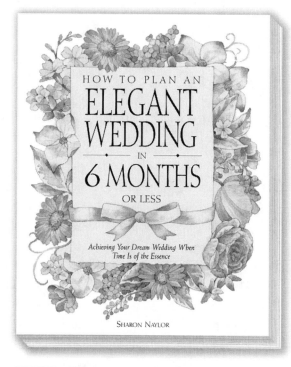

Let Nature Be Your Wedding Chapel

Whether you're thinking about exchanging vows on a sandy beach, a majestic mountaintop, or simply the friendly confines of your own backyard, you can enjoy the elegant, breathtaking wedding you've always envisioned. Inside, wedding expert Sharon Naylor takes you step-by-step through planning the perfect outdoor wedding day. You'll discover an array of tips, hints, resources, and answers to vital questions, including:

- **The best choices for location, time of year, and hour of day**

- **Practical considerations, such as space, privacy, and weather**

- **Suggestions for choosing outdoor-friendly wedding attire**

- **Information on regulations, permits, and other requirements**

- **And so much more!**

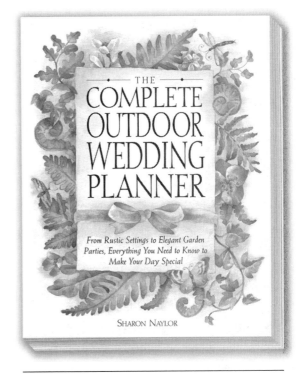

ISBN 0-7615-3598-5 / Paperback / 384 pages
U.S. $16.95 / Can. $25.95

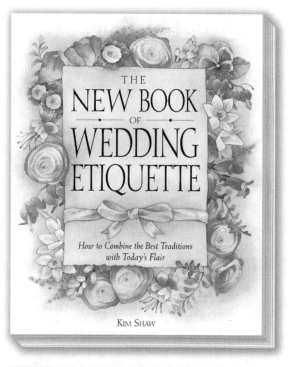

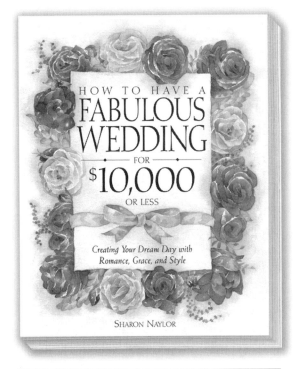

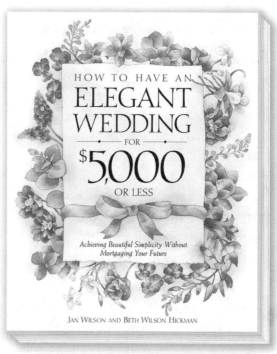